Mimi and Toutou's
Big Adventure

Mimi and Toutou's
Big Adventure

The Bizarre Battle of Lake Tanganyika

GILES FODEN

ALFRED A. KNOPF   *New York*   2005

THIS IS A BORZOI BOOK
PUBLISHED BY ALFRED A. KNOPF

Copyright © 2004 by Giles Foden
Illustrations copyright © 2004 by Matilda Hunt

www.aaknopf.com

Originally published in Great Britain by Michael Joseph,
Penguin Books, London, in 2004.

Knopf, Borzoi Books, and the colophon are registered
trademarks of Random House, Inc.

Library of Congress Cataloging-in-Publication Data
Foden, Giles, 1967–
Mimi and Toutou's big adventure : the bizarre battle of Lake Tanganyika /
by Giles Foden.— 1st American ed.
p. cm.
Originally published: London : Michael Joseph, Penguin Books, 2004.
Includes bibliographical references and index.
ISBN 1-4000-4157-0 (alk. paper)
1. World War, 1914–1918—Campaigns—Tanganyika, Lake.   2. World
War, 1914–1918—Campaigns—German East Africa.   3. Mimi
(Gunboat)   4. Toutou (Gunboat)   I. Title.
D582.T34F64 2005
940.54'237828—dc22   2004026403

Manufactured in the United States of America
First American Edition

For C.T.F. on one lake and D.A.J. on another

"Let us see, however," he said, "if there is not some assemblage of letters which appears to form a word—I mean a pronounceable word, whose number of consonants is in proportion to its vowels. And at the beginning I see the word *phy;* further on the word *gas.* Halloo! *ujugi.* Does that mean the African town on the banks of Tanganyika? What has that got to do with all this?"

—JULES VERNE,
Eight Hundred Leagues on the Amazon

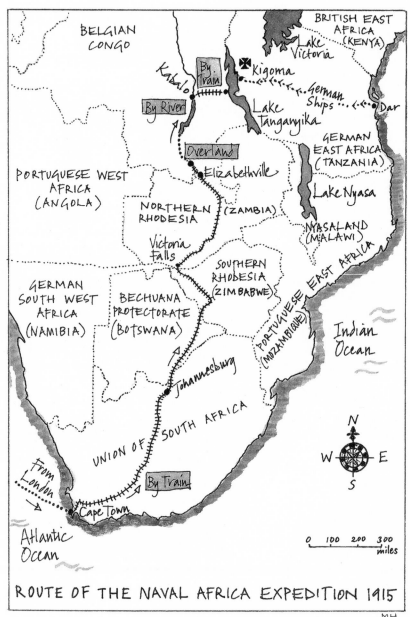

BELGIAN CONGO

BRITISH EAST AFRICA (KENYA)

Lake Victoria

Kabalo

By Train

✖ Kigoma

By River

German Ships

Dar

Overland

Lake Tanganyika

GERMAN EAST AFRICA (TANZANIA)

PORTUGUESE WEST AFRICA (ANGOLA)

Elizabethville

Lake Nyasa

NORTHERN RHODESIA

(ZAMBIA)

NYASALAND (MALAWI)

Victoria Falls

SOUTHERN RHODESIA (ZIMBABWE)

GERMAN SOUTH WEST AFRICA (NAMIBIA)

BECHUANA PROTECTORATE (BOTSWANA)

PORTUGUESE EAST AFRICA (MOZAMBIQUE)

Indian Ocean

Johannesburg

UNION OF SOUTH AFRICA

N
W   E
S

From London

By Train

Cape Town

Atlantic Ocean

0   100   200   300
miles

ROUTE OF THE NAVAL AFRICA EXPEDITION 1915

MH

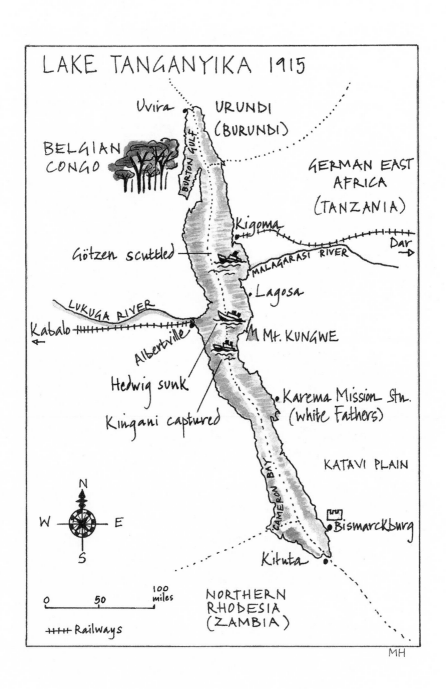

LAKE TANGANYIKA 1915

Uvira
URUNDI
(BURUNDI)

BELGIAN
CONGO

BURTON GULF

GERMAN EAST
AFRICA
(TANZANIA)

Kigoma

Dar

Götzen scuttled

MALAGARASI RIVER

LUKUGA RIVER

Lagosa

Kabalo

Albertville

Mt. KUNGWE

Hedwig sunk

Kingani captured

Karema Mission Stn.
(white Fathers)

KATAVI PLAIN

CAMERON BAY

Bismarckburg

N
W   E
S

Kituta

0   50   100
miles

++++ Railways

NORTHERN
RHODESIA
(ZAMBIA)

MH

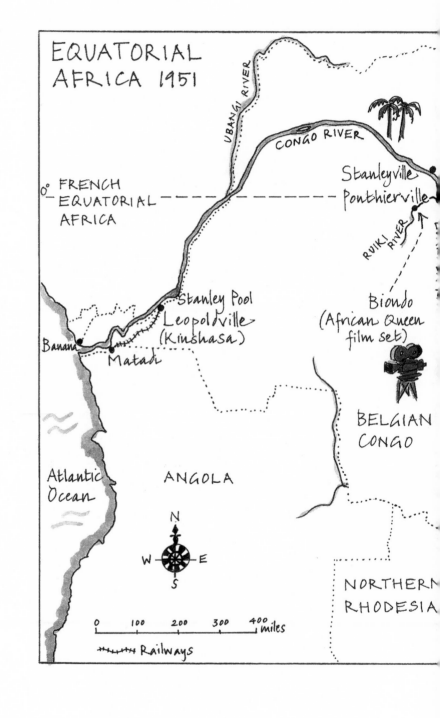

EQUATORIAL
AFRICA 1951

UBANGI RIVER

CONGO RIVER

0° FRENCH
    EQUATORIAL   - - - - - - - - - - -   Stanleyville
    AFRICA   Ponthierville

                                           RUIKI RIVER

                    Stanley Pool
                    Leopoldville
                    (Kinshasa)   Biondo
Banana   (African Queen
        Matadi   film set)

                                          BELGIAN
                                          CONGO

Atlantic   ANGOLA
Ocean

              N
         W   E
              S

                                          NORTHERN
                                          RHODESIA

0   100   200   300   400 miles

++++++ Railways

SUDAN
WHITE NILE RIVER
Lake Rudolf
Butiaba (African Queen film set)
UGANDA
Murchison Falls
KENYA COLONY
Lake Albert
Entebbe
EQUATOR
ake Edward
Nairobi
RUANDA
URUNDI
Lake Victoria
Kigoma
Ujiji
LUKUGA RIVER
Tabora
Tanga
Zanzibar
Kabalo
Dar es Salaam
RUFIJI RIVER
Lake Kisale
Lake Tanganyika
Mafia Island
ukama
TANGANYIKA
ankisia
MITUMBA MOUNTAINS
Fungurume
Elizabethville
NYASALAND PROTECTORATE
MOZAMBIQUE
Indian Ocean
MH

Mimi and Toutou's
Big Adventure

Prologue

There was plenty of game in the shooting grounds of German East Africa. That enormous stretch of territory between the Great Lakes of the continent and the Indian Ocean had not been over-shot. As had happened, in the hunter's opinion, in the country's neighbours, Kenya and Uganda. There the noble bongo, finest of African antelopes, was almost extinct, as was the white rhinoceros. These creatures were already entering the world of myth, like the unicorn. The hunter remembered another *âge d'or,* a genuine one. Yesteryear, when the delicate art of reading spoor had not been overtaken by the motor car and the repeating rifle.

Here in German East things were different. On his way to the lakeshore, for instance, the hunter had watched a white rhinoceros trot across the undulating grassy ridge in front of him. Even now, amid some trees nearer the lake, a cow elephant was pulling down ripening palm-fruits for her calf; rearing up and gripping the tree with her front legs, using her trunk like a spoon.

In spite of the reeds around him and the breeze wafting under the brim of his hat, the hunter felt the heat coming off the surface of Lake Tanganyika. On the shore he could see small, brown clusters of antelope dotted about in the haze. There were two types down there, he noted from his prone position: the shy, mysterious Sitatunga—whose splayed, webbed hooves kept them from sinking in swamps—and the more common Defassa water-buck or "Sing-Sing." *Cobus defassa* was a fine animal with a shaggy coat, good horns and a splendid carriage, but there was no point shooting it. Water-buck meat did not roast well.

The hunter pursued his profession in German East Africa, once known as Tanganyika. He had no hunting licence from the authorities, however, nor did he live there. He was after elephant. Not this gentle she-elephant plucking palm nuts, but one of the big tuskers, 20,000 pounds at least. He shifted in the bed of reeds, feeling the rifle's weight in his hand, Old Sol's heat through the crown of his hat: waiting, waiting . . . the principal occupation of a big-game hunter. It was not the glamorous career many held it to be. He watched a flock of spur-winged geese rise into the air above the reed-bed. Now they *were* good eating, but they could not be shot with a .475. His rifle was by no means a fowling piece; it would blow a bird into a thousand feathery fragments.

Why carry such a heavy weapon? he was often asked. They say choice of arms comes down to "shock" versus "easy handling" and it was his firm belief that, where elephants were concerned, shock was very much to be preferred, as much to protect oneself as to avoid wounding and slow death.

Watching the geese fall into a V formation in the sky, he reflected that he should have told his Holo-holo bearer to bring up his shotgun as well as the heavy-calibre rifle. Then he could have shot for the pot. His eye drifted down to the lake, so wonderfully calm today. He had known gales rise here many times in the past—

heavy storms that ripped up and down the water with terrifying ferocity. Tropical cyclones formed magnificent waterspouts in some seasons, rising miles high.

The lake's headlands and creek-banks were mainly covered with acacia scrub—fringed, as here, with reed and papyrus. Elsewhere, there was thick jungle and—no less dense—*miombo* forests studded with African teak and rare ebony. In some places along the lake, sheer granite slopes rose from the water up to a thousand feet. Raked by deep gullies, these cliffs were testament to the epic narratives that had formed Lake Tanganyika. It was the longest freshwater lake in the world, more than 400 miles long. Geological time—no longer so fathomless as heretofore, but still a sign of God's grace: the outward workings of his spiritual perfection—was the key to this beautiful inland sea.

Geology also explained those other great natural tanks of rainwater that extend down the backbone of the Rift Valley: Lake Albert, Lake Victoria, Lake Nyasa. All along this "vital and structural centre of Africa," as a certain missionary had once described the Rift to him, were what were termed "foundered valleys": valleys made not by the ground being pushed up, but by it falling away. Into these vast troughs—through swamp-choked estuaries, through clear, pebble-bottomed creeks, or tumbling down foaming chasms—the rivers and streams of the surrounding region had flowed for untold years. Once in the lake, the water had many of the characteristics of the sea, able to turn from green to grey to deep blue, its waves cresting white as they broke on the shore. With a surface area of 13,000 square miles, Lake Tanganyika was even large enough to attract the attention of the moon and produce tides.

As the cow elephant wandered away—her calf gripping her tail with its trunk—the hunter wondered how long the vast quantity of game could last. Modern civilisation, if that is what one should call it, was rushing into Tanganyika like Noah's flood and so-called progress was everywhere at hand.

Mainly a whip hand. Most Germans in the colony, which had

been established since 1885, carried whips as a matter of course. It was one of the reasons he hated Germans. But the Belgians across the water in the Congo were not much better and from time to time he recognised a vein of sadism in his own country's doings, too.

The hunter lived on the Congo side of the lake. Every few days he and his bearer—a member of the Holo-holo tribe—would sail over in a former slave dhow to take advantage of the more plentiful elephant on the German shore. Not paying permits and licence fees was another of his ruses. If a large animal was killed, he allowed his bearer's tribesmen—there were Holo-holo on both sides of the lake—to come and butcher it. The heart and the liver were considered great delicacies. For this reason, although the Holo-holo were mainly allied to the Germans, they kept quiet about his activities and even warned him of approaching German patrols.

The hunter ate some orange-flavoured biscuits purchased from a Russian grocer in Elizabethville, and then he must have dozed off. He awoke with a start at a splashing sound below and was surprised to see a large bull elephant with fine tusks washing or more properly cooling itself in the shallows of the lake, its grey flanks covered in black slimy mud. Cautiously, he eased himself into a crouching position, raising his .475. The elephant was slapping its sides with its trunk, plastering itself with the mud. The hunter was about to pull the trigger when it surged forwards.

He thought he had missed his chance, but the bull was merely heading for an island of floating vegetation. It began tugging at some young papyrus, tearing the bunched green shafts from the long-rooted plant and beating them over its back. The image which struck the hunter was that of a flagellant monk. He lifted his rifle again, noticing as he did so a smudge of grey cloud in the sky above his mark.

It was then that the animal seemed to sense him. Dropping the papyrus on the water, it turned its giant head and moved nearer, shifting its weight from one foreleg to another and raising its trunk in the air. The elephant stared in his direction, blinking, then lowered its trunk towards him. He could hear the breath vibrating as the trunk uncurled, its mottled pink tip opening and closing like a sea anemone. It was trying to smell him.

The hunter waited, not wanting to shoot while the elephant was on the move. Wounding it would only result in a rogue. But the bull was still swaying from side to side, as if haunted by some premonition of its death. A death the hunter was already beginning to calculate . . . a shot to the large mark of the heart or to the smaller one of the brain? The latter was trickier, since an elephant's brain is housed in one of the thickest skulls of any creature on earth. The relative advantages of a brain shot were, to his mind—*parrumpf!*

The elephant lifted its trunk, trumpeted again and flapped its ears. With astonishing speed for such a huge beast, it floundered out of the water and galloped into the bush. The hunter jumped to his feet, but knew the game was up. Volleying never worked with elephants, they should never be shot on the run.

He sat down disconsolately in the reeds. Only then, after the birds the elephant had sent wheeling into the air had settled again, did he hear what had startled his prey: a low *tuk-tuk,* a vibrating sound which came from the lake. The noise was mechanical in nature, so different from the usual bark of a baboon or call of a bird, those familiar Tanganyikan sounds, that he wondered for a moment if his imagination were playing tricks. But it wasn't; the sound grew louder. He lifted his field glasses.

The ship was painted white with a horizontal blue-grey line bisecting its hull. The smudge of dirty cloud he had noticed earlier was the exhaust from its funnel; the noise which had frightened the elephant was that of the wood-burning steam engine that drove the ship's screw propellers. From his hidden vantage point behind the reeds, the hunter watched as the vessel held steady along the shore, growing larger as she came closer. Low in the water, she gleamed in the sunlight, edging forwards. About her bows curled a foam moustache.

Beyond the bow-wave, eddies spread out and slapped against

the shore. Watching the impact of the wash in the reeds, the hunter wondered if the ship would come up this particular channel and if there was any danger of him being discovered. He peered through his binoculars. The name on the side was *Hedwig von Wissmann;* a vessel of nearly 60 tons in his estimation.

He saw the officers in their white uniforms, shining buttons on their chests, gold braid on their shoulders. He saw a pile of fire-wood on the deck, from which an African labourer extracted bundles to carry down to the boiler room. He saw a long pennant—emblazoned with the Iron Cross of the Imperial German Navy—streaming from the pole-mast. And he saw a gun: a gun that made his .475 look like a child's toy. He watched the barrel's erect shape as the *Hedwig* steamed by in profile, before turning for the horizon. Reflected in the lenses of his field glasses, the ship that ruled Lake Tanganyika continued on her tour of inspection.

Arriving some four weeks later back at his digs in Elizabethville—the capital of Katanga, the southern province of the Belgian Congo—the hunter heard in a bar from a commercial agent that war had been declared between Britain and Germany.

He had arrived in Katanga (once famous for its black-maned lions, but now dominated by the Star of the Congo copper mine) on 30 August 1914. By then, a British Expeditionary Force of seventy thousand men had landed in France and been defeated by the Germans at the battle of Mons. It had been an ignominious start to the conflict.

Under normal circumstances, the hunter would have been concerned with selling the ivory he had brought back from German territory, but that seemed unimportant now. He gazed out of the hotel window over the red-dust main street of Elizabethville, with its cafés and bordellos and engineering workshops. A detachment of African soldiers—*askaris* as they were known—was marching up the street, a Belgian officer at their head. The Belgians had come into the War as Britain's allies and these Congolese could be employed against the Germans. With the troops of their Force Publique spread throughout the colony (one of them a *compagnie cycliste*), the Belgians were hard pressed. But they had a chance to attack German East Africa—if only they could cross Lake Tanganyika.

This was now impossible. The last serviceable Belgian steamer on the lake had already been holed by the time the hunter arrived in Katanga. The 90-ton *Alexandre del Commune* had been allowed to leave the German port of Kigoma on the other side of the lake on 6 August. This was two days after the declaration of war, but the port authorities were still uncertain whether the Belgian Congo would remain neutral or not. On 15 August troops from the *Hedwig* had landed on the Belgian side; they had cut telephone cables and destroyed canoes and dhows. On 22 August, as the hunter had been making his way back through the bush to Elizabethville, the *Hedwig* had engaged the *Del Commune* at the mouth of the Lukuga River. In a two-hour battle, the Germans landed two shells on the Belgian ship, damaging its boiler and funnel. Thus disabled, it had withdrawn into the Lukuga.

After the German attack, General Tombeur, Vice-Governor of the Katanga Province, was ordered "to take all measures for the defence of Belgian territory" and to co-operate with British forces in Northern Rhodesia and elsewhere. But the presence of German vessels on Lake Tanganyika and the decommissioning of the *Del Commune* put the General at a major disadvantage. The fact that the *Del Commune* was no longer functional also meant that the British advancing to the south of the lake through Northern Rhodesia could not take offensive action. They had around five thousand men, of whom about half were African conscripts. Many were former policemen, the rest members of the King's African Rifles.

With roughly the same number of troops as the British—and the same division between what they called *polizei askari* and proper soldiers—the Germans had only a slight advantage. It was a naval advantage, the hunter realised.

For some concerted action to be possible, the Allied troops on the lake had to have access to ships. Counting back on his fingers, he worked out that the day the War was declared—4 August—was the very day he had seen the German steamer patrolling the lake. He took it as a kind of omen and with paper and pen he sat down to work out a plan to strike a blow for Britain in the middle of the African continent.

Chapter One

The rectangular patch of gravel in front of the Admiralty had been criss-crossed countless times since the outbreak of hostilities. It is entirely possible that the retired petty-officer doorman paid little attention to the guest who arrived on 21 April 1915. There were, after all, more important matters for a retired petty-officer doorman to consider; not least the impending departure from the Admiralty of the two dynamic but headstrong individuals who were running the place. Namely, the First Lord of the Admiralty Winston Churchill and the First Sea Lord Admiral Fisher. They were clashing bitterly over the military fiasco of the Gallipoli campaign. Both were great men; both would fall because of Churchill's plan to cut short the War with an invasion of western Turkey.

The visitor was tanned and fit and wore civilian clothes, but otherwise there was nothing remarkable about him. His profession sounded glamorous, however. He was a big-game hunter from Africa and he had an appointment to see the Admiral, Sir Henry Jackson.

The story the hunter told would set in train some of the strangest events of the First World War. Their conclusion would make famous—for a while, at least—the navy's most quixotic character since the days of the privateers. Like the hand-made cigarettes he commissioned, his personality was a particular mixture: one that involved as much cowardice as heroism, as much self-regard as self-belief.

This individual's name—inscribed in pale blue on those hand-made cigarettes—was Geoffrey Spicer-Simson and he held the rank of Lieutenant Commander. He was based in the Admiralty when the hunter paid his visit. The doorman would have known this, because the doormen of Whitehall know everything about the workings of government—especially in wartime, the only time when the Whitehall machine works properly. He would have known that Spicer-Simson sat in no great splendour in a barely furnished office somewhere high up in the building.

High up geographically, that is, because Spicer-Simson was actually in disgrace. And there was a good reason—several good reasons, in fact—why a trained naval commander had spent the first eight months of the War in a dusty office containing two chairs, two desks piled with papers and little else, except a stone fireplace without a fire.

Born in Tasmania in 1876, Geoffrey Basil Spicer-Simson was one of five children. Formerly in the merchant navy, their father Frederick Simson was a dealer in gold sovereigns in India who eventually settled in Le Havre, France, at the age of thirty-one. There he met eighteen-year-old Dora Spicer, daughter of a visiting English clergyman,* and on marrying changed his name to Spicer-Simson. In 1874 they moved to Tasmania, having some family there, and ran a sheep farm for five years. Dora didn't care for the colonial life, however, and in 1879 they returned to France. The children were sent to schools in England. The eldest, Theodore, became an artist, moving between France and the United States. The youngest, Noel, eventually joined the British army.

Geoffrey Spicer-Simson entered the Royal Navy at the age of fourteen, embarking on what for a considerable time would be a disastrous career. This was partly due to the eccentricities of his character. Boastful and vain-glorious, by the time war was declared he was well known throughout the officer corps. They generally avoided him. One reason for this was that he took every opportunity to show off his arms and upper torso, which were heavily tattooed with depictions of snakes and butterflies. He liked to brag, too, about his individual bravery in many dangerous adventures. Recounted with a distant, rhapsodic look, most of these tales were lies.

An expert on every subject (even in the presence of genuine experts), Spicer also enjoyed telling jokes (nobody laughed at them) and singing (he was invariably off-key). It is not surprising that his fellow officers thought of him as at best peculiar, at worst downright dangerous. It didn't help that he spoke in a curious manner. Nor that he tended to swagger and throw his weight around. In his groundbreaking history *The Great War in Africa* (1987), Byron Farwell describes Spicer as "a large, muscular, round-shouldered man with thin, close-cropped hair, a Vandyke beard, and light grey eyes, he affected a nasal drawl . . . He indulged in a proclivity for browbeating waiters and others serving on lower rungs of life than his own."

Spicer had always wanted to be a hero. After joining the training ship *Britannia* in 1890 as a cadet, he advanced some way

---

*William Webb Spicer, the rector of Itchen Abbas, near Winchester.

through the ranks, serving in the Gambia and on the China Station, where he made the first hydrographic survey of the Yangtse River. But a series of bumbling errors and catastrophic misjudgements had left him stuck in the naval hierarchy, the oldest lieutenant commander in the navy.

There was, for example, that time during the Channel manoeuvres of 1905 when he suggested it would be a good idea for two destroyers to drag a line strung from one to the other in a periscope-hunting exercise. He nearly sank a submarine. Or there was the time when, in an exercise intended to test the defences of Portsmouth Harbour, he drove his ship on to a nearby beach. He was court-martialled for that.

He was also court-martialled for sinking a liberty boat in a collision, after smashing his destroyer into it. Someone was killed. The incident was reported in the local papers. Lieutenant Commander Spicer-Simson had something of a reputation for disaster.

In August 1914, at the start of the War, Spicer was put in charge of a coastal flotilla consisting of two gunboats and six boarding tugs operating out of Ramsgate. He felt confident enough of the anchorage of his gunboats to come onshore and entertain his wife and some lady friends in a hotel. He could see HMS *Niger,* one of the ships in question, well enough from the window, could he not?

Fate answered this question with a resounding Yes.

Yes, from the window of the hotel bar Spicer could see *Niger* as the Germans torpedoed her. He could watch her sink, too, in just twenty minutes. And going down with her, he could see his hopes of advancement to the highest echelon of the navy disappear beneath the waves.

Such was the state of Spicer's fortunes on 21 April 1915 when a big-game hunter called John Lee arrived at the Admiralty with an appointment to see Sir Henry Jackson. Lee had great experience of Lake Tanganyika. He also had a scheme to bring it under British control. Britain had no ships on the lake and it was not an area Sir

Henry knew anything about, so he was happy to listen to Lee's plan and called for a map.

How did the War stand in April 1915 on the "forgotten front"? The conflict on the plains, lakes and mountains of Central and East Africa had almost slipped from the mind of the British authorities. On a wooden chart table in Admiralty House, Whitehall, Lee showed Sir Henry the lie of the land . . .

Here was German East Africa, comprising the present territory of Tanzania, Rwanda and Burundi. Here were Kenya and Uganda, under British control. So too were the Rhodesias Northern and Southern (now Zambia and Zimbabwe respectively). Further down was South Africa, which was British—though some of the Boers with whom Britain had fought a war between 1899 and 1902 could not be trusted. The South Africans had invaded German South West Africa (now Namibia) at the start of the War. Superior in numbers, by September 1914 the British South Africans had more or less overrun the South-west German territory, though a pro-German rebellion by Boer officers rumbled on until February 1915.

The Germans had more success in East Africa, mainly thanks to their force of *Schütztruppen*. These highly trained units of German officers and African *askaris* respected their commander, a military genius called Paul von Lettow-Vorbeck. In November 1914 he had repelled a British landing of troops from India at the northern Tanganyikan port of Tanga. This was "a major setback for British ambitions in east Africa," as Ross Anderson notes in his 2002 study of the battle—and it left many British guns and other supplies in von Lettow's hands. Another problem was the continuing existence of a big German cruiser called the *Königsberg,* which was hidden in the swamps of the Rufiji delta farther south near Dar es Salaam, the capital of German East Africa.

If we compare the German army marching into Belgium at the start of the War with the African experience a year or so later, we get a sense of how utterly different were the two theatres of conflict.

Here is journalist Richard Harding Davis describing the Germans entering Brussels, mesmerised by their massed grey uniforms:

> It is a grey-green . . . the grey of the hour just before day-break, the grey of unpolished steel, of mist among green trees. I saw it first in the Grande Place in front of the Hôtel de Ville. It was impossible to tell if in that noble square there was a regiment or a brigade. You saw only a fog that melted into the stones, blended with the ancient house fronts, that shifted and drifted, but left nothing at which you could point.

It was, Davis adds, "typical of the German staff striving for efficiency to leave nothing to chance."

In Africa, by contrast, von Lettow's *Schütztruppen*—cut off by British naval power from German supply lines—quickly became a raggedy, make-do outfit that depended on chance and thrived on opportunism. Motor fuel was improvised from cocoa; quinine was brewed from the barks of trees; ammunition was captured from the British. Hippopotamus were shot for their meat and fat, the latter being used to make candles and soap. As Hew Strachan points out (in *The First World War,* 2001), the most important difference between the two theatres was that the individual was not tyrannised, as he was on the western front, by the industrialisation of warfare.

Yet if there was a great material and psychological difference between von Lettow's rag-tag force and the Prussian Junker—the "road-hog of Europe" as Lloyd George once described it—they shared the same philosophy, the same sense of belonging to a military brotherhood. It was an emotional business, as the memoirs of one German captain reveal. Describing the moment when the German army crossed the Rhine into Belgium, Walter Bloem wondered: "Was it real or was I living in a dream, in a fairy-tale, in some heroic epic of the past?"

No stranger himself to such feelings of fraternal heroism, von Lettow had something else, too. Nous, you might call it: that quality of cunning which brings Odysseus home to Ithaca and saves the fox from the hounds. Like Odysseus, von Lettow did not follow a straight line. He made the British chase him all over Central and East Africa.

Nor would Spicer-Simson, on the great journey that was to come, follow straight lines. But he wanted to. He strayed from the path through error, showed nous not by design but by mistake. It was his dream, his hope, to be an epic hero. What kind of hero he turned out to be instead—well, that is what this book hopes to show. It is not necessarily the story of a career in decline, because there was nowhere left for him to fall. Much later, his friend Dr. Hanschell, who would accompany him to Africa, recalled Spicer's dilapidated office in the Intelligence Division of the Admiralty office:

> Light filtered through the upper part of a dusty window and showed its meagre furnishings—a filing cabinet, an empty fire grate with a bare yellow mantelpiece, and above it a signed photograph of His Majesty the King in a heavy frame. There were two swivel armchairs, and two desks piled high with papers—it appeared that it was only the room, and not Spicer, that was in the Intelligence Division, for the papers dealt with the transfer of Merchant Marine Officers and Seamen to the Royal Naval Reserve. A cracked teapot on a tray with two empty cups was perched on a corner of the mantelpiece.*

To Spicer at that time it must have seemed that the First World War was his last chance to make good and win the laurels he longed for. His sculptor brother Theodore Spicer-Simson was famous for his

*Peter Shankland, *The Phantom Flotilla* (1968).

portrait medallions of celebrities such as the conductor Toscanini and the philanthropist Andrew Carnegie. Why shouldn't he have his share of glory too? Why was he now stuck in a desk job in White-hall and not out on the high seas in the thick of the action?

John Lee, the big-game hunter, explained to the Admiral that the Germans had two steamers under military orders on Lake Tanganyika: the 60-ton *Hedwig von Wissmann* and the 45-ton *Kingani*. There were two petrol motor boats as well. One of them, the *Peter,* had been donated to the German forces by the Gesellschaft für Schlaftkrankheitsbekämpfung (The Society for the Fight against Sleeping Sickness). The Germans also had a fleet of dhows and a number of "Boston whalers"—wooden boats based on an American design that were originally brought to East Africa in the early 1900s.

Lee had also heard vague talk of another steamer (his spies among the Holo-holo tribe had definitely said the Germans had three big boats), but he made no particular mention of it to Sir Henry. Nor did the Belgian army intelligence report which Sir Henry commissioned as a follow-up. This omission, as it turned out, would have devastating consequences.

Lee's scheme to attack the German steamers was simple in conception, but difficult in practice: if two British motor boats could be sent to South Africa, up the railway to the Belgian Congo, and dragged through mountains and bush to the lake, they could then sink or disable the *Hedwig* and the *Kingani*. Taking control of Lake Tanganyika in this manner would allow Belgian forces from the Congo and British forces from Kenya and Northern Rhodesia to drive the Germans back to the eastern seaboard. That was the idea, anyway.

In one of the Admiralty's beautifully appointed rooms—all oak panels and heavy chairs and paintings of Drake and Franklin—naval experts quizzed Lee on why it was not better to take much bigger boats. The Germans had taken out the *Hedwig* in sections in 1900, they told him. Why could we not do the same?

The hunter explained that African spies told the Germans everything. If they heard that a big ship was being assembled on the lakeshore they would land and try to damage or destroy it, just as they had done with the Belgian ship *Alexandre del Commune*. This, and associated problems with the supply of parts, was why the Belgians were keeping back their biggest steamer, the *Baron Dhanis,* which remained in pieces at a railhead in the Congolese interior. After great energy and expense in transporting similar sections of a large warship to Africa, the same thing was likely to happen to a British scheme of this nature. The advantage of using light motor boats instead was that they could be put into action the moment they reached the lakeshore.

Accepting this argument, the navy then asked Lee why it was not possible to launch the expedition from British territory in Northern Rhodesia at the lake's southern end, thereby avoiding the likelihood of disagreements with the Belgians. Lee answered that the southern end of the lake was too far from the German base in Kigoma, 200 miles away. The issues were further thrashed out by the War Office, when it discovered that Belgian forces were currently spread out along Lake Tanganyika, trying to keep the Germans at bay. If the Allies could get command of the water, men could easily cross and start attacking the German railway, which came in to Kigoma.

Lee was right; it made sense to attack immediately opposite Kigoma and his route was the best one. Sir Henry ratified the plan, largely on a matter of principle. "It is both the duty and the tradition of the Royal Navy to engage the enemy wherever there is water to float a ship," he noted in a memo.

The only question remaining was who would command the Naval Africa Expedition? Sir Henry sought out candidates, but the service was short of officers. He drew a blank and promptly handed over control of the idea to his junior, Admiral Sir David Gamble. Despite its strategic importance, the war in Africa was still regarded as little more than a sideshow.

Sir Henry could not be blamed for handing on the baton of the Naval Africa Expedition. It must have seemed like a fanciful proposal compared to his other business at the time. The Gallipoli operation had put the navy under a great deal of pressure. Sir Henry had been personally involved in working out the detailed plans for a naval attack there—as opposed to a joint naval and military attack, which is what Churchill had favoured. Sir Henry's boss, the combative and cunning seventy-four-year-old First Sea Lord Admiral Fisher, believed only ships should be used. And Fisher had resigned on 15 May when it became clear that delays and disagreements were provoking errors of judgement. It was taken as read in the House of Commons that Fisher's opposition to landing troops meant the less experienced and impetuous Churchill was wrong to have insisted upon it. And so it seemed. Three days after Lee's visit, Australian and New Zealand troops had landed on the Gallipoli peninsula too late to prevent a strengthening of the Turkish position. Men were dying. Back in White hall, Sir Henry was appointed as the new First Sea Lord.

The affair provoked a crisis in the Liberal war leadership that went to the very heart of British politics. Two days after Fisher's resignation, Prime Minister Asquith announced in Parliament that a Coalition government would be formed comprising both Tories and Liberals. Part of the deal was Churchill's removal from his post as First Lord of the Admiralty, which was insisted upon by one of his fiercest opponents, the Conservative leader Andrew Bonar Law. A "teetotal, chain-smoking Scots-Canadian devotee of the chessboard,"* Bonar Law was one of many to loathe Churchill for crossing the floor and joining the Liberals more than a decade earlier.

---

*Graham Stewart, *Burying Caesar: Churchill, Chamberlain and the Battle for the Tory Party* (London, 1999).

Churchill, who at the end of the year would leave to serve in the trenches, was aware of the planned operation on Lake Tanganyika. Indeed, he would have a role to play in its endgame. But for now he was persona non grata in political circles.

All this was going on, more or less, while Admiral Gamble was planning the Naval Africa Expedition. He had yet to find somebody to take command. As a civilian, Lee was not eligible (though it was pointed out he had served in the Anglo-Boer War). The hunter gladly accepted the position of second in command and immediately set about organising the transport of the boats with South African Railways, and hiring African carriers to help haul them over the mountains in the Congo. He also began selecting members of the Royal Naval Volunteer Reserve (RNVR) who might be suitable for such a venture: men with experience of Africa and machinery.

As well as seeking out various specialists, Lee was also looking for people who could keep their mouths shut. As one of his recruits later recalled: "It was important that no news of the departure or object of the expedition should leak out and get to the enemy. Consequently, officers and men were put on their honour not to divulge, even to their nearest and dearest, where they were bound nor what was their mission."*

Meanwhile Gamble focused on the problem of finding a leader. It seemed a Royal Marines officer would be ideal for an expedition like this, and he began casting about. Most marines were on active service on the high seas, but he happened to look in on a certain major working in the Intelligence Division. Next to the Major—in an office with a cracked teapot and a photograph of the King above an empty grate—sat a man named Spicer-Simson. He was an ordinary naval officer. Or seemed to be.

. . .

*Frank J. Magee in "Transporting a navy through the Jungles of Africa in Wartime," *National Geographic,* October 1922.

"And how do you think I got the command?" Spicer later asked the expedition's medic, Dr. Hother McCormick Hanschell, in that same room one morning a few months later. "Simply by eavesdropping!"

The doctor had known Spicer for a long time. Their wives had been school friends and were reacquainted by chance when both couples were staying at a hotel off London's Russell Square. He knew Spicer well and he also knew, in the words of that brilliant naval historian Peter Shankland (who interviewed Dr. Hanschell at length shortly before he died in 1968), how "mischievous fortune seemed to invest everything he did with a faint tinge of absurdity." Everyone seemed to know this, actually, which explained why Spicer was the oldest lieutenant commander in the navy. Or had been. For the purposes of the Naval Africa Expedition, he'd been promoted to acting commander.

Given his chequered career, it is surprising that Spicer was ever considered for the post, let alone given it. Perhaps Sir David saw some streak of heroism in Spicer hitherto unperceived or perhaps, as seems more likely, there was simply nobody else available. In any case, promotion meant Spicer was at long last permitted to wear gilded oak leaves on his cap. He had coveted them for so long. And perhaps, while setting his newly adorned cap on his head the moment it came back from Gieves (later Gieves and Hawkes), the naval tailors in Bond Street, Spicer smiled at his mirror image. Things were going to turn out just fine. The years of romancing were over. At last he could be what he had always known he could be: the best of men.

Or maybe not. When Spicer invited Dr. Hanschell to join his African expedition, the Major who shared that spartan office tapped his temple while Spicer was speaking, implying he was mad. He was probably right. But Africa was an exciting proposition and a man had to do his duty in wartime. Dr. Hanschell accepted and his first responsibility the next day was to visit a Lieutenant Higgins, one of the men Lee had selected, who was ill.

Spicer had sworn the doctor to absolute secrecy, so when he

returned home the night after he had accepted the job, he told his wife only that he was joining Spicer on an expedition abroad.

"Oh, didn't he tell you, dear?" she replied. "You're going to Lake Tanganyika via Rhodesia and the Congo River. Amy Spicer-Simson telephoned me this afternoon and we had a long talk about it."

The following day Dr. Hanschell did his best with Lieutenant Higgins, but it was hopeless. The man had blackwater fever from a previous tour of duty as a mining engineer in Africa. He died the day after. It did not seem a good omen for the Naval Africa Expedition; but the doctor was a strict rationalist and did not believe in omens. Undeterred, he threw himself into the task of collecting the necessary medical supplies for the expedition.

They would be entering dangerous territory: tropical jungle, savannah bush, formidable mountains. Some of the most difficult terrain in the world, in fact, and it was blighted by malaria, the tsetse fly (*Glossina palpalis,* conduit of the sleeping-sickness germ) and a thousand amoebic horrors that made a home of the human gut. The doctor knew his amoebas. Prior to his appointment to the team, he had spent some time in West Africa's Gold Coast (Ghana) researching the causes of yellow fever. While there, he had contracted amoebic dysentery and it had never quite gone away.

Chapter Two

In London during the summer of 1915, Spicer embraced the Tanganyika project with gusto. All the torpor and guilty self-laceration of the past few years was forgotten at a stroke. Perhaps he knew this was his last chance—that there was no other way of becoming a hero than going to Africa and making a successful expedition.

First of all he fitted out the two motor boats that had been chosen for the operation. They were 40-foot motor launches, made of mahogany, both about eight feet wide. They had two propellers each, driven by 100-horsepower petrol engines. Originally designed as tenders for the Greek seaplane service, they were part of a batch of eight made before the War by the famous boat-builders Thorneycroft, who kept a yard at Twickenham on the Thames. One boat

was there, the other in Dundee, whence it was swiftly commandeered and brought up to London.

At this stage the boats were merely numbered, and it fell to
Spicer to name them. He suggested—they were very small—that
they be christened *Cat* and *Dog*. The navy was not amused, so
Spicer went back to the drawing board. They had to be named, after
all, for they would be the smallest ever vessels to be distinguished by
the title His Majesty's Ship. But what would follow the HMS? It
was just the sort of topic to which Spicer liked to apply his febrile
imagination: the same imagination that had so far blighted his
career with madcap schemes that ended in disaster.

But there was also another issue outstanding. There still weren't
enough men. In spite of the need for secrecy, further word was put
out among members of the RNVR. One by one, over a period of
weeks, hearing of the plan through diverse routes, prospective members of the team came to see Spicer at the Admiralty to be signed up.

The retired petty officer who kept the door at the Admiralty
grew to recognise members of "the Tanganyika Party," as he called
them. They were an outlandish lot, catching the eye as they went
back and forth for briefings.

Here was fifty-something Sub-Lieutenant Tyrer with his canary-
yellow hair, who'd previously been in the Royal Naval Air Service.
One of the earliest British aviators, he was addicted to Worcester
sauce—as an aperitif. Tyrer was a handsome man, but spoilt the
effect by wearing a monocle and addressing people with the prefix
"Dear Boy," even if (like the retired petty-officer doorman) they
were several years older than him.

Next up the steps was "Tubby" Eastwood, a short man with a
neat round face. He was once a travel agent at the offices of Thomas
Cook in Elizabethville in the Belgian Congo, which was on the
expedition's route. Taken on as the team's paymaster and Spicer's
confidential clerk, Eastwood was a genial fellow. He was also an
ardent Methodist and animal-lover.

A former racing driver, Chief Engineer Lieutenant Cross had twice won the Grand Prix, though he actually knew almost nothing about the workings of the internal combustion engine. Appositely named, he took offence easily and would become the butt of jokes during the expedition. Cross's senior Engine-Room Artificer (ERA) was John Lamont, a Glaswegian and an equally prickly character: he was a sportsman, too, having been a famous oarsman in Scotland before the war. Among the junior ERAs was one William Cobb. He and Lamont were the only ones who really understood how the boats' engines worked.

Lieutenant Wainwright would be Transport Officer. A Belfast man originally, he had worked on the railway that came from Beira in Portuguese East Africa (now Mozambique) inland to Rhodesia, where he had a cattle farm. He had been a labourer once, then driven locomotives, and he loved steam engines with a passion. Wainwright was in charge of the traction engines that would pull the boats part of the way. He was about forty-five, with a sharp nose and light brown hair. He would become known by the junior members of the expedition as "Old Loco Driver," but he was respected by everyone. Intelligent and inquisitive, Wainwright became great friends with Dr. Hanschell in particular.

Dr. Hanschell was born in Bridgetown, Barbados, in 1880. He was part of the Hanschell shipping and distilling family, makers of Cockspur rum. During his childhood there he became fascinated by the navy. He remembered fondly the time he had been allowed aboard HMS *Tourmaline* in the harbour and climbed to the top-sail, coming home with ship's tar on his hands and knees. He was later sent to Britain to be educated at Malvern College, Worcestershire. After qualifying at St. Bartholomew's medical school in London, he returned briefly to the Caribbean. He was Acting Port Medical Officer in Bridgetown in 1907–8. In 1913–14 he was a member of the Colonial Office Commission on Yellow Fever in the Gold Coast.

Prior to his appointment to Spicer's team, Hanschell was back in London and holding down two jobs. He was both Acting Medical Superintendent of the Seamen's Hospital in the Royal Albert Dock at Wapping and Senior Demonstrator at the School of Tropical Medicine. The doctor had a precise mouth, searching eyes and an odd way with sideburns, which were cut off at angles high above the ear. While working in London he had lived quietly with his wife in Muswell Hill. Spicer and his wife Amy sometimes visited—Amy bringing along her husband's socks to darn as they chatted in the comfortable front room.

Also on the team was Frank Magee. A "half-scalliwag Fleet Street adventurer," according to Dr. Hanschell, Magee had covered the Anglo-Boer War for the Northcliffe newspapers, the *Daily Mail* and the *Evening Standard*. One of Magee's first jobs was for Hannen Swaffer, the spiritualist and "Pope of Fleet Street," then with the *Daily Mirror*. Swaffer once told Magee to go and be the first to climb Mont Blanc that season. He was to plant a *Daily Mirror* flag at the summit for a picture story. Magee was given expenses of only £20. Reaching Chamonix, he realised the expedition would cost far more, so he sent a begging telegram to the *Mirror*. Swaffer wired back: "The greater the task, the greater the glory," but sent no money. Magee wired another telegram: "God Alps those who Alp themselves. Send £100."

The money was sent. A week or so later a report came back that Magee had been killed in an avalanche while climbing the mountain. Swaffer and his colleagues were just clubbing together to buy a wreath when the man himself walked through the door of the newspaper's offices in London. Asked by Swaffer what his thoughts were when the avalanche came sweeping down, Magee said: "I offered up a prayer that I might return safely to give you a kick in the pants for sending me on such an awful journey."

Magee carried a letter from Lord Northcliffe informing whomsoever it may concern that he had seen a great deal of active service. He was commissioned Petty Officer Writer and would take charge of clerical and photographic duties on the expedition. He would later write it up for the October 1922 issue of the *National Geo-*

graphic magazine. The other main sources for the story are Peter Shankland's *The Phantom Flotilla* (based on taped interviews with Dr. Hanschell) and a lecture given by Spicer himself to the Royal United Services Institute in London.*

Chief Gunlayer was to be James Waterhouse from Birmingham. Quiet and unflappable, he was self-possessed to a fault. You could never tell what he was thinking, which unnerved some members of the expedition. He was tall and dark, with bushy eyebrows and sharp lines either side of his nose and mouth. Waterhouse would take charge of the guns that were to be mounted on the motor boats—far too much weight for such small vessels, it might be supposed, but there was no point in going all that way and having insufficient firepower to finish the job. He would be assisted on the guns by Petty Officer Flynn.

Among the ratings was a tall, muscular fisherman from Donegal whose name has not survived in naval records, many of which were destroyed in a Luftwaffe bombing raid during the Second World War. This intriguing character appears at crucial moments in Shankland's account of the journey. His flaming red hair and very pale skin distinguished him among the crew—as did his habit, when speaking about his wife, of calling her "mother."†

Most of these men were recommended by friends and colleagues of Spicer or Lee. One or two, however, heard about the expedition through less orthodox routes. They included Tait and Mollison, two hulking Scotsmen who learned of the mission in a West End bar and went straight round to the Admiralty to volunteer. They were lance corporals of the London Scottish Regiment and had played for its rugby team. Tait had lost a finger at Ypres, and both men mostly wore kilts.

Some of the members of the expedition knew each other. Tait

---

*"The Operations on Lake Tanganyika in 1915," given on 28 March 1934 at 3 p.m. Reprinted in the *Journal of the Royal United Services Institute,* Vol. 79, 1934.
†It is possible he was William Carey from Buncrana, who later served on the royal yacht *Ilona* and died in 1918.

had certainly come across the eccentric, monocle-wearing Tyrer before, telling Dr. Hanschell that the barmaids at London's Criterion Restaurant called Tyrer "the Piccadilly Johnny with the glass eye." Perhaps it was at the Criterion that Tait and Mollison overheard talk of the expedition, which was supposed to be top secret. The two giant Scotsmen didn't speak much throughout the adventure. They simply carried out their orders and gave the impression they didn't care about much except their next meal, which they always consumed with great eagerness, whatever the ingredients. And so Tait and Mollison joined the rest of the expedition, most of whom were billeted in the old monkey-house at Crystal Palace.

The palace, at Sydenham in south London,* had become the headquarters of the Royal Naval Volunteer Reserve a week after the declaration of war. Thousands of men slept in hammocks in its courts and rooms, doing physical training and marching about among its statuary. It must have been a strange experience. Stray cats prowled in the echoey building, making hideous cries at night, and jokers put clothes and masks on the statues—Venus wearing slacks and Cupid sporting a beard. Vast chess championships took place in the Egyptian Court under effigies of the Pharaohs. In the evening the sailors danced to the Crystal Palace Band, doing hornpipes and rag-times with each other for half an hour before turning in.

As they left the Admiralty and went down the Mall, the Tanganyika party would no doubt have admired Brock's new statue of Captain Cook, who stood on a stone pedestal with ships' prows protruding at the sides. Cook was an inspiration, but he might also have made some of them think twice. After all, there was no less danger in their African enterprise than Cook had faced on the beach in Hawaii where he met his end.

---

*The Crystal Palace was originally in Hyde Park, housing the Great Exhibition of 1851, after which a group of enterprising promoters took it to pieces and transported it to south London. It burned down in 1936, possibly due to a fault in electrical wiring, leaving nothing but a tangled mass of metal and melted glass.

Only a fool would set foot in the Congo's pathless wilderness unthinkingly. Only a fool would believe that pitting HMS *Mimi* and HMS *Toutou* (as Spicer had finally christened the motor boats) against the Germans on the lake was not a truly desperate endeavour. The fact that it was an impossible adventure, a very British kind of stunt, did not lessen the probability that somebody would die. Even if, by some miracle, death were avoided, there was still the very real danger of fever and other considerable hardships.

As Hew Strachan points out: "East Africa was home to the anopheles mosquito, the tsetse fly, the jigger flea, the spirillum tick, the white ant, the scorpion, the poisonous spider, the wild bee, and the warrior ant. The range of larger fauna provided more than an exotic backdrop to the fighting. Soldiers, if sick or sleeping, were liable to be eaten by lions or hyenas; both elephants and rhinoceroses were known to attack patrols, with fatal consequences."[*]

It is perhaps indicative of how things would turn out that the expedition split up while it was still being assembled. John Lee returned to South Africa in the middle of May, before Spicer had even met him. The big-game hunter was accompanied by the reporter, Frank Magee. They were followed shortly after by two others, Douglas Hope and Reginald Mullin, respectively a captain from the War Office and a mechanic from the Thorneycroft yard. Hope and Mullin took with them a three-ton lorry, which they would put on the train from South Africa to the Congo. The advance party also carried some other "stores," as the navy phrase goes. These included thirty-six long "Marine's" rifles, three acetylene searchlights and some mines to blow up the stacks of firewood the Germans kept at various points along the lake to fuel their ships.

The Admiralty accepted the names *Mimi* and *Toutou* for the launches. As Spicer later explained to his crew, they meant "Miaow" and "Bow-wow" in French, but nobody found this quite so amusing as he did. In the meantime he had the motor boats

*The First World War (2001).

altered for the job in hand, cutting their height so they could go faster. Maxim machine-guns were mounted aft and three-pounder Hotchkiss guns fixed in the bows. The mounting of the Hotchkiss guns made the centre of gravity in the boats too high, so they also had to be cut down. This meant, says Spicer, "that the gun-layer, instead of standing at the gun, had to kneel down to fire it. Anyone who has ever handled a Hotchkiss gun will realise how much more difficult it is to fire from a kneeling than from a standing position."* Spicer had the petrol tanks lined with extra steel sheeting to deflect bullets—if they were ignited the wooden boats, with their ⅜-inch mahogany hulls, would go up in a flash. The sheets helped compensate for the weight of the guns forward.

To Spicer's design, the Thorneycroft yard made some special trailers on which *Mimi* and *Toutou* could be carried overland, and cradles in which the whole ensemble could be shipped by sea or rail. There was some disagreement between Spicer and the Thorneycroft engineers about the design of the cradles. Certain details, he says, "were altered by the experts, who assured me that the light wheels they put fore and aft and the six-inch-by-two-inch supporting beam would be quite adequate to stand any strains likely to be thrown on them. I had stuck out for a twelve-inch beam . . ."†

On 8 June it was agreed: the boats and guns would be tested on the Thames at Chiswick. *Mimi* and *Toutou* looked rather forbidding now with their forecastles removed and the big guns in place. Various members of the team, including Engineer Cross and the dour Chief Petty Officer Waterhouse, joined in the tests. Amy Spicer-Simson even went along for the ride. In a wide-brimmed hat she sat like Cleopatra in the bows of *Mimi* as the spray flew up on either side. *Toutou* followed close behind as they made their way downriver.

Spicer had obtained a licence to fire a practice shell from the

---

*RUSI lecture, 1934.
† Ibid

three-pounder into an old dockside (actually a disused yard of Messrs. Thorneycroft, the boats' manufacturers). What happened, when the moment came, would in some way set the tone for the whole expedition. As *Mimi* went past the dock at full throttle Waterhouse took aim and fired. The round hit its target—but the gun and Waterhouse flew off the boat and into the Thames. It had not been properly locked to the deck.

The following day *Mimi* and *Toutou* were driven to Tilbury to be loaded on board the liner *Llanstephen Castle,* bound for Cape Town on 15 June. The main party would join the ship on the day it sailed.

The week prior to their departure saw the various members of the expedition collecting the kit and personal items they would take with them. Dr. Hanschell had ordered his medical stores using an antiquated Admiralty stocklist. He was not very happy with the proposed material, as most of it came from a pamphlet entitled *Medical Stores as Supplied to Gunboats West Africa Station,* dated 1898.

Each member of the expedition was issued with a camp bed and a woollen Jaeger sleeping bag. Only Spicer had a tent—everyone else would sleep under the stars. Tarpaulins were ordered to protect petrol and ammunition from the heat of the sun. For his own protection, each man had a solar topi. Many African veterans believed these to be essential between the hours of 8 a.m. and 4 p.m., although lately there had been a movement in favour of the felt hat.

A Union Jack was ordered for ceremonial purposes and spare cutlasses in case any officer should lose his own. Meals were to be eaten off folding tables and chairs and the main source of protein was canned beef. Concerned about nutrition, Dr. Hanschell took precautions against beriberi by bringing plenty of tinned tomatoes, too. A large number of razor blades were also brought—as much for trading with the Africans as to enable the men to shave each day. A few bicycles were packed—up-to-date models with milometers— and some spare parts. Weapons included shotguns and .303 rifles. Spicer had a Webley revolver. He also took a pair of binoculars—an item that would be associated with him later, when Holo-holo tribesmen made his effigy in clay.

Unfortunately Spicer forgot to order food stores for Lukuga,* which he should have logged with the Director of Naval Victualling. However, he did remember to pick up a supply of personally mono-grammed cigarettes from the army and navy stores. He also had his own supply of sherry and vermouth. To trim his beard, the Commander took along his favourite set of cut-throat razors.

Tyrer had his cases of Worcester sauce and a liqueur glass from which to drink it. He packed some hair-dye, too: the canary-yellow shade was achieved by chemical means. Dr. Hanschell had a pair of long leather mosquito boots, a set of Jane Austen and the *Oxford Book of English Verse* (the 1900 Quiller-Couch edition). The Donegal seaman had pencil and paper with which to write to his "mother." Several members of the expedition brought slippers to wear in camp in the evening and white flannel shirts that could, similarly, be put on after a long day. Boots were generally leather, army-issue type, though some of the volunteers took along more modern footwear with crêpe rubber soles. Additional items included hurricane lamps, electric torches and compasses with luminous dials. Beads and lengths of cloth were also taken, in what was now a time-honoured tradition, for "trading with the natives."

Much to the bemusement of onlooking Londoners, the expedition paraded at St. Pancras railway station before taking the train to Tilbury. Spicer had designed a special uniform for such ceremonial occasions, consisting of army khaki tunics (short sleeved and belted at the waist), grey flannel shirts and navy-blue ties. Each officer, even Dr. Hanschell, carried a naval cutlass. Spicer insisted upon this, tearing a strip off the doctor when he questioned the point of a medic wearing such an item. Dressed mostly in this manner the men lined up under the Victorian Gothic portals of St. Pancras. The

*Their destination on the lake, it was later christened Albertville by the Belgians. It is now called Kalemie.

effect cannot have been quite what Spicer intended, given that the ratings were in bell-bottomed sailor's trousers or khaki shorts, and Tait and Mollison wore kilts. He marched up and down the line all the same, carefully inspecting each man.

This performance was repeated on the quay at Tilbury, whereupon Spicer marched his men up the gangplank of the *Llanstephen Castle:* to the suppressed laughter of the liner's merchant navy officers. Some of the passengers were not so amused, complaining to the captain at this use of the ship for military purposes. Surely it made them more liable to be torpedoed by German U-boats, as had happened to the *Lusitania* the previous month.

That event, which took more than a thousand lives to the bottom of the sea, puts the scale of the Naval Africa Expedition in some perspective. So, too, does the situation on the Western Front in June 1915 as Spicer's twenty-eight-man team was embarking. Every day, close-ranked units of troops were being cut to ribbons by machine-gun fire as they tried to advance over fields of mud. The mud was caused not by the weather but by the pounding of heavy shells. At Ypres in April the Germans had used poison gas for the first time, releasing it from canisters whose arrival through the air would send troops into panicked retreat.

It seemed as though the Germans were winning. Their dugouts, their steel helmets and most of all their guns were of better quality. In Africa, too, their superiority was evident, though their rifles were mainly old, puff-smoke things—1871-pattern weapons that used black powder and easily gave away a soldier's position in the bush. Still the Germans were victorious and for a very simple reason: their commander von Lettow knew what he was about and the British did not.

The battle of Tanga the previous November was a case in point. Two brigades of the Indian army dispatched by ship from Karachi, hoping to take the port of Tanga in the north of German East Africa at the end of their voyage, had suffered a shameful defeat because of poor organisation and bad planning. That battle was the beginning of a long, fiercely fought campaign by von Lettow, which would outlast the war in Europe.

The campaign had a naval element, as the British were trying to ensure naval supremacy in the Indian Ocean. Von Lettow, meanwhile, was desperate to supply his men from Germany. That June, he had only one way of protecting a cargo ship. It was the wily *Königsberg*, the heavily armed German cruiser, still hiding out in the sinuous green curves of the Rufiji delta. But the British were determined to take it from him.

The Admiralty had ordered the *Königsberg*'s destruction— orders picked up by the *Königsberg*'s radio operators on their own aerials. Forewarned is forearmed, as they say. Two shallow-draught British ships, the *Severn* and the *Mersey*—both originally intended for the Gallipoli landings—had arrived off the Tanganyikan coast on 3 June ready to hunt the German ship out of its river maze.

This operation would eventually involve Spicer's men in ways none of them could have anticipated as they boarded the *Llanstephen Castle* that bright June day in 1915. Their destination was nearly a thousand miles away from the *Königsberg* on the other side of German East Africa, closer to the copper mines of the Congo and the Mountains of the Moon than the crocodile-infested waters of the Rufiji.

Chapter Three

Vibrating at great volume—rocking and swelling, rumbling and gurgling—the *Llanstephen Castle* was making her own preparations. It was like something boiling in a saucepan. Down the side of the vessel, visible from her promenade deck, a foam of pumps disturbed the water. Fish gathered in the warmth, tumbling about in the exhausts, and young lads threw lines off the wharf, hoping to catch them. She threw up such a symphony of departure as was typical for ships of her class at that time. The siren sounded—a prolonged, ear-blasting note—and then a shout went up.

"Any more for the shore? Any more?" as the last non-passenger scrambled down the gangplank.

Those familiar with the ship would have noticed two strange shapes cowled in tarpaulin on the foredeck: *Mimi* and *Toutou*, late of Twickenham and Dundee, denied to the Greek seaplane service by wartime necessity. They were lying in their special cradles, which the ship's merchant seamen had lashed to the deck. These carriages were squares of timber "carcassing" that created a shell round the boats, with criss-cross struts on either side for extra strength. Inside the cradles, the boats' hulls sat on rubber tyres to protect them.

Half an hour after the gangplank had been lifted, the liner left her moorings. Towed by a tug, she was pulled out into the main stream of the Thames. The men of the Naval Africa Expedition watched the spectators at the pier fade into the distance and soon the grey buildings of the Tilbury docks were shrinking too. Then the lines of tugs and barges and even the cranes that had towered over them were gone. Soon England itself would be just a memory. Perhaps it was already, as the men's heads crowded with images of their destination: the dazzling seas, the orange suns, the acacia trees of Africa.

The expedition might also have been conscious of the voice of history at Tilbury—for it was here that Queen Elizabeth had reviewed English troops when the Spanish Armada threatened. But as the ship sailed, the voice that echoed loudest in their ears was that of Spicer. He was telling Dr. Hanschell not to worry about the expedition's medical supplies, which had not arrived in time to be loaded.

"We don't need more than a little quinine, do we? I never had more than that on the Yangtze or in Gambia. We can buy some more in Cape Town. The bar's open—come and have a drink!"

The doctor obliged, though he was still very worried about the missing drugs. And so, the Naval Africa Expedition—commanded by a man who had yet to reveal his more eccentric qualities—was on its way at last.

Suddenly it seemed terribly important to the Government. Maybe they had realised what Sir Henry had sensed: that control of Lake Tanganyika meant control of a vast swathe of Central Africa. Maybe they were beginning to see that unless Lee's plan worked, a nightmare possibility could emerge. If victorious in Africa, the

Kaiser could conscript hundreds of thousands of African troops—the *askaris*—to fight in the trenches of Europe. Many colonial troops already fought in the trenches, but complete strategic control of Africa would have taken this to an unprecedented level. There was even the spectre of a great army of *askaris* marching up through Egypt.

As the *Llanstephen Castle* left Tilbury a message arrived at the Admiralty from Winston Churchill's old enemy Bonar Law, now at the Colonial Office: *When would operations on Lake Tanganyika start? Can they be speeded up?* Von Lettow had been moving troops up and down the lake in steamers, attacking British and Belgian positions at will from his base in Kigoma, the lake's main port. One minute he seemed to be in Burundi, the next in Rhodesia. How was he moving about so quickly?

No one seemed able to answer this question, though the reason would emerge soon enough. The Belgians were more concerned about potential friction between their officers on the lake and Spicer than with giving the British the full picture. Through Bonar Law, they insisted the following phrase be inserted in Spicer's orders: "You will work in harmony with the Belgian Military Authorities, giving them such aid as may be in your power." However, by that time Spicer was well away, entertaining Dr. Hanschell in the bar.

As the liner approached the sea, the tug prepared to cast off. Watching through a porthole as he sipped his drink, Dr. Hanschell noticed a motor launch come alongside. A petty officer climbed up the ship's ladder and one of the crew began hauling up bundles of half-tied cardboard boxes in a net. The doctor realised they were his medical supplies and went outside to sign for them. The petty officer handed him an invoice, then climbed back down and sped off in his launch.

A relieved Dr. Hanschell returned to the bar with this news. Only later, when he opened the packages with Eastwood to check them against the invoice, did he realise that most of the medicines and other equipment he had ordered were missing. He retired to bed feeling rather bitter. There weren't even any splints . . .

At 17 miles an hour, with *Mimi* and *Toutou* safely tied to its deck, the *Llanstephen Castle* steamed south. Spicer's men were allowed a brief respite from their duties as they mingled with other passengers and settled into the pattern of life at sea on a liner. This was beautifully described by Winston Churchill, who had made the same trip to Cape Town just over a decade before, on another ship of the Castle line:

> Monotony is the characteristic of a modern voyage, and who shall describe it? The lover of realism might suggest that writing the same paragraph over and over again would enable the reader to experience its weariness, if he were truly desirous of so doing. But I hesitate to take such a course, and trust that some of these lines even once repeated may convey some inkling of the dullness of the days. Monotony of view—for we live at the centre of a complete circle of sea and sky; monotony of food—for all things taste the same on board ship; monotony of existence—for each day is but a barren repetition of the last; all fall to the lot of the passenger on great waters.

However, Churchill also admits that "even monotony is not without its secret joy":

> For a time we drop out of the larger world, with its interests and its obligations, and become the independent citizens of a tiny state—a Utopian State where few toil and none go hungry—bounded on all sides by the sea and vassal only to the wind and waves. Here during a period which is too long

while it lasts, too short when it is over, we may placidly reflect on the busy world that lies behind and the tumult that is before us.*

If the Utopia of the *Llanstephen Castle* had a king, it was Spicer. Every evening in the bar, he would hold forth on his skill in hunting big game. Dr. Hanschell, who had cheered up on discovering a beautiful brass microscope among his supplies, remembered one night in particular. It is a scene worth picturing . . .

Before his usual audience of cooing widows and impressionable young men, Spicer is looking glamorous in full-dress uniform. He has his cutlass buckled on and, in his hand, his silver-topped black cane as a prop. The lines of care around his eyes have been temporarily transformed. No longer do they express the dashed hopes of a man whose career has failed, but instead call to mind a life of adventure and an accumulation of escapes from tight spots in the great outdoors. They bespeak the wisdom born of experience—and this is Spicer's theme, which he warms to with thespian vigour. He is telling a tale of his days as a gunboat captain on the Gambia River in West Africa:

"The rhino threw up his head, breathing heavily with rage . . . In an instant, with a sound like thunder, he was pounding straight for me! You know I have my ammunition specially made for me and my finely tempered bullets went right through the animal from stem to stern, piercing lungs, heart, spleen and liver on the way."

The widows cluck in amazement while the doctor looks aside in embarrassment. He knows there are no rhino to be found in the Gambia, except perhaps in a zoo, if the Gambia had any zoos. But Spicer is untroubled by mere facts as the professional hunter in him gives way to the concerned zoologist.

"I was really sorry I had to kill him, for these animals are becoming increasingly rare, but of course I had to in self-defence.

*Winston Churchill, *London to Ladysmith via Pretoria* (Longman, 1900).

His horn was exceptionally long—about 27 inches, as I recollect. Anyway, it was so remarkable that I presented it to the Natural History Museum."

Dr. Hanschell was surprised that Spicer's nose did not grow equally long, Pinocchio-like, at this tall tale. Surely he ought to have been preparing for the task ahead, rather than indulging in such foolish exhibitions of boasting? The Commander didn't even have a proper map and had shown the doctor where they were going in a Bartholomew's school atlas, tracing a finger down the long blue streak of the great lake.

Throughout the nineteenth century control of Lake Tanganyika and the area around it had been in some doubt. A Congolese tribe, the warlike Holo-holo, had settled on the shore, ousting the other African tribes that had been there since ancient times. The Holo-holo were superstitious as well as fierce. Their supreme god was Kabedya Mpungu ("Remote in the Sky"), to whom appeals were made through witch doctors, secret societies and intermediary spirits. Until the arrival of the Arabs, the crossing of the lake by the Holo-holo was the biggest political change the region had seen. The Holo-holo were themselves reacting to the expansion of the Luba tribe in the Congo. They brought with them the practice of ordeal by poison and of drowning newborn babies whose top teeth happened to grow first. Arab slave parties began arriving on the lakeshore from 1820; they employed the Holo-holo to guard the slaves and shipments of gold and ivory.

And then the whites came. Among European travellers it was the British explorers Burton and Speke who first reached Lake Tanganyika. Starting from Zanzibar and following the caravan route, they arrived in January 1858. Not content with being the world's longest freshwater lake,* Lake Tanganyika is also the world's second deepest lake and the lowest point in Africa below sea level. It

---

*About 420 miles or, as Spicer put it in his lecture, "as long as England from Southampton to the Scottish border." The average width of the lake is 31 miles.

has evolved utterly separately, even from the other great African lakes of the Rift, and its depths contain innumerable unique forms of life. "It filled us with admiration, wonder and delight," wrote Burton on first seeing it:

> Beyond a short foreground of rugged and precipitous hill-fold, down which the footpath painfully zigzags, a narrow plot of emerald green shelves gently towards a ribbon of glistening yellow sand, here bordered by sedgy rushes, there clear and cleanly cut by the breaking wavelets. Farther in front stretches an expanse of lightest, softest blue, from thirty to thirty-five miles in breadth, and sprinkled by the east wind with crescents of snowy foam.

In the so-called scramble for Africa that took place in the last two decades of the nineteenth century, it was Germany that won Tanganyika and its lake. Britain seized neighbouring Kenya and Uganda. Through a series of sham treaties, the Belgians had already taken the Congo in the 1870s. Many of these treaties were arranged by Stanley, whose activities on behalf of the Belgian king Leopold had spurred on the other powers, especially Germany. Covering roughly the present area of Tanzania, plus Rwanda and Burundi, German East Africa was established in 1885. It would be administered by the Deutsche Ostafrikanische Gesellschaft (German East African Company) until 1890 and thereafter by the Imperial Government. On the far western side of the territory lay the inland sea of Lake Tanganyika.

Despite the takeover by the Government, German East Africa Inc. had proved a profitable enterprise. Between 1900 and 1913, the value of German exports from Tanganyika had risen from 4 million to 27 million marks. The products sent out of the country, in wooden crates bound for Hamburg, included cotton, sisal, coffee, tea and tobacco.

Of these, cotton was the most important. Indeed, its significance in the story of German East Africa cannot be overestimated, though to understand why takes some unpacking. One of the reasons is cotton's qualities as a material. A fabric with a long staple and great resilience, it can be mechanically processed more easily than wool, silk or linen. It was the first fabric to switch from hand- to machine-weaving in Germany, yet even as late in the Industrial Revolution as 1873 the Germans lagged far behind Britain and America in cotton production. By the turn of the century, establishing a secure national supply had become a matter of national pride for Germany, which never again wanted to submit to the indignities of having to pay hiked-up prices for cotton, as she had done during the Napoleonic wars and the American Civil War.

Even in peacetime, German industrialists like Karl Supf, a Bremen factory owner, resented having to pay what he described as an "annual tribute" to Britain and America. Powerful figures such as Imperial Chancellor Bismarck advocated independence of supply, and the Colonial Office and industrialists like Supf were constantly agitating for it.

They had a point. In 1900, 80 per cent of Germany's cotton was imported from the United States. The remaining 20 per cent they bought from the British: Germany's main rival for global power. It was decided that Germany would henceforth satisfy her cotton needs with production in the newly established colony of German East Africa. Supf, a colonial enthusiast, emphasised the political benefits of this new economic enterprise. Cotton could be a means of control: "Becoming economic master of our colonies depends basically on our succeeding to make the natives dependent on us. Indeed, the economic dependence of the inhabitants will make us real masters of our colonies. The introduction of cotton cultivation as a peasant culture seems to be a very appropriate means of teaching the natives to work while making them at the same time dependent on us."

German-American experts were brought in to oversee the new venture in Tanganyika. For four years from 1902, a harsh system of agricultural imposition was put in place, as native Africans were persuaded to grow cotton (from foreign seed) through a mixture of threatened and actual violence as well as punitive taxation—measures that eventually provoked the Maji-Maji rebellion of 1905–7.

One of the cotton-growing areas was to the north-east of Lake Tanganyika—the destination of Spicer and his men. Tanganjikasee, as the Germans called the lake, was well stocked with fish, hippopotamus and crocodile, but its main appeal was strategic. During the early 1900s, as the colony developed, the Kaiser was keen to extend his empire farther into Central and East Africa. He saw clearly how modern transport could bring remote regions as yet unconquered into his orbit. In 1904 he began building a railway through the centre of German East Africa. The *Mittellandbahn*, as it was known, would link the capital Dar es Salaam with the port of Kigoma on Lake Tanganyika—effectively connecting the Indian Ocean in the east to the Congolese border in the west.

No one doubted the *Mittellandbahn*'s importance. As *The Times* of Tuesday 29 December 1914 put it: "The great value of the railway as an economic factor lies in the fact that it borders on three great inland seas—Nyassa, Tanganyika and Victoria Nyanza—thus linking up the great lake system of Central Africa and the River Congo with the east coast ports . . . One thing is certain—had the great conflagration in Europe not taken place we should have clashed with Germany in Africa. Our Central African and the east coast trade would have been in jeopardy, and our power would have gradually declined east of the 25th parallel."

The railway was especially useful in the matter of transporting ships to the lake, which hitherto had required African labour. In 1900, setting off from Dar es Salaam, a team of 5,000 porters had carried the 60-ton *Hedwig von Wissmann*—the ship John Lee had seen—to Kigoma. This port town would later become the centre of German maritime operations in the west, under the command of

Kapitän zur See ("Sea Captain") Gustav Zimmer, the man destined to be Spicer's strategic rival on the lake.

This was the context in which Lee's plan was to be made operational. Not that Spicer regarded it as Lee's plan any more. He liked to intimate that he had already been studying just such a plan when Lee came up with his. Spicer had never met Lee, but he was quite prepared to hold forth on him to Dr. Hanschell in the early days of their voyage to Cape Town.

"Lee is one of those chaps one meets all over Africa," he told the doctor, "doing a bit of shooting, prospecting, contracting for native labour and so on—a bit of a tramp, in fact. What they call a 'stiff' over there."

As far as the Admiralty was concerned, who came up with the plan was immaterial. They just wanted it completed as soon as possible. At the heart of Spicer's orders was the instruction to capture, sink or otherwise disable the *Hedwig von Wissmann*.

It was supposedly a secret mission, although Kapitän Zimmer's memoirs reveal that he knew there was a British naval expedition on its way to the lake by late May 1915: before it had even set off! How this could be is still unclear. In any case, Zimmer had no good reason to fear any British boats, having a trump card up his sleeve. He was more concerned at rumours that the Belgians were trying to build an iron-panelled steamer, the *Baron Dhanis,* the parts of which were currently hidden inland. Zimmer had paid good money to the Holo-holo to find out where, but so far had drawn a blank.

Steaming south on the *Llanstephen Castle,* Spicer and his men were aware of little if anything of all this. They simply knew they had to get *Mimi* and *Toutou* halfway up Africa, then sink the *Hedwig*. Until then, they could relax. The weather was getting warmer and they would soon cross the Equator. After putting in at Madeira, where they took the opportunity to sample the island's famous fortified wine and to load plentiful supplies of fruit and vegetables, the day finally came.

It was a tradition on ships of the Castle line that fun and games were to be had when the Equator was crossed. These generally included an appearance by the sea-god Neptune, complete with trident. Churchill scorned such festivities and they were unlikely to have changed much in the intervening decade:

> Neptune and his consort boarded us near the forecastle and paraded round the ship in state. Never have I seen such a draggle-tailed divinity. An important feature in the ritual which he prescribes is the shaving and ducking of all who have not passed the line before. But our attitude was strictly Erastian and the demigod retired discomfited to the second class, where from the sounds which arose he seemed to find more punctilious votaries.*

A few days after they had crossed the Equator, Spicer's officers had just finished dinner when he invited them to his cabin. Once they were all inside he turned on them in fury, saying he had heard them talking about "Lee's Expedition." Such talk was to cease forthwith.

"This is no man's expedition!" he shouted. "It is the Naval Africa Expedition—that is its official title—and I am in command!"

He dismissed them at once and the doctor and "Tubby" Eastwood went for a walk on the deck. The setting sun was a beautiful sight on the western ocean as they leant over the ship's rail. Neither spoke as night fell. There was no sound, writes Shankland, who reported their conversation, save "the swish of water against the ship's side and the deep throbbing of the engines." Stars had appeared by the time Dr. Hanschell broke the silence.

---

*In his autobiography, *A Collector of Characters,* Spicer's artist brother Theodore remembered similar antics taking place on the family's sea voyage back from Tasmania: "That trip has remained in my memory, particularly the incident when Father Neptune came on board and tricks were played on those who had never crossed the equator before."

"What do you think of the ultimatum?" he asked Eastwood, meaning Spicer's threat to punish anyone who described their enterprise as "Lee's expedition."

"I was thinking," said the Methodist as he gazed up at the night sky, "that the hand of God is over this expedition."

"I've no information about that," the doctor replied, half-mockingly, "but of one thing I'm sure—that Spicer's hand will be over it."

"Tubby" Eastwood was used to Hanschell's atheist jibes by now. "It amuses you to play the Devil's Advocate, doctor," he said, "but I know you don't mean any harm."

A few minutes later Wainwright and a civilian passenger joined them. Wainwright's companion began pointing out the Southern Cross and the other stars that filled the magnificent panoply of the tropical heavens, when a voice was heard in the darkness. It was Spicer, correcting the civilian's reading of the night sky.

"You must forgive me if I don't agree," responded the passenger. "Stars are in my line of work, you know."

"Oh, indeed?" retorted Spicer. "I certainly wouldn't know it from what you're telling us. I am a Navigating Officer!"

Wainwright's companion studied Spicer as he emerged into the light, then simply turned and walked away.

"That was the Astronomer Royal of Cape Town," explained the doctor, as casually as he could.

"Is that so?" Spicer laughed out loud. "He'd make a damned bad Navigating Officer!"

Such stories spread like wildfire among the members of the expedition, rapidly eroding Spicer's authority. It was his stupid boastfulness about hunting that especially did for him. When he claimed to have carried a water-buck back to camp slung over one shoulder, having outstripped his native trackers, it only needed someone to point out that a water-buck was about the size of a pony for him to appear a figure of fun.

It didn't help that the Captain of the *Llanstephen Castle* clearly thought Spicer a complete idiot. One day, under Spicer's supervision, Lieutenant Cross and the other engineers had been starting *Mimi* and *Toutou*'s engines to test them. Some passengers were smoking nearby on the promenade deck and as he passed the Captain said, "No smoking here!"

"Whyever not?" inquired Spicer, sidling up.

"Because of the danger of igniting petrol vapour," explained the Captain.

"What nonsense!" said Spicer, in full earshot of his men and the watching passengers. "We're far out of reach of any vapour!"

"No smoking here!" the Captain shouted, so loudly people looked up. "Those are my orders!"

Spicer flushed, but for once he kept quiet—until that night in the bar. "You know what these Merchant Service fellows are like!" he told his juniors. "Actually, I could have ordered the Captain off the deck there and then. As a Commander RN on the active list in time of war, I can order any merchant skipper to turn his ship over to me."

Engineer Lieutenant Cross, who had witnessed the whole episode, chewed the side of his mouth as Spicer spoke. He now did this as a matter of course to stop himself from laughing or answering back. Spicer had already reprimanded him for "smiling in a disbelieving manner" on one occasion. This had resulted in an embarrassed pause at the dinner table, until Cross was forced to retract his smile in public and confirm that he entirely believed what Spicer was saying: that he had a certificate from the Admiralty authorising him to run the engine-room of a second-class cruiser. In effect, Spicer was claiming to be an experienced engineer.

"Bloody liar!" Cross muttered, once Spicer had left the table. It was becoming a common sentiment among Spicer's men who, with mounting dismay, continued on their way to Cape Town, where the African leg of their adventure would begin.

During the journey, British forces captured Bukoba, an important port on the other great African lake, the Victoria Nyanza. One can be sure that the full story of the victory did not come through on the *Llanstephen Castle*'s Morse set: drunken soldiers dancing about in looted German dress uniforms, or in stolen ladies' underwear, with spiked *Pickelhaube* helmets on their heads and cigars between their lips.

Some of the looters, writes Byron Farwell, "were scandalised . . . by their glimpses of the Germans' sex lives. One soldier discovered companion photographs of the German commandant: in the first he stood resplendent in full dress uniform beside a woman (his wife?) who was completely naked; in the second, the same woman stood fully dressed in formal attire beside the naked commandant."

Chapter Four

It was a cool day. The region at the tapering end of Africa where the Atlantic and the Indian oceans come choppily together was less turbulent than usual. There was no storm and the foamy line where the oceans met—or was it divided?—was barely visible. It must have seemed a good omen to those like "Tubby" Eastwood who put their faith in God's providence. The first part of *Mimi* and *Toutou*'s journey was over. There had been no attacks by U-boats or those surface raiders of the German fleet that still roamed the sea-lanes. The liner carrying the Naval Africa Expedition arrived safely in Cape Town, South Africa, on 2 July 1915.

The town was beautifully situated in the shadow of Table Mountain and since the War it had become a busy naval base. It was the headquarters of the British Admiral charged with keeping the crucial trade routes of the Indian Ocean free from German attack.

Most of the German navy was concentrated in the North Sea and the Pacific, but there was one serious threat in the African theatre. Farther up the coast, past the South African city of Durban and the coast of neutral Portuguese East Africa (now Mozambique), lay German East Africa, or Tanganyika as it was sometimes known.

Near the Tanganyikan capital Dar es Salaam, the speedy, three-funnelled German cruiser *Königsberg* was still hiding out in the swamps of the Rufiji delta. The ship's exact position had been spied out by a South African ivory hunter, Major Pieter Pretorius, who knew the Rufiji well. Disguised as an Arab trader, he had paddled up one of the delta's channels with an African assistant. Reaching the German cruiser, they boarded it with a basket of chickens for barter. As the exchange took place, they discovered that the ship's torpedoes had been sent ashore. Having disembarked, Pretorius spent a month taking readings of the tide and sounding the channel depths so that the *Severn* and the *Mersey* would have a clear passage.

The next few days would see the *Königsberg* attacked by the flotilla of British boats which was assembling near Mafia Island—a kind of mini version of Zanzibar off the German-held coast, all palm trees and Arab traders. From Mafia Island, with the help of some aircraft, an attack would be launched into the mangrove-choked channels of the Rufiji River where the *Königsberg* had been hiding for months. The mouth of the river, once the largest water-way on earth, formed an enormous delta about 500 square miles in extent. With mangrove trees occupying the greater portion of the coastline and sand filling up the channels, the Rufiji could only properly be navigated by light-draught ships, such as were assembling at Mafia Island.

It was this operation that preoccupied the British navy down in Cape Town and not the arrival of Spicer's expedition. Consequently, there was nobody there to greet them after their 17-day, 6,000-mile voyage. Tyrer stepped down the gangplank, squinting through his monocle, followed by Tait and Mollison in their kilts and all the officers carrying cutlasses and wearing the special grey uniform of the Naval Africa Expedition. Spicer made them parade on the quay once more, as the African stevedores carried off the ship's cargo. *Mimi* and *Toutou* were lifted off the *Llanstephen Castle* by crane, their mahogany hulls swaying in the freshening wind, the so-called Cape Doctor, which blew down from the north.

Spicer informed his officers that their hotel was on Adderley Street—a long, slightly rackety thoroughfare that stretched from the lower slopes of Table Mountain down towards the sea; nearby were some formal gardens laid out by the colony's Dutch founders. Spicer then told "Tubby" Eastwood, his round-faced confidential clerk, to find cheaper lodgings in the town for the ordinary sailors. He drew Dr. Hanschell to one side. They would be staying at the Mount Nelson, the town's most salubrious establishment.

Spicer and the doctor took a hansom cab up there from the docks. An African guard in a solar topi let them through the gate, above which the glorious mountain towered with its "table-cloth" of cloud. The cab horse trotted up Mount Nelson's cobbled driveway, which was lined on either side by majestic, thick-trunked royal palms. Another guard in a sun-helmet opened the door of the cab and Dr. Hanschell stepped out and stood before one of the grandest hotels he had ever seen. Surrounded by lush gardens and painted a creamy buff, it was a kind of Gothic folly: the last bastion of European sophistication on the southernmost tip of Africa.*

This pillared palace had a history, too. A young journalist called Winston Churchill had stayed there while covering the Anglo-Boer War, which had ended a mere thirteen years before. Were it not for the Gallipoli débâcle, Churchill would have been Spicer's ultimate superior, as head of the navy.

This wasn't the fallen minister's only connection to the battle getting under way in East Africa. In 1914, as First Lord of the Admiralty, Churchill had sent a glowing message to the crew of two

---

*The hotel, which still exists, was painted pink in the 1920s, probably because this colour reminded the Mount Nelson's Italian manager of the villas of his homeland.

of the light-draught ships now assembled at Mafia Island, HMS *Severn* and HMS *Mersey*. These "unseaworthy steel boxes" (originally intended as river barges for the Brazilian navy) carried very little fuel, but earlier in the War they had played an important role supporting the Belgian army off Calais and Boulogne. It was for this reason Churchill congratulated their crew, who, like Spicer's men, were mainly volunteers and reservists. They would have joined the Gallipoli fleet, but, pulled by tugs from Britain to Malta, they had been too slow to get there in time. Then it was decided they should be sent to East Africa to resolve the *Königsberg* problem, so they were tugged a further 5,000 miles to Mafia Island and the Tanganyikan coast. As it turned out, their fate was intimately connected with that of *Mimi* and *Toutou*, which had a no less curious journey ahead of them.

Once off the *Llanstephen Castle*, the two motor boats were put on to goods trucks in a railway siding, ready for travel. The special cradles that had held them on the deck of the boat were simply lifted on to the flat beds of the railway wagons and bolted down again.

After a comfortable night at the Mount Nelson, Spicer spent the following morning making a series of official visits to navy and government officials in the town. He took with him as his aide-de-camp Sub-Lieutenant Tyrer, complete with monocle and cutlass and canary-yellow hair. Meanwhile, Dr. Hanschell and "Tubby" Eastwood went to Lennard's the pharmacist to supplement the expedition's inadequate medical supplies.

Mr. Lennard supplied zinc-lined boxes to keep the medicines safe from rain and insects. He also advised not putting all of the painkillers in one box, all the quinine in another, and so on. It was always better to split up the supplies, he said, in case a box went astray. The old chemist, who had fitted out many safaris in his time, also counselled taking plenty of laxative pills. These, he informed them, would be in constant demand from the African tribes they would encounter on the way.

While further preparations were made for their journey up to the Congo, Spicer had time to ponder a report he had received that John Lee, whose idea the whole thing had been, was a drunkard and had been "blabbing" about their top-secret mission. In fact, many people knew about the expedition and the big-game hunter was probably innocent. However, the German commander Zimmer's memoirs make clear that his intelligence about the arrival of the expedition came around the same time that Lee appeared in the Congo in late May.

Lee had worked hard blazing the trail up in the Congo, if his companion Magee is to be believed. Four years after the War he described Lee's work in the *National Geographic*:

> While preparations were being pushed in England, Lee and I left for Africa on 22 May 1915, going ahead of the main body to select a route across the African bush from the point where the boats would be taken off the train. It was important that a route be free as possible from hills, gorges, etc, yet close to water, should be chosen, as our boats were to be taken over this trail intact, each drawn by a traction engine. Great difficulty was experienced in finding a suitable route over which to make our road, owing to the hilly nature of the country, as well as to the long stretches of marshland, the breeding ground of malaria-carrying mosquitoes. But at last a route was selected and thousands of natives were recruited from the adjacent villages and set to work under white supervision literally to carve a passage through the bush.

Spicer refused to accept any of this as true, even though Lee had been sending back reports of his own. He had to investigate, so on Tuesday 6 July Spicer left Cape Town by train for Salisbury in Southern Rhodesia (now Harare, the capital of Zimbabwe) to meet the British authorities there.

That same day the saga of the *Königsberg* came to a head in the east, on Tanganyika's Indian Ocean coast. Since October 1914 the German ship had been skulking in one of the Rufiji's channels and guns and troops had been put ashore for further protection. The British knew where she was: an officer had noticed that some coconut palms were moving above the tree level near the river mouth. They were tied to the *Königsberg*'s masthead as a primitive camouflage. But it was only with the arrival of shallow-bottomed boats like HMS *Severn* and HMS *Mersey* that she could be successfully attacked.

At about 5:30 a.m. one of the *Königsberg*'s officers saw two shadowy ships appear through the morning mist. They looked to be ungainly craft, but they were armed and clearly meant business. The German inshore guns began to fire—47mm field guns and small arms—but the *Severn* and the *Mersey* returned the compliment in heavier kind. A torpedo was launched against them from a tube on the shore, but it was blown up in the water by a shell from the *Severn*. Shortly afterwards, a British seaplane dropped bombs on the *Königsberg*—but missed, hitting some nearby mangrove trees. German troops were still firing on the *Severn* and the *Mersey* from the banks—a continuous hail of rifle and machine-gun fire—but the steel boxes made it through, the plates on their hulls rattling with a deafening din.

On board the *Königsberg* was Job Rosenthal, an *Oberleutnant zur See*. Along with other members of the crew he was eating breakfast on deck when the British attacked at 6:40 a.m. The alarm went up with the shout: "Clear ship for action!" *Severn* and *Mersey*'s guns began pounding them, their fire directed by spotter aircraft overhead. Smoke drifted across the water as the British fired shell after shell into the mangroves. They fell just short of the *Königsberg*, hitting a bank and throwing up a fountain of mud and bushes; or hitting the river and creating waterspouts. One of Rosenthal's colleagues shot himself out of fear, but the others fought back fiercely, dodging the moaning shells as they came. The suicide, a former merchant navy officer called Jaeger, took some time to die.

In the first hour of the battle, four men from a British gun-crew on the *Mersey* were killed when a German shell hit their casement. However, at about 7:50 a.m. a British shell hit the *Königsberg*, killing a sailor. Shortly afterwards another projectile tore off the foot of one of Rosenthal's colleagues, Richard Wenig. The *Königsberg* fired back, its shells landing perilously close to the British ships.

The day grew hotter, as did the fighting, which continued for hours. By about 3:30 p.m. the *Severn* and the *Mersey* had together fired 635 shells. The Germans kept returning fire, despite being hit four times. If a single German shell had struck one of the ungainly barges below the waterline they would have been done for. But none of the German salvos found its mark, except for the one which had killed the four men on the *Mersey*. At 3:45 p.m. the British commander, seeing that his men were tiring and the guns overheating, decided to withdraw from the delta to the relative safety of the open sea. The *Königsberg* had been damaged and wasn't going anywhere. Refuelled and rearmed, the *Severn* and the *Mersey* could return again soon enough.

Rosenthal and the other Germans on the ship knew this. After burying their four dead and sending away thirty-five wounded by paddle boat, they spent the next few days trying to repair the damaged ship, whose bunkers were beginning to fill with water. All combustible material was removed, along with any secret documents. Extra spotters were put up in the palm trees to watch for the return of the British. A telephone line was run from the lookouts to the ship. But the truth was that after eight hours of incessant firing, not to mention months of fever in the sweltering delta, German morale had been shot to pieces.

Away to the south-west, at a dinner table in Salisbury, skullduggery was afoot. Over the weekend of 10–11 July, Spicer stayed with General Edwards, the senior British officer in Rhodesia. Spicer persuaded the General that if the reports about Lee's drunkenness and loose talk were true, the Belgians should be asked to arrest him. If this sounds like an over-reaction to what was, after all, an unconfirmed report, the answer may lie in the fact that the report came from Sub-Lieutenant Douglas Hope, the Spicer appointee sent to the Congo in Lee's wake. Hope never even met with the big-game hunter and it seems likely that Spicer had planned all along to get Lee out of the picture. It was to be his expedition, not Lee's.

At about noon that Sunday, 11 July, the *Severn* and the *Mersey* returned to the delta to finish the job. There could be no surprise this time. Two British spotter planes flew above the ship with impunity.

Alerted by her own spotters in trees and on hills, the *Königsberg* fired salvo after salvo as the two barges approached—and fired with great accuracy. But the seamen on board the barges had learned how to control their flat-bottomed craft. They kept slipping moorings and edging out of range of the German guns.

At about 12:30 a shell from the *Severn* hit one of the *Königsberg*'s three funnels. It made a fearsome sound as it was shot away, the shell piercing the funnel casing and exploding. Up above, a British spotter biplane piloted by Flight Lieutenant John Cull swooped over, taking considerable small-arms fire. Cull's observer, Flight Sub-Lieutenant Arnold, radioed the *Severn* and told her the shot was on target. The British fired more rounds and seven hits were recorded in the next ten minutes.

At 12:45 the inevitable happened. The biplane was hit. As it stuttered down Arnold broadcast one last elevation correction to the gunners on the *Severn* before the plane somersaulted on the crocodile-thick water (this final correction was later revealed to have been of vital importance). Arnold fell out of the cockpit, over Cull's head, but Cull, who had not undone his belt, went down with the plane. He was only able to free himself by ripping his trousers and tearing off his boots. Bobbing to the surface, he was found by Arnold amid the wreckage and both men were picked up by a motor boat from the *Mersey*.

Half an hour later, the coup de grâce was administered to the

Königsberg. Rosenthal and the crew felt the shock of a series of explosions and a huge cloud of smoke billowed above the coconut palms as the ship burst into flames. The cry went up: "All hands abandon ship!" The men panicked as they clambered over each other through the flames, pushing aside anyone who got in their way, and swam for the shore. Many were seriously wounded.

The ship's first officer George Koch detonated three torpedoes and blew up the hull, to prevent the British from using her. However, it is thought there were still some wounded on board. It was about 3 p.m. when the British ships withdrew. Coming back down the three-mile channel to the sea, they were showered by shells all the way. The Germans might have been beaten, but they weren't giving up.

Rosenthal and his colleagues spent that night on the banks of the Rufiji in a terrible state. Injured and half-naked, they were bitten into paroxysms by the fat mosquitoes that make their home in African swamps. There was not enough food to go round, but more importantly, not enough morphine. Wenig, Rosenthal's fellow officer who had lost his foot in the first attack, came down with malaria that night. They slept rough on the river bank, lighting campfires in a vain attempt to ward off the insects.

From malaria or gangrene or both, Wenig was delirious by the time the ship's doctor amputated his leg near the knee a few days later. By that stage Rosenthal and the other survivors had begun salvaging the ship. The *Königsberg* was beyond repair, but her guns were still functional. Unbolted from the hull, they were brought ashore. Von Lettow-Vorbeck, the German commander, ordered that they be dragged back to Dar es Salaam, to which task four hundred Africans were promptly put. The loss of the *Königsberg* was a blow to von Lettow, but at least he now had some serious artillery to distribute round the colony. He sent two of the *Königsberg*'s 4.1mm guns down the railway to Kigoma on Lake Tanganyika—which is where *Mimi* and *Toutou* were heading.

Back in Cape Town, a week after the *Königsberg* was destroyed, the motor boats were ready for the off. Wrapped in tarpaulins (each emblazoned with "S.A.R.": South African Railways), *Mimi* and *Toutou* had been brought out of their siding and their crews were itching for action. On 16 July a telegram from Spicer to Wainwright told them to get going. Having informed the Admiralty that he was going up into the Congo alone to look for Lee, Spicer instead headed for Bulawayo, which was on the railway from Cape Town to Elizabethville.

Wainwright marshalled the rag-tag band of sailors—there was no parade this time—for the 2,500-mile journey. This strange band of misfits and naval reservists assembled, their days of leisure over: Dr. Hanschell had been studying maps in Cape Town museum; Cross had been visiting friends and showing off his Spicer-Simson uniform; Tyrer had picked up his Piccadilly habits as best one could in a colonial city, strutting about with his monocle and cutlass.

Shankland records the mood of excitement among the more junior members of the Naval Africa Expedition as they embarked on this second leg of their journey: "The ratings had been generously entertained by the people of Cape Town and when their special train started on the long journey north, morale was good. They already felt like heroes!"

Many of them had never left Britain before, so the African landscape in all its varied forms made quite an impression. Nevertheless, the names of some of the places they passed would have been familiar, made famous during the Anglo-Boer War. The *Daily Mail,* the first mass-circulation newspaper—with its brilliant correspondents such as George Steevens, an Oxford don who abandoned academia for a life of adventure—had been founded on news of the war. So as they rocked northwards and the steam-whistle blew at successive stations, the crew would have recognised place names from the most exciting event in their youth.

Mimi and *Toutou* "were carried on goods trucks astern of the passenger coach in which they travelled," writes Shankland, and because of the fire risk, "Wainwright posted seamen on the tarpaulins, which covered the boats, with instructions to brush off any sparks that might fall on them from the wood-burning engine."

Bridging the Orange River, the special train went up through South Africa past the mining town of Kimberley, which had been made famous by the activities of Cecil Rhodes. Kruger's Boers had besieged it during the war. Next came another river, the Vaal, another siege town—Mafeking—and the mining and financial centre, Johannesburg. The train proceeded to pass into the Bechuanaland Protectorate (now Botswana), going along the eastern edge of the Kalahari Desert, before crossing the border into Southern Rhodesia and arriving at the junction town of Bulawayo. From there it would continue north-west up to the coal-mining area of Wankie and the border of Northern Rhodesia (now Zambia).

By the time *Mimi* and *Toutou* were heading north to Bulawayo, en route to Lake Tanganyika, Lieutenant Job Rosenthal, formerly of the *Königsberg*, had already received his marching orders. He, too, was to travel by railway (though a different one) to Lake Tanganyika (though to the opposite side), where he was to link up with Commander Zimmer, who was in charge of naval operations on the lake. Zimmer already had one Job in his fleet: the Captain of the *Hedwig*, Job Odebrecht. Now, in Job Rosenthal, he had another. So, with a feeling for symmetry, he made him captain of the *Kingani*, the *Hedwig*'s sister ship.

The *Königsberg*'s guns were to follow Rosenthal by rail down the *Mittellandbahn* and would be mounted on a new German warship called the *Graf von Götzen*, which Zimmer commanded in person. The *Götzen* was the jewel in the German fleet on Lake Tanganyika—and all the more remarkable for having been spirited there under the nose of the enemy. Spicer knew nothing at all about this ship and neither did the Admiralty. At 1,200 tons, she was roughly 20 times the tonnage of the one Spicer had been sent to sink (the *Hedwig*) and 150 times the tonnage of *Mimi* and *Toutou*.*

---

*See Catalogue of Vessels, p. 243.

The disparity would certainly have given Spicer pause, had he known, as would the news of Rosenthal's posting as captain of the *Kingani*. Rosenthal had, after all, seen serious action in the Rufiji. After what had happened to Wenig and the rest of the *Königsberg*'s crew, the Brits could not reasonably expect any mercy from Rosenthal. On arriving in Kigoma, he immediately took out the *Kingani* on raiding parties. According to Colonel L. B. Cane:

> the *Kingani*, a small wooden steamer of fifty-five feet that had come by train from the Indian Ocean, later destroyed two ancient British steamers, possessing neither engines nor boilers, whose hulls were lying at the southern end of the lake. They also raided Bismarckburg (now Kasanga), and captured four machine-guns and over ninety miles of telegraph wire from a Belgian company there, and bombarded and attacked various other lake stations.*

If a tiny wooden steamer could have such an effect, what more could the *Hedwig* and the *Götzen* do?

How Spicer didn't know about the *Götzen* is a mystery one can only attribute to the parlous state of communications in Africa and numerous misunderstandings between the Belgian and British governments. The German supership had been launched in Kigoma on 8 June—the day Spicer had made his practice run on the Thames in *Mimi*, with Engineer Lieutenant Cross at the wheel.

As it happens, Spicer met Cross the moment he arrived in Bulawayo. The rest of the Naval Africa Expedition had arrived before their Commander and were lunching at the railway hotel in the town. Finding a pony in the yard tethered to a post, Cross had mounted it and started riding round and round. The other men began to tease him, but unbeknown to them Spicer had arrived.

***Tanganyika Notes and Records* (1947). In fact, the *Kingani* had a wooden deck and superstructure, but a steel hull.

Striding forward in his naval uniform, he loudly ordered Cross to dismount, adding that horse-stealing was a crime punishable by hanging in Rhodesia.

As Cross did so, the assembled and well-lunched company began to make comments about a new medal ribbon on Spicer's chest: the Africa General Service Medal. He may well have heard their whispered remarks, but by chance an African messenger boy chose that moment to run into the station yard clutching a piece of paper and yelling, "Captain Cross! Telegram for Captain Cross!"

Spicer froze. "I can readily understand that an Engineer Lieutenant RNR would want to be thought an army captain," he said, "but as he is now serving under an RN commander and in an RN expedition, I, Commander Spicer-Simson RN, must order in future that Engineer Lieutenant Cross, Royal Naval Reserve, will bear that in mind and keep his army preferences until he has left the navy."

It seems Cross's friends in Cape Town had mistaken his peculiar uniform for that of an army officer, which is what the three pips on his shoulder suggested. However, Spicer's outraged snobbery was entirely typical and his men must have hated the sight of his tall frame by now as he strode out of the yard. Cross could be a tricky customer—it was readily agreed he was hard to get on with—but Spicer's posturing merely alienated him from the rest of the expedition.

It did not bode well for the future. They all had a very long way to go and, when they got to Lake Tanganyika, a very big job to do. Even for fast, manoeuvrable craft such as *Mimi* and *Toutou,* sinking the *Hedwig* would be no mean feat. But as they climbed back on to the train at Bulawayo, bound for Elizabethville in the Belgian Congo, via Northern Rhodesia, Spicer's men had no inkling that the *Hedwig* was the least of their problems.

Chapter Five

The border between Southern and Northern Rhodesia (now Zimbabwe and Zambia) was at the town of Livingstone, the site of Victoria Falls. Like all travellers of the period, the crew of *Mimi* and *Toutou* would have disembarked to watch as *Mosi-oa-Tunya*—"the Thundering Smoke"—plunged down into a gorge far below, dispensing 4,000 cubic feet of water a second. Even the most earthbound of souls, like the two hulking Scotsmen, Tait and Mollison, could not have failed to be moved by such a sight.

There was not yet a statue of David Livingstone gazing out from under a pith helmet over the water's mile-wide expanse, nor a plaque referring to his "discovery" of the Falls. But Wainwright and the others would have been alert to the explorer's residual presence, which was (and still is) considerable in the Zambezi region. It would not have been lost on Dr. Hanschell, after his careful study of maps in Cape Town, that Livingstone had arrived sick and tired in 1869 at Ujiji on what was now the German side of Lake Tanganyika.

Today Livingstone's meeting at Ujiji with Henry Morton Stanley in 1871 is often the only thing people know about him. In 1915 that story formed part of a wider picture, at the centre of which was Livingstone's (then outspoken) opposition to slavery. "The strangest disease I have seen in this country," he wrote, "seems really to be broken-heartedness and it attacks free men who have been captured and turned into slaves." As Dr. Hanschell and the Tanganyika party crossed over from Zambia into the Congo, they were passing through an area that had been central to the supply of the slave system. It had only really stopped within the last thirty years, in spite of legislation and the hunting down of traffickers. Long after slavery had been outlawed internationally, it continued locally as an agricultural and domestic arrangement.

Travelling by rail through the thick scrubland of the Katanga Province, Spicer and his men reached the town of Elizabethville in the Belgian Congo on 26 July. They were now more than 2,000 miles from Cape Town—and more than 8,000 miles from London. In terms of distance, the greater part of *Mimi* and *Toutou*'s trip was over. But the real journey was only just beginning.

The landscape near Elizabethville was dotted with anthills, some as high as 40 feet. Elizabethville itself barely existed. Built to serve the Star of the Congo copper mine, it consisted of a line of corrugated-iron shacks along a red-dust road. Most of the buildings were barns for storing mining and railway equipment, or light industrial workshops for mending it. There was a single whitewashed villa where the Vice-Governor-General lived, a few brothels and drinking dens, and a flea-pit hotel. It was here the following morning that Lee and Magee turned up out of the bush, to present themselves to Spicer.

Magee has left an account of the work they had done, and one can imagine Lee telling Spicer much the same thing:

Where slopes were too steep they were levelled down.
Bridges, constructed from timber growing on the spot,
were thrown across river-beds. Giant trees, when blocking
our path, were uprooted with dynamite. Rocks and boul-
ders were treated in a similar manner. Our biggest problem
was a dried-up gorge, 40 yards wide and about 20 yards
deep. This we completely filled up with tree trunks. Thousands of trees were cleared out of the way. The enormity of
this task may be appreciated better by the reader when he
learns that so dense was the growth of the bush in some
sections of the route that it was possible to travel for several days at a time and get only an occasional glimpse of
the sky through the tangled foliage overhead. So the 146-
mile roadway was pushed ahead, making, as it progressed,
an unavoidable climb over a plateau 6,000 feet above sea
level.

Spicer waited until Lee had handed over his survey maps and
contracts for labour before dropping his bombshell. He informed
him that he had been accused of insulting the Belgian flag while
drunk and of giving out information about the expedition to all and
sundry. Lee vehemently denied the accusations—adding, according
to Shankland, that "if everyone knew that the expedition was
bound for Lake Tanganyika it was for the very simple reason that
there was nowhere else it could possibly be going to."

This was true. It had been the case even down in Cape Town,
where Dr. Hanschell and "Tubby" Eastwood had been surprised
how easily people had worked out what they were up to. But this
cut no ice with Spicer. He ordered Lee to return to Cape Town
and await disciplinary proceedings from the Admiralty. Without
another word, the seasoned big-game hunter collected his wages
from Eastwood, the expedition's paymaster, and disappeared. From
this point on, the progenitor of the Naval Africa Expedition drops

out of history. If he was related to the Lee family of Mangwe near Bulawayo, he may well have returned there.*

When Eastwood told the other officers of Lee's departure, the mood turned against Spicer. Lee's brutal dismissal cast something of a pall over a dinner at the hotel that night, given by the British residents of Elizabethville in Spicer's honour. But if he felt the strain, Spicer didn't show it. Instead, he took great pleasure in telling the other diners of his skill at climbing the rigging of old sailing ships. Then, writes Shankland, "he embarked on a long story of how he had bagged a man-eating tiger while snipe-shooting in the Southern Provinces of China."

There was a broken-down piano in the corner of the hotel restaurant and the moment he had finished his tall tale, Spicer sprang up and announced he would sing. One of the expats volunteered to accompany him on the piano and so the officers of the Naval Africa Expedition were treated to the sound of their commanding officer labouring through "Swanee River."

> *That's where my heart is turning ever.*
> *That's where the old folks stay.*
> *All up and down the whole creation,*
> *Sadly I roam,*
> *Still longing for the old plantation,*
> *And for the old folks at home . . .*

The pianist halted at this point, perhaps embarrassed at the spectacle he was making of himself, but Spicer continued, running through every verse and chorus.

> *All round the little farm I wandered*
> *When I was young,*

---

*John Lee of Mangwe was a famous big-game hunter of a previous generation who settled in Northern Rhodesia around 1861. He married a niece of President Kruger and fathered many children. He had at least three other wives while in the Mangwe area.

Then many happy days I squandered,
Many a song I sung.
When I was playing with my brother
Happy was I.
Oh! take me to my kind old mother,
There let me live and die . . .

This sorry performance met with desultory applause, where-upon everyone quickly rose from the table. Dinner was over. "Tubby" Eastwood and Dr. Hanschell returned to the barn in which they had been billeted, while the rest of the expedition slept on the train. Only Spicer stayed in the hotel.

The following morning, most of the expedition moved on to Fungurume, a hundred miles up the line. Their destination was now common knowledge, writes Magee, describing their send-off:

The members of the expedition were fêted by the Belgian populace, who, however, were not a bit optimistic about the outcome of our efforts to reach the lake. Among the sporting fraternity of this township the betting against our getting through was 100 to 1. However, "It's dogged as does it" was our watchword and we left the Belgian town full of hope and bearing the good wishes of the townsfolk, who turned out in force to see us off.

Spicer, Eastwood and Dr. Hanschell stayed behind in Eliza-bethville. On the advice of the local Belgian medical officer, the doctor insisted fly-whisks were bought for every member of the expedition, to ward off the dreaded tsetse. Eastwood bought twenty-eight of them at Elizabethville market, including one for Spicer. It turned out the Commander had already, off his own bat, acquired a fancy number with a lion-skin handle.

Three native assistants were also employed: Rupia, who would help Dr. Hanschell; Tom, who would be Spicer's valet; and Marapandi, an older man who had trained in a mission in Nyasaland,* who would help Eastwood in his work as clerk and paymaster. Marapandi was also a fellow worshipper of the stern Methodist God whose hand, Eastwood believed, was always hovering over their enterprise—ready to lift them to salvation or dash them down to that place where tormented souls forever fuel the flames.

On 5 August—nearly two months after they had set out from England—Spicer, Hanschell and Eastwood rejoined the others at Fungurume, deep in the Belgian Congo. Fungurume was the rail-head in Cecil Rhodes's abortive Cape-to-Cairo project; the end of the line. In fact it was just a few sheds in the jungle, with piles of steel railway track and wooden sleepers lying here and there, under the watchful eye of a French-African railwayman known only as "Monsieur."

"Here the expedition detrained the boats and started its gru-elling journey through the heart of the Dark Continent," reads a caption in Magee's *National Geographic* article. To the right and the left of them was rough bush; in front of them, massive and for-bidding, lay the Mitumba Mountains, which they would have to cross. The day they arrived, the stores lay along the track in a hope-less mess. Ammunition and petrol tins became dangerously hot under the sun and there was hard work ahead. Still in their wooden cradles, *Mimi* and *Toutou* had to be lifted off the train into Spicer's special trailers. There had already been some damage: parts of the boats' undercarriage had broken during the rail journey, in spite of the protection afforded by the rubber tyres between their hulls and the wooden cradles.

While the boats were being unloaded (with the help of a small crane lent by "Monsieur"), Spicer and Dr. Hanschell went ahead in a lorry to check the work Lee had done on the road. There were two native labour camps on the route. One of these was run along strict

---

*There were many Nyasas in Elizabethville at this period; they were perceived as an élite by the Congolese.

lines by a Mr. Locke—an old Africa hand, ex–Boer War, in dark shirt and riding breeches. The other was the fiefdom of a Mr. Davison. He was the more flamboyant character, the doctor recollected: "He wore white ducks [strong linen trousers] and an enormous cowboy hat." The two camps were more or less villages, complete with women and children. The Africans under Locke and Davison had worked hard levelling the ground. They had also gathered firewood for the steam-tractors that were due to arrive from Northern Rhodesia, their job being to drag *Mimi* and *Toutou* over the mountains. In his lecture, Spicer typically ascribes the gathering of African labour as due to his personal charisma: "The white man, for certain reasons, is not greatly esteemed on the Belgian Congo; however, the natives learnt that we were a different sort of white man, and within two days I had 1,400 natives available."

In the afternoon, once the expedition's own camp had been established and latrines been dug, Spicer decided that a parade was in order. A Union Jack was hoisted up a tree in front of Spicer's tent and, with their cutlasses pointed outwards at 45 degrees, the officers inspected the men, each of whom held his rifle up in front of him. All wore solar topis. According to Shankland, Spicer made a speech at this point, reading aloud the King's Regulations and reminding the expedition that they were there for one purpose only: "to get *Mimi* and *Toutou* through to Lake Tanganyika and then, when they had sunk the *Hedwig von Wissmann,* to get home again as soon as possible.

"And we have another enemy more deadly than the Germans," he continued. "I mean tropical diseases. Very special precautions are necessary, which will be explained to you in detail by Surgeon Hanschell. Every man in this expedition, in matters of health and hygiene, will unquestioningly follow his instructions. All drinking water will be boiled. Fly-whisks will be issued today, and it will be the duty of every man to whisk flies off his neighbour, irrespective of rank."

Dr. Hanschell himself was the first to fall sick. His old bugbear—that amoebic dysentry he'd caught on the Gold Coast, which had never quite gone away—had returned with a vengeance. He spent the next few days hobbling between his small tent and the latrines.

Spicer was the only other person to have a tent (a much bigger one than the doctor's). The rest slept in the open air in an area at the beginning of Lee's road, nestling in their sleeping bags next to the dumps of petrol and ammunition, which were now covered with tarpaulins. Rupia, Tom and Marapandi camped a quarter of a mile away, along with the other African auxiliaries and their wives and children. Farther beyond camped Locke and Davison's labour gangs, their firelights gleaming in the darkness. Locke's gangmaster came from a family of witch doctors, which is why his men were so well organised. Years later, Dr. Hanschell would remember that first night in the true bush: how drum-beats and melancholy chants from the direction of the road-builders' camp had filled his ears as he fell into an uneasy sleep.

Chapter Six

On 6 August 1915, sixty-seven days from London, *Mimi* and
Toutou were ready to make their overland journey. Forty feet
long, eight feet wide and almost fifteen feet high (taking into account
the trailers), they looked impressive as they lay at Fungurume, the
valley gateway to the Mitumba escarpment. Today, when the trap-
pings of modern, so-called civilisation extend into almost every
nook and cranny of Africa, for better or worse (or, indeed, both at
the same time), it is hard to imagine the visual impact that the two
vessels must have had as they rested between the trees. As Magee
points out, almost any Western item was regarded with a kind of
reverential awe and was much sought after by the local chieftains.

> The prevailing mode among these petty potentates seemed
> to be obsolete uniforms of all armies. One old chief, I

remember, was attired in an old British militia tunic and a pair of spats, his crowning glories being an opera hat and a pink sunshade. I was aware that a big business in out-of-date uniforms is carried on between traders and these tribes, but the origin of the spats and pink sunshade puzzled me somewhat . . .

Fungurume was where the real business began and time was against them. They had to get over the Mitumba range before the rains came and obliterated the roads and bridges being built. This was no idle worry. Of the paralysing effect of the rains, an army officer wrote of the Moshi-Arusha road, "Its state was indescribable, the wet black cotton soil poached to morass. It was hard work for an unladen man to go two miles an hour." Wainwright, the transport manager, had witnessed in the Transvaal how the African rainy season could act like a tidal wave, sweeping all before it, and this made him especially conscious of the need for urgency. With almost 150 homemade bridges to cross or build and 146 miles of rough terrain to cover (including a climb of 6,000 feet over the Mitumbas), they had about eight weeks before the weather would break. Even sentinel showers could prove a problem, for as Magee observed, "one good rainfall would render useless our stacks of wood fuel all along the route."

The first bridge was in sight, thanks to Lee's good offices. It consisted of logs laid across a stream, over which the red soil of the region had been shovelled and flattened—red because the soil round Fungurume is said to contain the greatest density of copper on earth. Spicer's men were ready and an armed guard of African *askaris,* supplied by the Belgians, was on hand: huge men, who marched in bare feet and displayed magnificent discipline. They wore bandoliers and fezzes and carried old-fashioned single-shot rifles. Native carriers had gone on in front, each bearing on his head a load of about 60 pounds. "Provisions, ammunition and petrol for the motor boats were all transported in this fashion," says Magee, "our string of native carriers extending in single file for miles." The lorry, carrying further provisions and general camp gear, had been sent on to select suitable camping spots.

During these preparations a thin, blond-haired man wearing khaki shorts and an Australian-style slouch hat cycled into camp. His name was Arthur Darville Dudley and he was a friend of John Lee. He was exhausted, having ridden 200 miles down bush tracks to join them. Lieutenant Dudley had seen service in the Anglo-Boer War and spoke several Bantu languages. He belonged to the Rhodesian Rifles, a force of volunteers composed mainly of farmers and settlers. Disrespectful of hierarchy and liable to wear whatever uniform they could lay their hands on, they were nevertheless generally regarded as tough and useful fighters.*

Meanwhile, *Mimi* and *Toutou*—or "Mimmie" and "Tow-Tow" as the ordinary seamen called them—stayed put. The steam traction engines and ox-teams that would pull them had not yet arrived. Spicer grew frustrated and, calling back the lorry, had it fixed to *Toutou's* trailer. P.O. Mechanic Mullin climbed in to the cab and stepped on the accelerator, but the lorry's wheels simply spun round in the soft earth road. Spicer refused to give up. He ordered some of the native labourers to be brought back and together with the regular members of the expedition they attached tow ropes to *Toutou* and were able to drag her about 150 yards towards the bridge. The same procedure was applied to *Mimi* the following day, then *Toutou* was pulled the remaining 200 yards to the first bridge.

As they were about to cross, Spicer decided to check the special trailers Thorneycroft's yard had made for him. They had large rubber wheels in the centre and two smaller wheels on manoeuvrable

*Not everyone was of this opinion. One of the volunteers in the Rifles was Arthur Harris (later "Bomber" Harris of Second World War fame), who proclaimed that the colonial troops he rode with were, on average, with remarkably few exceptions, "damned bad horsemen and damned bad shots." It is possible Dudley may have felt the same. A nervous, impatient man, he was also energetic and conscientious. On discovering that before his career in the Boer War, Dudley had been a regular naval cadet, Spicer made him his executive officer.

castors at the front and back, mounted on transverse wooden beams, six inches thick. However, on inspection it was found that both these beams had started to split.

"I told the experts that the six-inch beam was not strong enough!" shouted Spicer at the surrounding trees. "It should have been a twelve-inch beam!"

Mimi showed similar damage. Spicer sent Wainwright and Eastwood back to "Monsieur" at the railhead to see if the broken trailers could be repaired. They purchased two wooden ox-wagons from the railwayman and replaced the broken wheels using pieces from the wagons. This all took another week, by which time the traction engines had arrived by train: they were enormous steam tractors with extra-large steel wheels at the back and a tall funnel at the front.

The huge wheels were intended to give clearance from the uneven ground and the engines had steel boilers in which water was heated by a timber-fuelled furnace. Each locomotive came with a ten-ton trailer usually used to store wood for the boiler. They had laid stacks of wood along the entire length of the route, however, so the trailers were instead loaded with bags of meal to feed the African labourers.

The ox-teams that were supposed to supplement the pulling power of the road-locomotives had not yet arrived, but Spicer was impatient to get going. On 18 August they set off once more. The steam whistles of the locomotives blew and the African carriers chanted and beat their drums as *Mimi* was towed on to the bridge. Within seconds of the first tractor coming on to it, however, the earthwork and timber of the bridge collapsed into the stream below. There was pandemonium as the second locomotive was disconnected from *Toutou* and put to work hauling *Mimi* and the other steam engine out of the broken ford.

It was Wainwright who came up with a solution: they had to lay the logs in the stream in the same direction as the current and pile them up until they were level with the road on either side of the gorge, making something more like a causeway than a bridge. The African labourers were set to work cutting down suitable timber and after a few days *Mimi* and *Toutou* were ready for a second attempt.

They began at six in the morning. At first all went well. *Mimi* crossed without difficulty, but then she stuck on the opposite side, unable to build up enough steam to climb a bank beyond the gorge. So another causeway was built that sloped up on to the bank. *Toutou* crossed on this with the second traction engine, which then helped pull *Mimi* and the other tractor up over the obstruction. Spicer tried walking alongside the engine as it crossed, but soon jumped off: "It was like trying to walk on a spring mattress."

By then it was about 3 p.m., but there was no time for celebration. Belching smoke, the two locomotives tugged their eight-ton burdens farther down the road, crashing and bumping and causing considerable consternation among the Africans who emerged from the bush to watch. Eyed at first with fear, then with wonder or simple curiosity, Spicer's team pushed on up that seemingly interminable mountain road. The lorry went on ahead with a small team to erect tents and prepare the evening meal, lighting a fire to welcome the workers and ward off wild animals.

They had almost reached the camping point, six miles from the railhead, when disaster struck again. *Mimi*'s locomotive slipped off the edge of the road and began to fall away, the earthwork sliding to one side, unable to carry the engine's weight. Stuck at an angle, the tractor had to be disconnected from *Mimi* again and pulled by cable by the other engine until she was upright once more. The expedition continued a little farther and then at last they could camp for the night.

It had been an exhausting day and their troubles were increased by the discovery that the adapted trailers were starting to buckle under the weight of the boats, just like their predecessors. For once Spicer kept his cool, perhaps realising that his furious outbursts were bad for morale. He tried to remain calm and collected throughout the day's difficulties, chain-smoking his personally monogrammed cigarettes—COMMANDER G.B. SPICER-SIMSON, R.N. printed in blue letters up the stem. He kept these in his revolver holster and also affected a long cigarette holder. Smoke wreathing his Vandyke beard, he went around encouraging the men, which they considered quite out of character.

The days that followed were much the same, as they raced against the rains under the penetrating glare of the African sun. Curiously enough, says Spicer, "some of my men suffered from snow-blindness at this time," even though they were not far from the Equator. The fact was, he noted, "that the whole of the surface soil in the district is full of mica, and the brilliance of the reflection of the sun off that material produced the same effect as snow." Moreover, "having cut down the trees we were deprived of their shade."

Another obstacle they had to overcome was wandering swamps—"swamps which actually move about," as Spicer mysteriously put it. They look like water lilies on the surface of rivers (the Belgians called them "water-cabbage") and sometimes grew in such bulk that "they form a kind of barrage" until the force of the water rolls them up and deposits them on the shore. "Sometimes when we had built our road we found that it was in the path of one of these wandering swamps, and the traction engines could not get through because their fire-boxes were so low that the fire would have been put out. Then we had to build another road round the swamp."

Tormented by insect bites, the expedition pulled and pushed their way through the bush. Up ahead the native carriers could be heard singing as they jogged along behind the lorry, carrying crates and bundles on their heads. The locomotives heaved and panted in their wake and yet more tribesmen emerged from the bush to stare at the steel monsters. Bringing fruit and vegetables and chickens and goats as gifts, they were held spellbound by the magic of cable and harness and the lurching, heaving motion of the tractors and *Mimi* and *Toutou*.

Shankland goes into some technical detail about these locomotives, which had been made by Burrels of Thetford and Fowlers of Leeds. They could do 90 miles a day on a good road, apparently, and had been customised for working in Africa. "To guard against sparks setting the bush alight," writes Shankland, "they had ash-pans specially constructed to hold water, and baffles and screens fitted to the smoke-boxes. They seemed to have been well cared for, and every bit of brass about them glowed like polished gold." Although Spicer later described them as "ordinary agricultural traction engines," Wainwright—who was in special charge of the tractors—cooed over the two machines as if they were a pair of oversized kittens.

The engines were hardly kittens when it came to noise, however. Their growling, jerking passage, says Magee, disturbed "the slumbers of herds of elephants and other denizens of the bush . . . driving them from their lairs." Bored with their tinned bully beef, some members of the expedition shot buck, wild pig and guinea fowl for the pot. At night could be heard, as if registering his own dietary interests, the roars of a particular lion—perhaps one of the black-maned ones for which the Katanga was once famous—who dogged their every step.

After building yet more causeways and levering the engines out of the holes into which they invariably became stuck every day, Spicer's men finally reached the village of Mwenda Mkosi on 28 August. They had covered the 30 miles from Fungurume in ten days. It was pretty good going, but they still had more than a hundred miles to go, and they hadn't even begun the climb into the mountains yet.

As they entered Mwenda Mkosi—a typical kraal of straw-roofed huts arranged in a rough circle—the trailers carrying *Mimi* and *Toutou* finally collapsed. Spicer had anticipated this. He ordered Wainwright and Cross to bring forward the locomotives' fuel trailers and raid them for their undercarriages. It meant the expedition halting at the village for a while.

They made their camp near a river, about half a mile from Mwenda Mkosi. Every evening Dr. Hanschell led a party of Africans to draw water in five-gallon oil drums, which were then boiled over the camp fires to make tea and to fill their water bottles. These were covered in felt to keep them cool and they were the men's constant companions for the next few weeks, knocking at their thighs as they walked. Tea, which they all sat round drinking on folding tables and chairs, was the highlight of the day. "Tubby" Eastwood had acquired a chimpanzee during the journey, which he christened Josephine. The Paymaster's servant, Marapandi, would often find himself serving tea and bread and butter to Josephine as well as Eastwood.

The bread, says Shankland, was not very pleasant because the self-raising flour that was part of the expedition's supplies was no good. "Eastwood made inquiries around and found that not one of the party knew how to use it. Spicer was indignant. He called them a bunch of land crabs and asserted that every seaman knew how to make bread, with self-raising flour or without. He gave the cooks precise instructions how to do it, but the result was the same—hard biscuit."

Spicer shrugged it off as he shrugged off everything else, with a wave of his lion-handled fly-whisk. All that mattered now was getting through to Lake Tanganyika. Every night the *ngoma*, or African tom-tom, broadcast this single-minded goal through the primeval forest, as one man's manifest destiny was related from tribe to tribe. The story of Spicer's mission went through ever more fantastic permutations, mile after mile, beat after beat, until, by the time it reached the Holo-holo living on the lakeshore, Spicer had been elevated to something like a god.

Chapter Seven

While they were held up at Mwenda Mkosi some expedition members pursued other tasks. Tyrer, the Piccadilly Johnny with the monocle, was sent on ahead to make further surveys of the route. Meanwhile, the lower ranks were put to work splitting up the 20 tons of meal that had hitherto been carried in the steam engines' trailers. The carriers, who now numbered almost a thousand, would each have to bear an extra load. Meal (known as *posho*) was made from the ground root of the cassava plant and was their daily food ration.

According to Magee, many of the tribes that supplied the porterage were former cannibals, though the tone of one caption in his *National Geographic* article bears all the hallmarks of imperialist fantasy: *The ordinary diet of the native consists of a manioc or cassava flour made into a paste, and a meat stew concocted of everything, from ants and grasshoppers up to man. Indeed, "food that once talked" is a special delicacy, though indulged in but secretly and rarely nowadays.*

As well as food, the porters had to carry a great many boxes and crates. These included Spicer's folding X-pattern camp bed (complete with mosquito net) and several washstands with enamel basins and canvas covers. There was also a large tin bath with a lid and canteens for plates and cutlery. Cups and plates had covers of green baize to prevent breakages. Every night large "chaguls"—canvas water-bags about the size of a Labrador dog—were hung in the trees filled with leftover water from Dr. Hanschell's boiling operation. There were also the guns to carry, which were stored in padlocked steel boxes.

The doctor's medicines added to this considerable load. A typical medicine chest of the period contained:

Quinine bihydrochloride in 5 grain tabloids
Potassium permanganate solids
Boracic acid and zinc sulphate solids
Iodoform powder
Tincture of iodine
Aspirin tabloids
Zinc ointment
Epsom salts
Lint, cotton-wool, iodoform gauze (unbleached), bandages, scalpel, dissecting and dressing scissors, artery forceps, silk ligatures, surgical needles, a glass syringe, a one-ounce measure, a probe and a vulcanite dredger

At Mwenda Mkosi Dr. Hanschell was frequently consulted by the locals, who came to him in droves. "When they heard of the Great Medicine Chief," recalls Magee, "the natives flocked from their villages, bringing their sick and their lame with them. But the doctor could attend to only a few, as his supplies of hospital requisites was limited." Fortunately, adds Shankland, "the adult natives mostly wanted purging pills [laxatives]. Those who had tried them brought their friends along for some, explaining with expressive pantomime their wonderful effect. Each received a large white pill and a small blue one with a cup of water, and the others watched solemnly while he swallowed them."

A good deal of shooting took place. The doctor himself bagged two guinea fowl and more intrepid souls brought back bigger game, including eland and impala and the blue wildebeest, or brindled gnu (*Connochaetes taurinus*), which was a feature of the region. It is probable that some zebra were shot and their flesh fed to the porters. Zebra fat was also used as a dubbin substitute to grease boots on safaris and perhaps some members of the expedition kept the animals' skins, which were not only pleasing to the eye but had some domestic use. They would have taken some curing, however. A Tanganyikan government handbook dated fifteen years after the expedition notes, "The hide looks well on the floor, but it requires endless labour to reduce it to pliability." It adds, "The noses make pretty slippers."

Buffalo was another favourite and Spicer hoped to bag one when he set out from camp one morning with a shotgun in one hand and a rifle in the other. He said he would be back for lunch, but as Shankland reports: "He wasn't. By and by, about three in the afternoon, Dudley took out a search party and found him not far from the camp, sitting on top of a large anthill. His clothes were torn, he was badly scratched and in a vile temper.

" 'Why has nobody heard my shots?' bellowed Spicer from his mound of dried earth. 'Doesn't anybody keep watch?' "

It is astonishing that he caught nothing whatsoever, for as Magee's article points out, in those days it was "a simple matter to step out into the teeming jungles or prairies of Africa and obtain an unlimited supply of game for food."

Spicer's inability to bag any game at all was yet another reason for his men to laugh at him behind his back. The situation was given added piquancy by the fact that he had lately been setting up targets for the men to fire at, to improve their aim when the day of battle finally came.

"It's easily seen," Spicer had remarked to Dr. Hanschell while watching them, "that none of these men were trained in sail. When I was a midshipman in the training ship *Volage,* I would stand on the quarterdeck with a rifle and shatter a bottle, six times out of six, that was swinging from the weather yard-arm."

One day—as the doctor told Shankland during the long interviews they conducted in London's Muswell Hill in the early 1960s—a young ox was brought into camp. Spicer took it upon himself to shoot the animal, calling for Waterhouse to bring him a rifle and load it. Various members of the camp accumulated to watch the slaughter. Spicer's first shot, taken from a standing position, disappeared into the nearby bush. He crouched closer to the oblivious beast, which was munching grass about three yards away, and fired again. The shot hit one of its horns, making it vibrate with a thrumming noise.

Turning towards Spicer, the ox "lowered its horns and waved its tail in the air. He got up, very red in the face, stood right in front of it and fired a bullet into its forehead at point blank range. It fell to the ground at his feet."

"It's just the same with buffalo," said Spicer as he handed the rifle to Waterhouse. "You've got to face up to them. It's only when they lower their heads to charge that they expose the vital spot!"

They stayed for five days at Mwenda Mkosi before the trailers were ready. During this period Dr. Hanschell was called out to treat a Greek pedlar who had come down with tick fever and was laid up at a Belgian government rest house. He made the eight-mile trip on a bicycle and was chased by a pack of baboons for almost the entire journey. He was terrified as they bowled along beside him, grunting and baring their teeth. But he arrived safely and gave the Greek—"a tall thin bearded white man with fierce glaring eyes, yellow face and long black finger-nails"—an injection, then collected the ticks stuck to the walls in a tobacco tin.

Back at camp, he told Spicer of his ordeal with the baboons. Spicer was unsympathetic and launched into a tale of how he used to shoot them from his survey boat going up the Gambia River, to prevent them raiding peanut plantations, which they dug up with their claws.

"We saw hundreds of them," he said. "I got tired of firing at them with a rifle, only one round at a time, so I changed over to my double-barrelled shotgun. I bagged so many with buckshot that I had a letter of commendation from the Governor. I preserved the pelts of the finest in Cooper's Sheep Dip—there's lots of it out in the Gambia you know—and I had a fur coat with a little cap to match made of them for my wife. It was the envy of all the other women! None of them could get one like it!"

The Greek pedlar—or *smous,* as they are known in South Africa—turned up at Mwenda Mkosi village a few days later, bringing imitation wrist-watches, tinned meat and old clothes. According to Shankland, one of the expedition's bearers bought a gold-laced tunic that had once adorned a hussar.

"Who's that dirty stiff walking about the camp?" asked Spicer, on seeing the pedlar.

Dr. Hanschell explained about his mercy mission into the bush.

"You don't deserve much credit for keeping a thing like that alive!" said Spicer, walking away.

Falling into conversation with the Greek, the doctor asked him if he understood the mysteries of self-raising flour. He did and showed the cooks, and thenceforth the bread rose and the expedition's diet improved.

Spirits rose, too, on 2 September when the ox-teams arrived, having been driven all the way up from South Africa:

Three columns of dust were seen coming along the road, [writes Shankland] and out of the dust three wagons appeared, each drawn by eight pairs of oxen. They were magnificent beasts with wide upturned horns which measured six feet from tip to tip. The leading teams were driven by a tall young Boer wearing a broad-brimmed hat, open shirt and long dust-coloured trousers. He walked beside the first wagon, shouting continuously and cracking a long whip: it was so long that he could reach any of the oxen without leaving his position. A Zulu "Voorlooper" walked in front, guiding the team by means of a leather thong, or "riem," attached to the horns of the leading oxen.

As luck would have it, the trailers were ready on the same day the oxen arrived. This time without the benefit of Monsieur's crane, Wainwright anxiously supervised the lifting of *Mimi* and *Toutou* on to the trailers, which were now made up of parts from three separate vehicles. *Mimi* was first to be swung up in slings from tripods. Using block and tackle and the steam engines' cables for traction, Wainwright carefully lowered the ropes in his pulleys until *Mimi* hung above her newly fashioned carriage and then, ever so gently, settled her down.

The following morning, *Mimi* and *Toutou* went forth: although not at the front of the caravan, but at the back, for they were the slowest of the party. The lorry went first, ferrying back water from streams up ahead in case the boilers should run out. Next came the African porters with their supplemented loads, chanting as they planted one foot in front of the other, followed by the *askaris* marching at an easy pace—then the extended families of both: wives with babies wrapped in cloths on their back and young children capering and calling out. The oxen came next, then finally the traction engines pulling *Mimi* and *Toutou*, puffing away as they thundered over the uneven ground, which a dozen labourers busily strewed with branches in a vain attempt to improve the going.

One thing that gave them trouble was the ant-lion, a small ant-eating insect. It dug cone-like holes in sandy ground into which ants would tumble. Unable to climb up the rolling sides of the cone, they would then be consumed by the horned and whiskered bandit which emerged from the bottom of the hole. Spicer was fascinated by them: "These holes would measure as much as 3½ feet in diameter, and were usually of some depth. Occasionally they were near the surface and, if any weight was placed on them they gave way. The danger was that, if a wheel dropped into one of these holes, the propeller shaft of the boat, which projected well below the stern, might be damaged. Eventually we got the natives to tap the ground ahead; with their finer senses, they could scrape off the surface growth, thus marking the places to be avoided."

Despite the irregular surface, the new trailers held firm. The cables took the strain and the two giant Scots, Tait and Mollison, walked alongside, making sure that the limbs of overhanging trees did not clip the boats' rudders or tear loose the forecastles. Farther up the ragged line, the Boer driver cracked his whip, yelling in Afrikaans when the oxen slipped and floundered. As the party moved forwards, the men and animals and machines made a procession several miles long, the smokestacks of the tractors and dust-clouds from the oxen marking its passage from afar. And so all day long, and for days afterwards, *Mimi* and *Toutou* went forth.

Chapter Eight

Each morning, as the smell of woodsmoke filled the camp, those who hadn't done so the night before filled up their water bottles from Dr. Hanschell's chaguls. They then queued up for tea and porridge, to fortify themselves for the day ahead. Some time previously, in the early hours before daylight, the porters had gathered up embers from last night's dying fire and wrapped them in leaves, in order to preserve them for the next stopping-place. The porters had then stoked the fire for the breakfast cook-up, before heading out of camp, leaving the *muzungu*, or white men, to wake in their own good time. This they would generally do to a deafening dawn chorus of tropical birds.

The servants Tom, Rupia and Marapandi might bring the senior officers tea in bed. Spicer, Dr. Hanschell and Eastwood would then get up and attend to their personal ablutions. Part of these included

Spicer's shaving with his cut-throat razors. Tyrer combing his yellow hair and fixing his monocle in his eye had once been a familiar morning sight—but there had been no news of Piccadilly Johnny for some time.

As usual, Tait and Mollison would roll towards the porridge pot like the biblical giants Gog and Magog. Their deliberate lumbering methods, says Shankland, "infuriated Dudley, who, as a cadet, had been taught to jump at a word of command, race to the mast-head and down again, and work to a stop-watch. Tait and Mollison refused to be hustled. They would gaze with patient wonder at the thin dry gesticulating Dudley, and what they thought of him nobody knew, for Tait spoke little and Mollison practically not at all."

Each new day was another step forward on the great task. Using one of the milometers, it was established that since leaving Mwenda Mkosi they averaged six miles a day. It was slow going, and hot too. *Mimi* and *Toutou*'s hulls were beginning to warp under the sun, in spite of their tarpaulins.

Something in the men prayed for the rains against which they were racing. They longed—as the trees and shrubs seemed to do—for the cataclysmic downpour of the second rainy season, which would begin in October, less than a month away.

The prevailing landscape was now the dry tree-savannah known locally as *miombo*. Seldom exceeding 50 feet, the spreading crowns of its *Pterocarpus* species covered vast areas on either side of Lake Tanganyika, playing an important part in the region's economic life. Bushbuck, sable and roan antelope abounded here, with lions in customary attendance, ready to pounce from the yellow grasses.

Small rodents such as the hyrax also thrived in this habitat, and were sometimes hunted by setting alight long lines of brush to drive them into nets. However, most of the fires that swept through the region were the result of natural combustion—except for a few caused by human error.

After talking about bread with the *smous,* Dr. Hanschell had braved the baboons once more to cycle back to the tick-infested rest house where the pedlar had stayed. Judging it unfit for human habitation, he decided to burn it to the ground.

It came first as a crackling noise on the wind, accompanied by a faint smell of burning. This grew stronger and before long the expedition could see a curtain of smoke rolling towards them over the savannah at a rapid pace. By the time it was half a mile away there were licks of orange flame at the men's feet. This was deadly serious. Realising they could be engulfed, Spicer ordered a firebreak to be lit for about a hundred yards. It went up quickly, scorching the men's faces and producing far more smoke than the steam engines' exhausts. Within a quarter of an hour, the charred, smouldering line of the firebreak was engulfed by the bushfire.

Spicer flicked his fly-whisk, weighing his options. The main worry was *Mimi* and *Toutou.* They would go up like matchsticks if the fire came near. And it was near. Flames leaped wildly into the air around the locomotives and the boats, and the men choked in the thick smoke as they tried to protect them. Spicer moved the entire expedition on to the still-smoking, blackened ground of the firebreak: the massive wheels of the engines, the oxen's hooves, the boots of the naval volunteers and the bare feet of the labourers, all crowded on to this narrow strip of hot grey ash. Anyone wearing shoes with crêpe rubber soles began to feel them stick. Yet the barefoot porters seemed unconcerned, the skin on their feet hardened by years of tramping through the bush.

Round about them, spinning through the smoke, whirled clouds of white egrets and other birds snapping at the myriad insects being driven out by the flames. A zigzag of brown and grey rodents could also be seen in the unburnt grass, frantically climbing over stalks and tussocks of earth to escape the heat. Buzzards swooped down and grabbed them as they fled.

This massive fire barely merits a mention in Magee's account. "Bush fires annoyed us a good deal," he writes, "and we frequently had to make a hurried shift to avoid being burnt out." Perhaps his brevity indicates just how harrowing it was—so much so that he doesn't want to relive it in print. One certainly gets a more powerful sense of the danger from Dr. Hanschell's account (as related by Shankland):

Suddenly the wind changed. Instead of carrying the fiercest of fire straight towards them it blew the flames slantwise towards the road they had come up, and passed only 150 yards from them, blistering their faces. The smaller flames petered out on reaching the line where the new fire had been started. A great gust of wind followed, swirling smoke and ashes in their faces and showering them with bits of burning grass and embers: men climbed up onto the boats and beat out those that showered on the covering tarpaulins. Soon the danger was past and they all stood with eyes streaming and blackened faces with *Mimi* and *Toutou* in a burnt-out desert, with here and there a clump of trees still smouldering.

The bushfire bonded the men and in the ensuing period they all put their backs into the work. But they were soon to be challenged again. Having fought the fire, they were now short of water. Travelling across the plain beyond Mwenda Mkosi, making for the foothills of the Mitumbas, they had encountered many dry spots. It was assumed these had caused the fire, though the suspicion was raised that it might have been Africans in the pay of the Germans (certainly Zimmer's memoirs suggest they knew the "top-secret" mission was on its way, though he mentions no such countermeasures). At this stage nobody seems to have suspected it was the rest house that Dr. Hanschell had burned down.

Water was growing scarcer and scarcer, and the *miombo* began to feel like a desert. The lorry brought back just enough water to quench the thirsty boilers of the steam engines, and the men frequently had to sacrifice their drinking and washing supply for the same. Occasionally, they were driven to seek out rare patches of swampy ground where they would dig down deep and squeeze the mud through mosquito nets to extract the moisture. But for the time being, there was just enough.

There were plenty of other difficulties. The traction engines kept tumbling over on their sides. Or they bogged down in streams. Or sand silted up their boilers. There were bridges to build, rivers to ford, trees to uproot with dynamite. What's more, the oxen that helped shift the engines when they got stuck began to die—from tsetse fever, tick fever, exhaustion. There was nothing the Boer driver or his Zulu assistant could do.

Contrary to everyone's expectations—including his old adversary, Engineer Lieutenant Cross—Spicer kept his cool. Only two signs of stress showed: the constant smoking of the monogrammed cigarettes in his long holder and the nervous tic of letting his beard grow for two days, then shaving it off again, week after week. "Throughout all these difficulties and apprehensions," writes Byron Farwell in *The Great War in Africa,* "Spicer-Simson remained calm and confident, undismayed by present difficulties or thoughts of future problems. Micawber-like, he trusted to his luck, sure that something would turn up—as, indeed, frequently happened."

Without warning one day a sunburnt Belgian officer emerged from the scrub at the head of a column of *askaris.* He introduced himself as Lieutenant Freiesleben* and explained (for he spoke fluent English) that he had been sent by the Vice-Governor-General of the Katanga back in Elizabethville. Some of the men in his column, he announced, could supplement the expedition's existing guard, provided Commander Spicer-Simson was willing to accept them. The

---

*Freiesleben was actually a Dane in the Belgian service. Coincidentally, a man of the same name was the river captain Joseph Conrad was sent to relieve on the trip up the Congo in 1890 that inspired his *Heart of Darkness* (1902). In the novella he is called Fresleven.

new *askaris* unhooked their bandoliers, set up their rifles in tripods and sat down on the dusty ground, tired out after their hard march. They wore shorts, so their knees were covered in tsetse bites or with ticks they had gathered as they passed through the long grass.

As *Mimi* and *Toutou* were laid up for the night, a sentry was posted. The oxen were driven out to pasture by the Boer and his Zulu, and the steam locomotives—their boilers emitting strange pings and clanks as the heat dissipated—were washed down and their gauges checked. A broken gauge glass would spell disaster, as steam would escape through it and the metal plates in the combustion chamber below the boiler would buckle. While these nightly chores were completed, Freiesleben was invited to join the officers' mess.

At first he declined, then changed his mind. He turned up at the little dining area the British officers had created under some trees carrying two bottles of wine, and he proved to be very convivial company. During dinner, accordingly to Shankland's account, Spicer gave his formal reply to the Belgian officer. He thanked the Vice-Governor-General for sending men to guard *Mimi* and *Toutou* as they got closer to the German lines, and accepted the extra troops to protect the expedition.

Freiesleben burst out laughing (he had very white teeth, Dr. Hanschell recalled).

"You think we are here to protect you?" he asked. "No, *mon Commandant*, we are here to protect the Congo from you!"

His cigarette-holder poised halfway to his mouth, Spicer was for once rendered speechless and it fell to Dr. Hanschell to step into the breach.

"I don't think the Congo is in much danger from us," he said. "We're nearly all amateurs, you know, except for the Commander."

"Exactly!" replied Freiesleben triumphantly. "That's precisely the point. You English have a genius for amateurism. That's what makes you so dangerous. It's always pretty obvious what professionals are going to do, but who but amateurs could have dreamed up an expedition like this?"

Spicer recovered his voice. "You appear to think better of our prospects than most of your colleagues," he said. He was probably thinking of the Belgian sporting gentlemen in Elizabethville who had laid 100 to 1 against them making the lake.

"Yes," agreed Freiesleben. "I think twenty-eight English amateurs with guns in their hands are capable of any folly—of any heroism—and no government in its senses would allow them to wander about unwatched. We'll be very relieved to get you out of the Katanga again, I can assure you. You nearly took it over once, with fewer men than that!"

Spicer was perplexed. "You really can't believe that we have any designs against our allies?"

"Perhaps not. I can only say that you English amateurs have been quite good in the past at taking other people's colonies."

Freiesleben turned his sunburnt face to the doctor. "And when we heard that you were already burning down government property, the Vice-Governor-General thought it was time someone should investigate."

At this, the doctor's own face went rather red.

A few days later, on 4 September, with Freiesleben's men protecting their flanks, the expedition reached a place called Mobile Kabantu. Here, on an expanse of sandy ground surrounded by dense scrub, Lee had built them a thatched barn in which to store material as they prepared for their ascent of the Mitumbas. The mountain range towered above them all as *Mimi* and *Toutou* arrived at the new camp. Beyond the ridge, storm clouds were rumbling, as if some great mountain god were warning them to go no farther.

That evening, as the expedition were buttoning themselves into their sleeping bags, there was a furious cry, followed by the sound of rifle shots. Spicer's boy, Tom, sprinted into the bush as his master shot at him six times from his tent.

Chapter Nine

At breakfast Spicer explained that Tom had scratched his cherished razors by rubbing them in sand. The poor boy, who had somehow escaped the volley of shots, had only been trying to win his master's favour by sharpening them. It is said (though only by white authorities) that Tom did not seem any the worse for his near-death experience. He still poured the tea with a smile as the team prepared for another day's work. The day in question was 5 September 1915—eighty-two days since they had left London—and they were about to ascend the Mitumbas.

Things started well. By the end of the day they had climbed 14½ miles up the mountainside on their narrow, winding road. On the 6th they had to wash out the boilers of the steam engines, which were silted up with muddy water, the supply of which remained a problem. On the 7th they reached the biggest of the bridges that Lee had built in expectation of their passage. It was 108 feet long and 32 feet below was a dried-up river gorge. Like the first bridge, which needed to be rebuilt, this one was made of timber—about 500 tons worth, said Wainwright, who was in charge of the transport train.

The bouncing pathway of logs covered with soil held up well. Pulled by the first locomotive—attached by a steel cable—*Mimi* slowly crossed the gorge. The engine was in the process of mounting the other side, which came up from the bridge at quite an incline, when the cable began to fray and suddenly snapped. The customised trailer carrying *Mimi* careered back down to the bridge, striking it with such force that the trailer bounced to one side and stopped—hovering over the rocks in the old river bed below—with one wheel in mid-air.

There was chaos as men rushed to grab the cable, while another length of twisted steel was run out from the steam engine and attached to *Mimi*. Slowly they managed to haul her back on to the bridge. The locomotive's wheels ground the dust as she dragged *Mimi* up the incline; the men put wedges of timber under the trailer's wheel to stop it rolling back should the cable break again. Eventually the slope was too steep. They uncoupled *Mimi*, moving her to one side, and brought the second engine over and hooked it up to the first. But even with both traction engines attached (a procedure Wainwright called "double-banking") the gradient was too much. The soil was simply too soft for the wheels of the steam engines to get a grip, in spite of their six-inch treads.

After a brief discussion it was decided to bring up the oxen. The Boer herded them over the bridge and beyond the two linked engines. There were thirty-two animals yoked side by side, the Zulu pulling a leather cord attached to the front yoke and the Boer standing alongside with his long *sjambok* whip. He spoke to the oxen in "horse-whisperer" fashion, calling each one by a special name. The meaning of the Afrikaans words *Engelsmann* ("Englishman") and *Rooinek* ("Redneck") was obvious enough to the expedition, but they found much of what the Boer said was incomprehensible.

The beasts were attached to the front of the first locomotive, so that the chain now ran: oxen, first traction engine, second traction engine and finally *Mimi* on her trailer. The other trailer, bearing *Toutou,* was still back down the mountain, below the bridge. In the rough soil on either side of the road stood Spicer—smoking obsessively, he simply let Wainwright take charge—and those members of the expedition not directly involved with the transport, such as Dr. Hanschell. They were joined by dozens of Africans who had come out of the bush to watch the fun. Shankland takes up the story:

> The oxen, with backs arched and hooves gripping the soft surface better than the wheels, seemed at times to be dragging the two locos and *Mimi* and her trailer as well. *"Engelsmann! Rooinek!"* the Boer shouted. *"Boschmann! Chaka!"* and as each ox heard his name he hurled his weight forward, but he got the lash just the same—it seemed to the doctor that *Engelsmann* and *Rooinek,* because of their names, got an extra vicious lash.

This struggle continued for another day, as mile by mile they crept towards the top of the Mitumbas. Every hour threatened the arrival of the rains, which would make their ascent impossible. Neither wheels nor hooves would be able to cope with deep mud. When the steam engines and the oxen failed to do the job, another method was used, known as "cabling." The locomotive was uncoupled and driven several hundred yards up the slope into a specially dug pit. A hawser was then attached to a drum on the engine and *Mimi* and *Toutou* were drawn up.

Near the top of the mountain range, however, neither cabling nor double-banking was feasible: the road was too winding for the first, too narrow for the second (there was no room for the steam engines to go back and forth without falling over). Magee describes the method devised by the ingenious Wainwright to get round this problem:

A stout tree was selected about 20 yards ahead of the spot where the boat stood on its carriage in the trail. A block and tackle—that is, a pulley block with rollers, such as is used aboard any ship—was fixed to the tree. One end of the rope was attached to the boat carriage, the other end passed through the pulley block and attached by a cross-bar to the rearmost pair of oxen. The oxen faced downhill, in the opposite direction from and parallel with the boat.

Spicer later took personal credit for this plan. "Then the idea occurred to me of balancing the weight of the oxen against the eight tons or so which had to be pulled up . . . and in that way the boat came slowly up."

Drawn in this manner, 50 yards at a time, *Mimi* and *Toutou* reached the top of the mountain. There, 6,400 feet above sea level, they came to rest on a pleasant meadow-plateau. The African bearers could lay down their loads at last, unwinding the thin cotton blankets with which they protected their heads from the heavy wooden crates and steel boxes they carried. Repairs were made to the steam engines and the trailers—*Mimi* and *Toutou* were intact, that was the important thing. The naval volunteers could congratulate themselves on a job well done and even Spicer was pleased, though he knew they still had a long way to go.

Crossing the 20-mile plateau was easy enough, except that now a great many lions surrounded the camp at night. On 12 September they reached the other side and saw far down below them the Lualaba, or Upper Congo, River, on which they would soon enough continue their journey. Or so they thought. In fact, going down the Mitumba plateau proved no easier than climbing up it. On the first day the hawser broke and the leading steam engine, suddenly relieved of its burden, shot downwards, unable to stop. Slewing wildly, it struck a tree, almost catapulting the driver out of his seat. It was a lucky escape, for he narrowly avoided a drop of several hundred feet into the gorge below. After that, *Mimi* and *Toutou* were lowered down the steeper gradients by teams of men, until they reached places where the steam engines could take over again. Sometimes, says Spicer, the gradient was so steep they had to bury a "dead man," that is, "several blocks of timber 20 feet long—about 8 or 9 feet in the ground, with a wire strapped round them and brought up to the surface, thus acting as an anchor; then by means of a hawser and bollard we managed to ease the traction engine gently down the slope."

And so the precarious descent continued, hindered considerably by the constant search for water for the engines' boilers. They tracked down only slimy pools here and there, until one day the inevitable happened. The engines ran out, but before the expedition's drinking water was plundered once more they discovered that more than four hundred people—including porters, road-builders, camp servants and the naval volunteers themselves—had a mere ten gallons left to share. There was nothing left for the oxen, who had begun to paw the dust in frustration.

Three parties of water-scouts were sent out, one under Dr. Hanschell, who returned with a few petrol tins full of what was really more mud than liquid. But the day was saved by Wainwright, whose party returned with 150 African women. On their heads were balanced clay pots full of water, which they had carried up from a natural well some eight miles away.

The women had to make the trip several times before the steam engines had been filled and the African labourers had quenched their thirst. The Europeans had to wait until Dr. Hanschell had boiled theirs in his five-gallon drums. Smelling the water, the oxen began to bellow loudly. Only when they, too, had been watered could the women finally put down their pots. It is unclear whether they were ever recompensed for this astonishing act of mercy. According to Hanschell (via Shankland), "Each received a generous length of cloth as payment and reward," but Magee maintains the women were commandeered: "That the gentle susceptibilities of white folk may not be unnecessarily aroused by the fact that the native women were 'rounded up' to fetch water, it may be said that the work in this country is done by the women of the native villages, while the men loaf—sad yet true."*

Thirsty, sun-bleached and aching all over, Spicer's men reached Sankisia at the foot of the plateau on 28 September. Almost six weeks after they had begun their journey, *Mimi* and *Toutou* were nearing water once again. The Boer was paid for his services and released—now he had to lead his oxen all the way across the mountains. As for the steam engines, they were cleaned, oiled and put into storage.

The Belgians had built a railway in this part of the country using supply routes up the Congo River of very much the type described by Joseph Conrad in *Heart of Darkness*. Eighteen miles of track linked Sankisia to the river at Bukama, where the Congo was known as the Lualaba (the name changed at Stanley Falls, farther north). A trading-station for ivory and diamonds, Sankisia did not have much going for it, but it was connected to the telegraph system and this enabled Spicer to contact the Admiralty about the food supplies he had forgotten. He requested they be sent from Kinshasa, the Atlantic Ocean port in the far west of the Congo, where the Liverpool-based firm of Lever Brothers (later Unilever) had a depot.

From Kinshasa, writes Conrad in *Heart of Darkness*, the river makes its way across the Congo, "resembling an immense snake uncoiled, with its head in the sea, its body at rest curving afar over a vast country, and its tail lost in the depths of the land." Once they had loaded the boats onto the train and reached Bukama, just two hours away, Spicer's men would be at the tail end. But whether Spicer himself, that "obscure conqueror of fame," that "exalted egoist" (the phrases are from another of Conrad's novels, *Lord Jim*), would be able to see through the next stage of their journey was still uncertain.

---

*In his lecture Spicer says: "We bribed the women by supplying them with gaudy waist-cloths—in that place a woman is regarded as over-dressed if she has two articles of clothing."

Chapter Ten

On 1 October 1915 at around 2 p.m. a train carrying *Mimi* and *Toutou* and their crews arrived over a skeletal iron bridge at Bukama Station in the central Congo. Under the bridge ran the Lualaba River, on which our expedition would make the next leg of their journey. Down by the water were some desolate sheds and a dingy shop selling cheap goods. The place was thick with mosquitoes.

Dr. Hanschell sensed it would be unwise to stay too long: everything about Bukama spelled fever. In any case, Spicer was eager to be off. He had shown some good sense in hiring a river-pilot called Mauritzen, a stocky, fair-haired fellow who wore a straw hat and a white suit. Like Freiesleben, he was a Dane in the employ of the Belgians. Mauritzen was a trained hydrographer, expert at charting rivers and seas—a skill Spicer shared . . .

The Dane looked on as *Toutou,* still in her wooden cradle, slid down some iron rails into the river. The cradle was knocked away with hammers and to everyone's relief she floated clear. But for how long? queried Mauritzen. He explained to Spicer that the river was very shallow farther down and its sandy bottom could sometimes shift, making it difficult to follow charts. He suggested raising each motor boat on eight empty petrol drums, four on either side, with grass-filled sacks between the hull and the drums for protection.

It worked: *Toutou* "drew" less (sat more shallowly in the water). An extension was fitted to the rudder so that she could still be steered. Her engine was started—that worked, too. By 5 p.m. *Mimi* was afloat as well, the white ensign (the red cross on a white ground that is the flag of the Royal Navy) fluttering at her prow. It was only then that they discovered both boats had sprung leaks and *Mimi* and *Toutou* were hastily hauled up the rails on to dry land.

The journey upriver would not start for another week. They had to wait for the supplies to go on ahead, as well as mend the leaks—the mahogany boards that made up the sides of *Mimi* and *Toutou* had warped in the intense heat and their seams had opened. This necessitated, writes Magee, "taking out the engines, caulking the seams, and submerging the boats, which then resumed their normal seaworthy condition." While this was being done the stores and camping equipment, along with other material, were transferred into immense dugout canoes, carved from tree trunks. The largest of these could bear three tons and were big enough to carry the pieces of the motor boats' cradles, which would be needed later in the journey.

On 3 October, Tait—the Scot who lost a finger at Ypres—was separated from his bosom pal Mollison and sent on with a company of *askaris,* at the head of a flotilla of canoes, with orders to transfer stores to depots ahead. Tait's flotilla also carried *Mimi* and *Toutou*'s special cradles. Three days later the motor boats followed, towed by river barges propelled by Congolese paddlemen. Spicer considered it too dangerous to use *Mimi* and *Toutou*'s engines, the probability of a collision with a sandbank at speed being all too likely. In a canoe at the front of this floating caravan sat the pilot, Mauritzen, wearing his white linen suit, panama hat, and carrying a rifle across his knees.

Not long after they set out, *Mimi* struck a sandbank. Dragging her loose took several hours, as all of her heavy equipment had to be unloaded. Leaving their own craft, the paddlemen helped lift her free, the naval volunteers using mangrove poles to lever her prow. This manoeuvre was frequently repeated in the course of their journey, which was full of bends and backwaters. Mauritzen was also well aware of the dangers of hidden rocks or submerged branches. Spicer agreed, saying he had encountered many similar "snags" in the Gambia.*

When the going was good, the volunteers simply soaked up the atmosphere, marvelling at the green mansions that rose up either side of the river. They were in the real jungle now: the deep forest that had once formed an immense equatorial belt across Africa's middle. The thick-girthed trees, heavy with moss and liana, seemed to carry within them the observances of previous generations; and they remembered also, or so it seemed, a time when there were no human eyes to observe them. Hiding in the ancient groves were several varieties of bamboo and palm trees, including those bearing "palm nuts," from which oil was produced. Here and there, nearer the bank, were clumps of giant hibiscus flowers, which closed their red petals at night, and pockets of white maduras from which poison for arrow-tips was extracted by local tribes.

Of these at first there was no sign. The only human sound was the occasional chant from the oarsmen beating time as their blades dipped in and out of the water and the boats heaved forwards. The volunteers mainly kept silent, awed and not a little humbled by the majesty of the surrounding forest. Only when something remarkable was seen—like the gleaming shells of turtles on the water's

---

*In Conrad's *Heart of Darkness* such "snags" appear as a distinctive shape disturbing the fairway of the river. As Marlow says: "I caught sight of a V-shaped ripple on the water ahead. What? Another snag!"

surface—did one of them pipe up. There were also hundreds of snout-nosed crocodiles basking on the river bank or winking from the shallows. They posed little danger, but Mauritzen kept his rifle handy all the same. Far more deadly were the hippos that lived in the river, he explained, as they thought nothing of rising under a boat to overturn it.

The main sound on the Lualaba River was birdsong—the croak of hornbills nesting in hollow trees or the eerie cry of a fish-eagle as it dived to scoop its prey from the water. The men could see partridges and guinea fowl near the bank and the occasional heron stalking through the shallows. But most noteworthy were the hummingbirds: red and blue and emerald, they hovered next to the boats, their wings a blur of colour. They were joined by black-and-white kingfishers swooping to and fro over the dark swirling water.

On that first day the expedition covered only three miles. They hit sandbanks or mudbars fourteen times before turning in and setting up camp on the river bank. In the pitch-blackness of the night many of them lay awake listening to the grunted conversations of hippos, the chattering of baboons and the famous "laughter" of hyenas—but insects were their greatest bugbear. The men always tried to eat before dark, otherwise their candles and hurricane lamps would attract hordes of "flying things," as Magee calls them in the *National Geographic*. "A plate of soup, a few minutes after being placed on the table, became a seething mass of floundering insect life."

The morning sun revealed a different landscape along the river: high grass and palms fringed the banks for miles, breaking occasionally to reveal acres of open savannah where antelope grazed and elephant came down to the river to drink. Fortunately there were fewer snags on this stretch. Overtaking Tait and his flotilla of canoes on that second afternoon, the men with *Mimi* and *Toutou* must have thought themselves in a kind of paradise, though some spoiled it by taking potshots at the animals on the bank. Again Conrad's words come to mind: "In the empty immensity of earth, sky, and water . . . incomprehensible, firing into a continent."

The day ended with a terrible discovery. It left those involved very shaken, but once again Magee omits to mention it in his narrative—perhaps not wishing to offend the "gentle susceptibilities of white folk." Dr. Hanschell, on the other hand, left Shankland in no doubt as to what had happened:

> Towards evening a gap appeared where they could get ashore. They landed, scrambled up a steep bank, pushed their way through dense undergrowth and found them-selves in a deserted village, abandoned like many others in the district because of the ravages of sleeping sickness. A stockade surrounding the village had sprouted into a thicket and all the exit paths were blocked by grass standing eight feet high. The roofs of the huts had fallen in, wooden bowls and earthenware pots lay among the rubbish, and an unfinished piece of weaving hung in a primitive loom. As they approached, a cloud of flies rose droning and hovering over their heads: rats scuttled away from under their feet. Human bones lay all around, cracked open by hyenas to get at the marrow.

The expedition spent an uncomfortable night in this grove of death.

The next day the insect peril followed them to the water. No sooner had the cool of dawn lifted—a moment presaged by a dread-ful hum in the distance—than a vast cloud of tsetse flies swept downriver. The Congolese stopped paddling and started beating them off their bare backs with swatches of cloth. Spicer's men used the fly-whisks purchased in Elizabethville. The pain of the tsetse bite is "like the prick of a red-hot needle," notes Magee, and the whisks had to be employed with some force: "The flies can bite through clothing quite easily, and actually have to be knocked off, it being impossible to shake them clear."

While they were being bitten the paddlers lost control of the boats—they slewed sideways—and it took some time for the order of the convoy to be re-established. Once the cloud of flies had lifted, the paddlers dipped their long blades back in the water and, to the rhythm of their chant, began heaving forwards again. They hardly went ten yards, however, before the dreadful hum would be heard again and once more they would all be switching and swearing.

The flies became so bad that Spicer decided to risk using *Mimi* and *Toutou*'s 100-horsepower engines. They had struck deeper water now and it seemed safe to assume they were less likely to hit anything. The petrol drums were cast off from the keels of the motor boats and the barges that had previously pulled *Mimi* and *Toutou* were now taken behind them; it was their turn to be towed. For probably the first and only time in their lives the paddlemen could hitch a ride, and it was with wonder that they watched the high-powered engines churn through the silver-black river. The extra speed meant they were able to leave the tsetses behind.

The following day, scratching at their bites, Spicer's men spotted more animals in the papyrus reeds and grass along the bank. Inevitably, some of them wanted to shoot again and this time Spicer allowed them to unload their Enfields into the bush. One gets a sense of what this must have been like from the travel journals of Evelyn Waugh, who made the same journey (albeit in the opposite direction) fifteen years later:

> The captain employed his time in inflicting slight wounds on passing antelope with a miniature rifle. Occasionally he would be convinced he had killed something; the boat would stop and all the native passengers disembark and scramble up the side with loud whoops and yodels. There was difficulty in getting them back. The captain would watch them, through binoculars, plunging and gambolling

about in the high grass; at first he would take an interest in the quest, shouting directions to them; then he would grow impatient and summon them back; they would disappear further and further, thoroughly enjoying their romp. He would have the siren sounded for them—blast after blast. Eventually they would come back, jolly, chattering, and invariably empty-handed.

With no doubt similar delays, *Mimi* and *Toutou* made their slow progress upriver. As the sun was setting, somebody spotted a steamer. Its smoking chimney above the reeds gave away its position. After a mile or two of struggling in its wake, the expedition pulled alongside. It was a vessel of the Belgian company that ran the Congo, its deck populated by a medley of African passengers and their livestock, together with a few white traders, as well as mailbags and other freight. Most of the room was taken up with stacks of wood for the boilers. The ship's sides were grimy with river muck, but its name, *Constantin de Burlay,* was rather romantic.

They were not well received. The captain, who came to the white-painted rail to inspect them, spoke only Flemish. Nevertheless, profanities are a universal language. A "burly, choleric unshaven individual," according to Shankland, Captain Blaes was not very amenable to Spicer's mimed suggestion that their stores be loaded aboard the steamer. In fact, he retreated to his cabin, whence "the volleys of *Gotfer!* and *Gotferdomme!* that issued . . . sounded very like English goddams."

Eastwood took over the negotiations. His blandishments, translated into Flemish by the steamer's purser, were relayed to the indignant Captain Blaes. Eventually the patient Methodist prevailed. It was agreed the *Constantin* would wait for Tait's party to arrive and that the stores would be loaded on to the steamer's lighter (a small boat she towed behind).

In the morning *Mimi* and *Toutou* continued upriver, Mauritzen joining Spicer in *Mimi* at the front of the procession. The crocodiles were larger in this section of the water and the men kept their rifles ready; but if they were ever in danger it was from a nearby hippopotamus, which opened its massive mouth to reveal bright pink gums and fearsome, tusk-like teeth. One crunch of its powerful jaws and the boats would be reduced to splinters. The men wanted to squirt some lead into its mouth. Some took a few shots, but missed and an argument broke out, Dr. Hanschell objecting that it was cruel and unsporting. Spicer took his side and ordered everyone to cease fire. The creature followed them for hours all the same, its head just above the water as it pursued them without a sound.

Winding through floating clumps of light-green vegetation, the expedition progressed under the relentless sun (everyone wore a solar topi now). Sitting or lying on the boats, the men watched slender palms and massive baobabs scroll by on the bank. This was the Africa they had always imagined—but more so, so much more so. Every now and then tributaries flowed off into the forest wilderness and it was here that elephants often appeared. Wreathed in creepers and grasses, these mighty beasts would spread their ears and, lifting their trunks, trumpet at the boats as they went by. *Mimi* and *Toutou* also passed more villages, from some of which the inhabitants would emerge, standing tall and proud on the bank above, hands on hips, disdainful of strangers.

For many members of the Naval Africa Expedition, products of their own period in history, the Africans were little more than beasts. Like someone staring into a thick fog, they could not see the humanity there. The people on the shore and the animals on the shore were one and the same: simple embodiments of the wilderness—pawns in the romantic primitivist game the white man had been playing with Africa for the past forty years. It all happened remarkably quickly. In 1875 only a tenth of Africa was under European control; by 1895 only a tenth was not.

However, some exceptional individuals can see through the fog of their time. David Livingstone could, with his never-faltering concern for African people. At this juncture, Spicer's expedition was passing through a region that the great Scottish explorer had charted a generation earlier. It was the Congo basin, a vast trough of alluvial soil surrounded by dripping hill-slopes. But when Livingstone was travelling here, he thought the Congo-Lualaba was either a northern branch of the Zambezi or (which he rather hoped) part of the Nile. It was a time of great hardship for him. His followers had deserted him and stolen his medicine chest and he was suffering from ulcers on his feet, while also struggling with bouts of pneumonia, dysentery and cholera. Every joint in his body was swollen with rheumatic fever from constant exposure to the wet. Eventually, he had to attach himself to a party of Arab ivory hunters, who turned out to be slavers and thieves, kidnapping and murdering wherever they went.

"I am heart-broken at the sight of human blood," he wrote in his moving *Last Journals,* his hand shaking with fever as he tried to steady the pen on the paper.

Earlier in his journey, Livingstone had spotted from some mountains a wide expanse of water and christened it Lake Liemba; it was in fact Lake Tanganyika. Like Waugh in 1930, he was coming from practically the opposite direction to Spicer's expedition, but he was passing through the same forests as the Naval Africa Expedition and they had not changed much in the intervening half-century:

Into these primeval woods, the sun, though vertical, cannot penetrate, except as sending down their [*sic*] pencils of rays into the gloom. The rain-water stands for months in stagnant pools made by elephants' feet, and the dead leaves decay on the damp soil. One feels himself the veriest pigmy before these gigantic trees; many of their roots, high out of the soil in the path, keep you constantly looking down, and a good gun does no harm to the parrots and guinea-fowl on their tops. The climbing plants, from the size of a whipcord to that of a man-o'-war's hawser, make the ancient path the only passage.

Near to where he wrote this, Livingstone heard of how the great river—the Lualaba, or Nile, as he was now erroneously convinced it was—spread into a large lake and joined with another river, the Lufira. It was at precisely this junction point that Spicer's men found themselves on the morning of 11 October 1915. First they had to navigate through a swamp, and as the channels between the beds of tangled reeds grew narrower and narrower, Mauritzen argued it was dangerous to keep using *Mimi* and *Toutou*'s engines. There was too great a chance of their propellers gathering up strands of vegetation and twisting the shaft to the engine.

Their brief holiday over, the Congolese paddlemen were once again put to work. As they paddled through the reeds—sometimes getting out to tug the boats through by hand, as Bogart and Hepburn would do during the filming of *The African Queen* thirty-six years later—enormous numbers of birds flew up from their nesting places in the marsh. Not just the kind of waterfowl familiar to Europeans—ducks, geese, herons and cormorants—but great African monsters like the Maribou stork, the pelican and the crested crane.

Eventually *Mimi* and *Toutou* emerged from the swamp and into Lake Kisale, where the current of the two rivers converged. The lake was famous for its floating islands, which were inhabited by fishermen. In his record of the explorations of Stanley and Livingstone, John Geddie describes the methods of Kisale fishermen:

> The matted growths of aquatic plants fringing its shores are cut off in sections, and towed to the centre of the lake. Logs, brushwood, and earth are laid on the floating platform, until it acquires a consistency capable of supporting a native hut and a plot of bananas and other fruit trees, with a small flock of goats and poultry. The island is anchored by a stake driven into the bed of the lake; and if the fishing become scarce, or should other occasion occur for shifting his domicile, the proprietor simply draws the peg, and shifts

his floating little mansion, farm, and stock, whither he chooses.*

Another type of floating dwelling greeted Spicer and his team. Coming faintly over the lake could be heard the tinkling of a piano and looking out across an expanse of rippling blue water, over a bed of white sand, they eventually spied a barge on which had been built a small house.

"It's my place," Mauritzen explained, coolly inviting Spicer and Dr. Hanschell to lunch.

The music stopped as they climbed aboard and a young blonde-haired woman in a white dress and sandals emerged on deck.

"My wife," added Mauritzen. As they embraced, a native servant fetched drinks and cigarettes. Spicer and the doctor followed the Mauritzens through to the cabin of their houseboat, where there were comfortable armchairs and pictures on the walls.

Lunch was delicious—fish from the lake, naturally—and they were both slightly dazed by this sudden display of civility after months of hardship. Having eaten their fill, the two hydrographers pored over charts and maps, while the doctor discussed music and literature with Mrs. Mauritzen. She was a very gracious woman, cultured as well as good-natured, and he later remembered it as the best day of the whole expedition.

Mimi and *Toutou*'s engines were started up again in the afternoon and Mauritzen kissed his wife goodbye. On leaving the lake the expedition continued for five miles upriver to the village of Kadia. Here they were flagged down by Captain Holmquist, the Belgian river superintendent, who told them it was too dangerous to continue farther. There were rocky outcrops in the river bed that might rip out the launches' hulls. There was nothing to do but wait for the unsavoury Captain Blaes and the *Constantin de Burlay* to

---

*John Geddie, *The Lake Regions of Central Africa: A Record of Modern Discovery* (Edinburgh, 1883); a book to be distinguished from Richard Burton's earlier volume of a similar name.

catch them up, hoping they might be able to load the boats on her deck.

But when he arrived Captain Blaes remained "extraordinarily uncouth and incommunicable," according to Dr. Hanschell. He was still unshaven and the contrast between him and Spicer, who was obsessed with the presentation of his facial hair, could not have been greater. Despite Tom's best efforts to ruin his cut-throats and the difficulty of finding suitable campsites along the river, Spicer had continued his peculiar practice of letting his beard grow, then shaving it off. These shaves were complicated affairs employing the full regalia of washstand, soap-stick and circular mirror.

Quite apart from the Captain's unwillingness to help, the *Constantin*'s cranes were too small to lift *Mimi* and *Toutou*. As usual it was Wainwright who came up with a solution. They would put the motor boats on the steamer's lighter, using tree trunks as a kind of bridge from the banks. He immediately sent some of the ratings into the forest to cut down trees for the job.

They laid the tree trunks out into the river in a line and the cradles and other stores were meanwhile removed from the lighter. *Toutou* was put back into her cradle while still in the water and brought close to the river bank. With pulleys and a large complement of African labour, the motor boat was pulled up the ramp of logs onto the bank. The ends of the logs were then lifted and placed onto the deck of the lighter.

One of the men involved was the red-haired seaman from Donegal, who may or may not have been William Carey. Stripped down to his shorts, he waded into the water to raise each log-end one by one. His muscular physique and porcelain-pale skin, as well as his distinctive red hair, brought coos of admiration from the womenfolk of the village, who had lined up on the bank to watch.

Seeing this, Spicer was outraged and perhaps a little jealous. "Disgusting!" he shouted. "Go and get some clothes on! Where do you think you are? Back in Donegal?!"

It was another Spicer "performance" and one that the ratings

would recall later in the expedition, when their leader began stripping off for male and female alike. But for the time being they had
serious work to do: it wasn't until the morning of 16 October—a
week after they had arrived at Kadia and ten days after they had
begun their river journey—that the motor boats had been properly
secured on the lighter and the *Constantin de Burlay* was ready to
leave.

By this stage, Captain Blaes was hopping mad. The business of
getting *Mimi* and *Toutou* on board had put him a week behind
schedule. He was a boozer, the expedition reckoned, and they didn't
think much of his passengers either. They included four convicts—
shackled at the neck and under the guard of an armed *askari*—and
several East European traders in dirty white linen suits. To these
were added a crowd of African families with children and livestock
and bags of provisions. The ship's cargo included several elephant
tusks and—tied to the side, still wriggling—a young crocodile.
Spicer's lecture about the expedition seems to suggest they actually
locked Blaes in his cabin at some point during this period, though
for form's sake the Belgian is transformed into a native caretaker:
"Dudley invited him into the captain's cabin to discuss the situation
and have a drink. He had arranged to be called away by one of his
engine-room staff, and as he went out he locked the caretaker in . . ."

The *Constantin* left just after 7 a.m. and her progress seemed to
confirm the expedition's opinion that the captain was a drunkard.
His method of sailing was to ram the steamer into the bank whenever a bend was approaching. He'd then let the current carry the
steamer round 360 degrees before continuing. They all burst out
laughing the first time this happened (Spicer's laugh, as ever, being
the loudest), but when the procedure was repeated at every bend in
the river they realised Captain Blaes was doing it on purpose. Perhaps he wasn't so blind drunk as he seemed; perhaps it was simply
the best way to get the *Constantin* downriver.

For all that, the steamer ran aground at 9:15 a.m. near the village of Mulango. Whatever they did—putting the engines into

reverse, throwing out anchors and hauling on them—she wouldn't budge. Captain Blaes's response was to retire down below, saying they would have to wait until the rains came and the river level rose, lifting the steamer from its resting place.* As the Belgian drank himself into a stupor in his cabin, Mauritzen went on to the bridge and began directing the crew. By 6 p.m. the *Constantin* was free of the sandbank.

That evening the men camped onshore in a clearing in the village. Much to Dr. Hanschell's dismay—for he believed venereal disease had been transmitted into the area by Arab slavers—many of them went with the women of Mulango that night. According to Shankland, the ladies were "bold and handsome, some of them, and dressed only in a few beads and a scrap of bark-cloth fore and aft." Some of the servants attached to the expedition began acting as procurers on their masters' behalf, running between them and the bare-breasted tribeswomen until a price had been agreed. Fortunately Spicer, who had gone to bed, saw none of this.

The convoy set off again after an early breakfast, back under the command of a hungover Captain Blaes. They had gone only a few more miles when, to everyone's fury, the *Constantin* snagged again. This time there was really no budging her. It suddenly seemed obvious enough why the Captain had resorted to the bottle and never bothered to shave. His job must have been sheer hell, if the steamer ran aground so often, and he clearly loathed himself as much as he loathed the job.

Like the riverboat captain whom Joseph Conrad deputised for during his trip up the Congo in 1890, Captain Blaes was probably half-sick with fever and dysentery, too. As an employee of the Société Anonyme Belge pour le Commerce du Haut Congo, Conrad travelled up as far as Stanley Falls on a steamer called the *Roi des Belges*. The name of the boat was no accident: nominally independ-

---

*A similar scenario gets Allnutt (Humphrey Bogart) and Rose (Katharine Hepburn) out of a fix in *The African Queen*.

ent, the Société was really a creature of King Leopold II, like every-thing else in the so-called Congo Free State at that time. Conrad fell ill himself during his four months in the Congo and grew despon-dent and world-weary, so it is easy to see how Captain Blaes had turned out the way he had. "Everything is repellent to me," Conrad wrote to his aunt. "Men and things; but especially men. And I too am repellent to them."

As the expedition sat in the river above Mulango, Wainwright sucked on his pencil, wondering how they would get *Mimi* and *Toutou* back into the water. The Lualaba flowed past on either side of the *Constantin de Burlay* and round her lighter, which carried *Mimi* and *Toutou*—from which heel-kicking vantage point Dr. Han-schell, Cross and the rest watched the waters heading north-northwest towards Stanley Falls. They were stuck fast. Surely this couldn't be journey's end after they had come so far?

Just then they spotted the smokestack of another paddle-steamer travelling in the opposite direction. Within minutes the *Baron Jansenn* hoved into view. More of a barge than a ship, it drew less water than the *Constantin* and would be able to float clear of the rocks and sandbanks that seemed to cover the river bed.

And so it proved, once Eastwood had brokered a deal between the two captains. Money changed hands, but there was no shortage of that. Eastwood had been given a great deal of petty cash for just such an emergency. The *Constantin*'s lighter, with *Mimi* and *Toutou* on board, was pulled behind the new steamer. The only losers were the mainly Congolese passengers on the *Baron Jansenn,* with their livestock, pots and pans and poultry. As it was now turning round and going back to Kabalo—the end-point of the expedition's river journey—there was little point in them staying on board. Nor was there much use in boarding the beached *Constantin de Burlay,* to wait with Captain Blaes and his bottles for the rains to come. A good few of these stranded passengers must have cursed Spicer and his men as they disappeared upriver.

Chapter Eleven

Winding through the forest, the Lualaba River passed a clearing where a few mud huts could be seen. There were also some barns made of mud, but roofed with corrugated iron instead of straw. Next to these dismal structures was a boatyard in which were stacked the rusting brown ribs of a large steamer. Together with its rivets and side panels, they looked like the bones of some ancient creature dug up from deep in the Rift. Each panel was painted with a number. Nearby, a railway siding cut away into the dense jungle. The only other building was a prison: a high-walled, grey-stone compound, its interior divided into small cells.

Viewed through a haze of mosquitoes as they pulled alongside in the *Baron Jansenn*, it was a depressing place to disembark. The sweltering heat made the whole scene feel extremely claustrophobic. Undergrowth threatened the torpid encampment on every side and even the ground on which they stood was little more than a kind of coarse vegetative mat, composed in the main of the same sort of weeds as the islands they had skirted on their way upriver.

This gloomy circle of hell was called Kabalo and the Naval Africa Expedition reached it at about 3 p.m. on 22 October 1915. When Evelyn Waugh landed there while globe-trotting in 1930, it hadn't improved much:

> It was just before sundown when we reached Kabalo, a place of forbidding aspect. There was no platform; a heap of wood-fuel and the abrupt termination of the line marked the station; there were other bits of line sprawling out to right and left; a few shabby trucks had been shunted on one of these, and apparently abandoned; there were two or three goods sheds of corrugated iron and a dirty little canteen; apart from these, no evidence of habitation.

Waugh, who came up by train from Lake Tanganyika—making the same journey as Spicer's men, but in the opposite direction—then turns his attention to the river:

> In front of us lay the Upper Congo—at this stage of its course undistinguished among the great rivers of the world for any beauty or interest; a broad flow of water, bounded by swamps; since we were in the rainy season, it was swollen and brown. A barge or two lay in to the bank, and a paddle-steamer rusted all over, which was like a flooded Thames bungalow more than a ship. A bit of the bank opposite the railway line had been buttressed up with concrete; on all sides lay rank swamp. Mercifully, night soon came on and hid this beastly place.

As Wainwright worked out how to disembark *Mimi* and *Toutou* and to ready them for the final stretch of their journey, which would bring them to Lukuga on the shore of Lake Tanganyika, the men wandered round Kabalo. The numbered iron fragments in the shipyard turned out to be bits of the *Baron Dhanis,* the "hidden" Belgian warship that had yet to be assembled. The Germans regarded it as the greatest threat to their naval power on the lake, even though it still lay in pieces; but as John Lee had explained to the Admiralty, the Belgians dared not take the *Baron Dhanis* to Lukuga, lest the Germans bombard her from the water. Despite her rusty appearance, the *Dhanis* was actually brand new. She had been at Kabalo for a year, waiting for a boiler. It was still in Antwerp, which had been captured by the Germans. The British Admiralty had sent out two twelve-pounder guns for the *Dhanis,* but since there was little likelihood of them being employed in the near future, the Belgians had taken the guns to Lukuga to use as shore batteries.

It took three days for *Mimi* and *Toutou* to be hauled on to flat-bed wagons at the rear of the train that would take them to Lukuga. On 26 October Spicer's men took their own places on the hard seats of two wooden carriages. The line was extremely uneven and the ride was so bumpy as to make it difficult to read or do anything except clutch on to something and stare out of the window. At first the country was relatively featureless: miles and miles of tall yellow grass on either side of the tracks, some of it as high as the carriages. They stopped from time to time to take on firewood for the 70-ton locomotive that pulled them along.

Then the landscape changed dramatically. The train rocked its way up into some sandstone bluffs. Reaching the top it assumed an alarming angle and plunged down into the Lukuga Valley. Below them for nearly 200 miles—sometimes foaming angrily over rocks, sometimes sluggish and clogged with water-plants and creepers—flowed a river that was at the very heart of the mystery of Lake Tanganyika. As much as the Nile—with which it was mistakenly connected by Livingstone—Lake Tanganyika was the Holy Grail of the great European explorers of Africa. Despite its vast size, it proved strangely difficult to find. But added to this, nobody quite understood how it was connected to the great river-systems surrounding it.

It was a question that Spicer, as a trained hydrographer, had considered and discussed with Mauritzen. Their discussions were footnotes to a grand tradition. While Livingstone believed that the Lualaba River and the much smaller Lukuga were at the headwaters of the Nile, Stanley was convinced they both fed into the Congo, whose source (he reasoned) must be Lake Tanganyika. But exploring the lake in his wooden sailboat, the *Lady Alice,* in 1876, Stanley found the situation to be rather more complicated. Instead of flowing out of Lake Tanganyika, as he had expected, the Lukuga River was actually flowing in, through a marshy intermediate zone. Stanley calculated that the level of the lake was rising and, with characteristic egotism, he reckoned that after thousands of years it was now at its limit. Just a little more rain, he said, and it would pour out over the swamp. As John Geddie puts it in *The Lake Regions of Central Africa,* it was extremely magnanimous of Lake Tanganyika to delay "the ceremony of turning on the water" until Stanley had arrived to witness it:

> This is a fascinating theory, but perhaps a more obvious one is to be preferred. Tanganyika is too old not to have discovered this chink in its side long ago. In its time it has had several levels, and in point of fact it alters its floodmark at least once every year with the rainy and the dry seasons. The Lukuga gap probably represents the fracture of an earthquake, or a hole which the imprisoned waters had broken out and escaped by in some former age, and which has been its safety-valve in its later history. When the Tanganyika has water to spare, it empties it westward; when it has not, it keeps all its supply to itself, and generally preserves a very fine balance between inflow and evaporation.

It was towards this occasional contributor to the Congo and unique hydrological phenomenon that the Naval Africa Expedition made its precarious way on 26 October 1915. Perhaps among the members of the expedition only Spicer understood the Lukuga River's significance. He may well have read the account of its discovery written by his naval predecessor Lieutenant Cameron, who explored Lake Tanganyika in 1874, while in search of Livingstone.*

After descending into a wooded area above the river, the train came to a halt. This was Kilu, said the Belgian engine-driver, where they would swap locomotives. For the remaining 40 or so miles of their journey, *Mimi* and *Toutou* would cross gorges on rickety wooden bridges that would not support the 70-ton locomotive, so a smaller one would be hooked up. In the event, the driver also ordered *Toutou* to be uncoupled. Both boats would be too heavy for the trestle bridges, he explained, and he would only take *Mimi* for the time being. So *Toutou* was shunted off into a siding along with the big locomotive.

Over the high rocks, to which the track clung with all the tenacity of a mountain goat, the tiny train chugged its way, continually dipping in and out of gulches. Where the gulches became gorges there were wooden bridges constructed from long poles driven into the rocks and fastened with guy ropes either side. At any moment the train might have plunged down one of these deep ravines and the driver stopped before each bridge to inspect its fixtures carefully and see if it was safe. Sometimes the gorges were more like tunnels. On one of the bridges the vertical clearance was so slight they had to remove the boats from the carriages and slide them along the tracks on their cradles. This was done, says Spicer, "by lowering them onto sleepers laid across the rails, which were

---

Across Africa (London, 1877). Meeting Livingstone's servants bearing the dead body of their master, Cameron explored Lake Tanganyika before proceeding westwards to the Atlantic, becoming the first European to cross equatorial Africa. He was later an author of adventure stories for boys.

well greased." The engine then pulled the boats slowly through. Even so, Spicer adds, "We had only 7 inches clearance at the top." There were no less than thirty-three bridges, so even though the distance they had to travel was relatively short, their journey took most of the day.

Not far from Lukuga—the Belgian encampment on Lake Tanganyika—the line petered out. The train simply came to an abrupt halt on a piece of bare track. All of the rail and sleepers had been used up. There was a sort of station in the bush, consisting of little more than a few huts, a water-tank and a pile of firewood. From behind this modest establishment, a quaint and ragged personage greeted them, looking like some figure from the *commedia dell'arte.* It was Sub-Lieutenant Tyrer, otherwise known as Piccadilly Johnny, he of the monocle and the addiction to Worcester sauce. In the intervening months, however, his bottle of yellow hair-dye had run out and his hair was now as white as snow, with a beard to match. The other members of the expedition stared at this tatty individual in astonishment. Seemingly oblivious to their scrutiny, Tyrer informed them they would have to walk the remaining two miles to the lakeshore. It was almost evening by this stage and too late to see Lake Tanganyika, so *Mimi* was hidden in a siding, in case the Germans came looking for her, and the expedition set up camp.

Dr. Hanschell awoke the following morning to find that Spicer had already set off for the lake. The locomotive was being prepared to return up the line to fetch *Toutou,* accompanied by some of the men; the others had gone with Spicer to Lukuga. Dr. Hanschell and Eastwood, finding themselves with nothing to do, decided to walk to the lake. Despite their very different religious beliefs, they were now firm friends. So it was with a sense of companionship as well as mounting excitement that they climbed the hills surrounding the vast expanse of water they had travelled so far to conquer; its presence was heralded by a change in the light over the brow of a range of hills some miles off. As they climbed, the weather broke with a warning thunderclap and a sudden flash of lightning. Finally the rains had arrived, it seemed, pattering down on the cane and dry grass in round fat drops.

The moisture was borne in by the monsoon winds from the Indian Ocean—the same journey Burton and Speke had made, when they first saw Lake Tanganyika, after a long and arduous march from Zanzibar. The weather became milder at the final moment, but Eastwood and the doctor had nothing like the sunny conditions under which their predecessors had seen the lake: its characteristic aspect of dazzling water reflecting every tint of land and sky. As they climbed the final hill, the change in the light they had perceived in the distance became the thing itself: a vast grey panel of water. It was as if an enormous slate had been sunk in a trough far below the level of the undulating tableland over which they had climbed.

Atheist and Methodist stood in awestruck silence on a red sandstone cliff in Belgian territory. The opposite side of the lake was under the control of the Germans. All that could be discerned of it was the hook-like summit of Mount Kungwe, home to the resident spirit of one of the tribes on the German side, a vengeful deity who demanded great sacrifices of his followers.

The Holo-holo thrived on both sides of Lake Tanganyika and were then the dominant tribe in the area. They had informed Lee about German activities on the lake, but they had also spied on the Belgians for the Germans, for which a great many had been hanged. Some of this information consisted of news about the expedition's progress up the Lualaba River, on the banks of which lived several Holo-holo clans. Fortunately, the Germans had been too preoccupied with the apparent threat of the *Baron Dhanis* to pay attention to the muttering forest drums.

Once Eastwood and Dr. Hanschell had descended from their bluff, they crossed another line of hills, hiking up and down through basins of land until they reached the Belgian headquarters at

Lukuga. This lay next to a swampy river about a mile wide, its banks choked with a profuse growth of arum lilies and papyrus.

On one bank of the river, amid tall grass stalks, could be seen the iron hulk of another steamer, this time with shell-holes in its side.* On the water were various small vessels manned by the Belgian navy. Nearby, on a little plateau, was the Belgian camp and another they had built for their British visitors: a series of mud-walled, thatch-roofed huts around a level piece of ground. Eastwood and the doctor found Spicer sitting in a chair in the largest hut, legs crossed and hands busy with needle and thread. He was making himself up to Vice-Admiral and sewing on a flag to prove it.

---

*The *Alexandre del Commune,* which had been disabled by the Germans earlier in the War.

Chapter Twelve

Mimi and *Toutou*'s great journey was over. Now they had to prepare for battle. Spicer had his Vice-Admiral's flag—white with a red circle in the corner—run up a pole in the centre of the camp. He ordered the men to smarten themselves up and parade, reminding them that they still had the most important part of their mission ahead of them—the sinking of the *Hedwig von Wissmann*—and they could not afford to let standards slip, as they had on their long journey here. He added that *Mimi* and *Toutou* would be kept hidden in the bushes back at the railway siding until a suitable safe harbour could be constructed for them. "This will be your next job," he said in conclusion, his eye wandering to East-wood's chimpanzee, which had hooked an arm round the ankle of one of the men in the front rank.

Finding and making a safe harbour proved to be Spicer's first flashpoint with the Belgian senior army officer, Commandant Stinghlamber. This stiff-shirted individual had given Spicer what Byron Farwell describes as "a correct but unenthusiastic welcome." There was an immediate tension over who was higher in rank. Strictly speaking, Spicer was a grade higher than Stinghlamber, as a Belgian army commandant is equivalent to a British army major, whereas a British navy commander is equivalent to a colonel. But the Belgians can be forgiven their confusion: quite apart from the *folie de grandeur* of the Vice-Admiral's flag that now flew outside Spicer's hut, the Englishman's epaulettes had been wrongly sewn by Spicer's African valet, Tom. As Shankland explains: "They were perhaps confused by the fact that Tom, unaware of the important difference between a pip and a crown, on transferring them to Spicer's clean shirt had made him a Lieutenant on one shoulder and a double Major on the other."

Stinghlamber had begun building a harbour in the mouth of the Lukuga next to the camp, but Spicer thought there was a better place a little farther south. The Lukuga mouth, he maintained, was an unreliable place to float boats. As Stanley had discovered, the river could become blocked, stopping and starting as the rains prevailed. This hydrographer's argument cut no ice with Stinghlamber. Spicer retaliated by saying that unless the Belgian concurred, he would take *Mimi* and *Toutou* to the British port of Kituta in Northern Rhodesia (now Zambia), 200 miles to the south. In the end, Stinghlamber capitulated, not wanting to lose the "two little cruisers automobile," as he called them.

Despite this difference of opinion, within a week of their arrival Commandant Stinghlamber hosted a dinner for Spicer and Dr. Hanschell at the Belgian mess hut. Joining Stinghlamber as host was Commandant Goor, an extremely tall, thin man in charge of the Belgian fleet on the lake, such as it was.

Flying ants flitted about the hurricane lamps hanging from the rafters as Spicer and the doctor were introduced to the other guests. Apart from officers of the Belgian army and navy, they included

Monsieur Jadot, the Area Engineer (a Rabelaisian figure, according to the doctor), and a missionary from the Catholic Order of the White Fathers, who was also good company. Female African servants in print dresses waited at table.

Spicer and Jadot probably had much to talk about. Like Spicer, the Belgian engineer had spent much of his earlier career in China. There he built a 750-mile railway, including a bridge spanning the Yellow River that was at the time the longest bridge in the world. On behalf of the Katanga mining company, Jadot had directed the construction of the railways upon which Spicer's men had travelled. He was later commemorated in the town of Jadotville, an important mining centre 75 miles north of Elizabethville.*

All the Belgians, even the frosty Stinghlamber, were suitably impressed by Spicer's lively account of *Mimi* and *Toutou*'s journey, which he launched into the moment they began eating. But as Shankland points out, "Spicer distressed the Doctor by speaking as if he had overcome all the difficulties by his own ingenuity—he mentioned neither Lee, nor even Wainwright who had got the boats to Lukuga for him."

Goor explained to Spicer the current naval situation on the lake. The Belgian flagship was a rectangular petrol-driven barge called the *Dix-Tonne,* which was armed with two cannon. Goor's other main vessel was a *glisseur,* or motor boat, called *Netta.* She was a light, flimsy creature, he admitted, able to carry only a single machine-gun. He also had at his disposal a Boston whaler with an outboard motor, which he called *la vedette* ("patrol boat"). There were also the vessels he wanted to bring into commission: the *Baron Dhanis,* which they had seen rusting at Kabalo, and closer to hand the hulk of the *Del Commune,* which had been bombarded by the *Hedwig.* (The *Del Commune* was named after Alexandre Del Com-

*Uranium from the mines of Jadotville was used in the bombs dropped on Hiroshima and Nagasaki. The town's last claim to fame was when 150 Irish UN troops were besieged there during the Congolese civil war of 1961, holding their position against 3,000 Katangan soldiers until they ran out of ammunition, food and water.

mune, an official of the Société Anonyme Belge pour le Commerce du Haut Congo, with whom Joseph Conrad had planned to make a second expedition upriver twenty-five years earlier, after his famous *Heart of Darkness* journey. It never took place, after Conrad fell out with Del Commune's brother.)

The meal progressed. Goor wanted to continue his naval briefing with information about the German boats that *Mimi* and *Toutou* would face, but Spicer seemed more interested in trotting out his own stories than in gathering intelligence. It was some time since he'd had a captive audience and he rose to the occasion. He provided himself with an entrée by asking Monsieur Jadot if there was much game to be found round these parts.

"Plenty before the War," replied the engineer distractedly (for he was mainly interested in the African girls serving them), "but we've been short of meat and now there's little left to shoot."

"What a pity," sighed Spicer. "The hunting of big game is a passion with me. It's given me some of the most exciting moments of my life. I once had a remarkable day's shooting in the Galapagos Islands . . ."

Dr. Hanschell recognised the signs, remembering them years later as he recounted the episode to Shankland. Spicer's dove-grey eyes were beginning to mist over as he slipped into one of his preposterous reveries.

"The wild cattle were really wild—not used to being hunted— you had to kill, not wound. The first to fall, I remember, was a huge black bull with wicked-looking horns. I dropped him at 40 yards, but before I could go up and examine him, two more were thundering down on us. I bagged them with a left and a right."

An embarrassed silence fell round the table and the doctor smiled to himself, remembering the ox whose horn Spicer had winged—at a distance of just a few feet—back in Mwenda Mkosi. How long ago that seemed now . . . Looking up, he saw Spicer raise his liqueur glass to the light.

"Just the colour of my wife's hair," said Spicer, studying the deep-red liquid intensely. "She'll be a rich woman one day," he added. "Every time I return from one of my adventures in China or Borneo, I bring her a pearl—she has quite a famous string now."

He then launched into a long account of his near-fatal experience sinking a German cruiser off the Kent coast. As it ended— "One's actions in such cases are purely instinctive"—Dr. Hanschell reflected on Spicer's psychological condition, for he knew that the only action Spicer had seen in European waters was watching HMS *Niger* go down from a hotel window. He later told Shankland:

> There was no doubt that while he was telling it Spicer believed the story, and that all his past humiliations and failures were blotted out of his mind. For a brief moment, surrounded by a group of admiring listeners in the heart of Africa, he really was the hero he would have liked to be, and that perhaps only a malicious fate had so far prevented him from being.

Fate would test Spicer again soon enough. Not the Graeco-Roman variety with scissors and thread, nor—despite a missionary's presence at dinner that night—the Providence of a Christian God. In the eyes of the local tribes, Mkungwe, the *nzimu,* or spirit, of the mountain opposite, under which the Germans kept a stock of wood to refuel the *Götzen,* was a much more powerful arbiter of man's destiny.

Mount Kungwe, Mkungwe's seat, was a vast granite tower rising to a height of 8,620 feet. At its summit goats and chickens— and, if the stories were to be believed, human beings—were sacrificed by the local people to determine future outcomes. If you sailed or camped near Mkungwe, it was customary to cry: "You big devil! You big king! You kill all men; let us go by." If you did not, as had been proved on many occasions, you would die. Or, at the very least, your luck would run out.

Chapter Thirteen

The sun rose over Lukuga the morning after Stinghlamber's dinner party. It shone across Lake Tanganyika to Mount Kungwe beyond—the holy mountain whose priests were solitary, rogue-male baboons, whose acolytes were bounding bands of screeching hyrax. The expedition would have heard the eerie cries of these dassies, or rock rabbits, one of the most extraordinary sounds of the animal kingdom. As the naturalist Richard Estes memorably puts it, "The call starts with a series of spaced cracking sounds, likened to the rusted hinge of a huge gate slowly opening, followed by a series of expiring screams suggesting a soul in torment."

Despite the shower that had greeted the expedition, the rains seemed to be holding off a little. The weather was glorious, in fact; the sun's rays made the high sandstone and granite cliffs of the lake's precipitous shores gleam like shields of gold. The foliage that clothed the cliffs luxuriated in its own greenness. Here and there the bluffs were broken by a small pebble or sand beach, upon which dugout canoes were drawn up, carved from huge trunks with axe and adze and infinite labour. In the villages behind the beaches—there were not many—stood the odd oil palm or banana tree and some small huts. Covered with drooping straw, the huts had the shrouded appearance of old-fashioned beehives.

Had any of the members of the expedition taken a walk that morning—on 28 October 1915—this is pretty much what they would have seen, before hurrying back to the mess for breakfast. As usual Josephine, Eastwood's chimpanzee, joined them. As an honorary human being she now wore a bib and had her own cup and saucer. Marapandi, Eastwood's servant, was just pouring tea when a cry went up. A German boat had been spotted on the horizon.

Everyone ran to the top of the bluff for a better view. Eastwood and Dr. Hanschell joined twenty or so others on the hill of granite, below which were scattered peculiar rock formations piled up in a fantastic manner. "Enormous masses of rock," wrote Verney Cameron in 1874 as he searched in vain for Livingstone, "vast overhanging blocks, rocking-stones, obelisks, pyramids and every form imaginable. The whole is overgrown with trees jutting out from every crevice or spot where soil has lodged and from them hang creepers, fifty or sixty feet long, while through this fringe there are occasional glimpses of hollows or caves."

It was from this dramatic viewpoint 800 feet above the water—"more like a design for a transformation scene in a pantomime, rather than a substantial part of Mother Earth," as Geddie described the same place—that members of the Naval Africa Expedition first sighted the enemy.

The German ship was a wooden paddle-steamer, about the length of a tug, but narrower in the beam. Mounted amidships was a small gun, a six-pounder, around which stood a curved steel shield. Next to the gun, sticking up through a kind of awning that covered most of the ship, was a dirty smokestack. In all truth she didn't look much of a challenge as she steamed down the coast; but she was still twice as long as *Mimi* or *Toutou*. Squinting through his field glasses, Dr. Hanschell noted that the gun of the *Kingani*—for that was the name of the ship—was trained on them where they were lined up on the cliff. There was less than a quarter of a mile between them. He looked around to ask Spicer what he thought, but the Commander was nowhere to be seen.

The Belgian guns were, in their turn, trained on the *Kingani*: the twelve-pounder guns that had been sent by the British for the *Baron Dhanis*. But neither side fired. The Belgians were waiting for Commander Goor to appear from the mouth of the Lukuga in the *Dix-Tonne*, his river-barge. The *Kingani* was out of range by the time he emerged, struggling through reeds and mudbanks in the oddly shaped *Dix-Tonne*, or "Fishcake," as the Belgian garrison nicknamed it.

As the watchers scrambled down from the bluff, Josephine's undomesticated cousins began chattering in a nearby ravine, just as Cameron had seen them a little over forty years before—"suddenly the long creepers began to move, as some brown object, quickly followed by another and another, was seen. It was a party of monkeys swinging themselves along, and outdoing Leotard on the flying trapeze; and then stopping, and hanging by one paw, they chattered and gibbered at the strange sight of a boat."

Eastwood rejoined his chimp (Josephine cried if left alone too long) and Dr. Hanschell located Spicer on the veranda of his hut. Seated on a wooden chair, he was studying the *Kingani* through his binoculars. Spicer said nothing then, but over the next few days he explained to the doctor his theories of speed versus power and their relation to naval engagements. He concluded that the odds against *Mimi* and *Toutou* were rather high.

Meanwhile work was under way on the harbour for the British boats, to protect them from the weather as much as from German attacks. It was also agreed that a second British camp should be built on a cliff above the harbour. The site itself would be called

Albertville, in honour of the Belgian king. The name was still used a decade and a half later when Evelyn Waugh dropped in and gave the Belgians a dose of his trademark satire:

> It was raining again before we reached harbour and moored against an unfinished concrete pier, where dripping convicts were working, chained together in gangs. Albertville was almost hidden in mist; a blur of white buildings against the obscurer background. Two rival hotel proprietors stood under umbrellas shouting for custom; one was Belgian, the other Greek. Officials came on board. We queued up and presented our papers one at a time. The inevitable questions: Why was I coming into the Congo? How much money had I? How long did I propose to stay there? Where was my medical certificate? The inevitable forms to fill in— this time in duplicate: Date and place of father's birth? Mother's maiden name? Maiden name of divorced wife?

Members of the Naval Africa Expedition built the harbour Waugh would eventually sail into, using heaps of rock that lay about by the railway track near where *Mimi* and *Toutou* were concealed. The track was extended by taking up pieces of rail that had already been laid and placing them forward, which enabled the engine to bring the stone down to the shore. While this was under way, Spicer went out with Goor in the *vedette,* making hydrographic measurements of the Lukuga.

At breakfast a day or two later, someone told the doctor he'd seen the Commander wearing a skirt. Hanschell assumed they were pulling his leg, for they knew he was friends with Spicer. But at that moment Spicer appeared, framed in the doorway. He was indeed wearing a skirt. It was made of lightweight khaki and came down to his knees. The doctor studied the garment. It was not a kilt, as worn by Tait and Mollison; it was most definitely a skirt. Spicer sat down at the breakfast table, joining Josephine and the humans. Tyrer's monocle nearly popped out of his eye and nobody knew what to say.

"I designed it myself," Spicer announced eventually, in response to the questioning stares. "My wife makes 'em for me. Very practical for the hot weather."

Chapter Fourteen

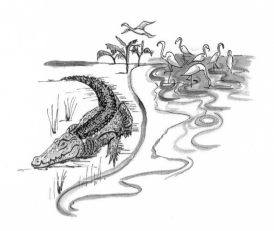

Spicer's skirt became a familiar sight during the first week of November, as he decided to join his men working on the new harbour. It had to be finished soon so that *Mimi* and *Toutou* could be brought out of hiding and sink the *Hedwig*. The Sea Lords had made no mention of the *Kingani*, the ship the expedition had seen from the bluff, and in communications they professed themselves entirely satisfied with Spicer's progress. However, it was during this period that Spicer's peculiarities came to the fore.

Building the harbour was tough work. As the men piled up the blocks they had to wear shoes in the water, because the stones cut their feet. Several of them suffered severe sunburn and blisters. Along with his twenty-eight men and some two hundred African labourers—many of them Holo-holo—Spicer worked with his sleeves rolled up. This allowed the tattoos of writhing snakes on his arms to be seen, which fascinated the Holo-holo tribesmen and their families, who came along to watch. As Shankland reports: "A crowd of women, children, *askaris* and hangers-on, kept at a respectful distance by a native corporal, gazed at him all day long with cries of pleasure and amusement."

What the Donegal seaman whom Spicer had bawled out for taking off his shirt on the Lualaba thought of this is not recorded. Spicer's skirt blew up in the wind from time to time, Marilyn Monroe–style, leaving nobody in any doubt that there were tattoos all the way up his thighs as well. Laughing as they looked on, Stinghlamber and his officers began calling him *le Commandant à la jupe*.

This caused more friction. Spicer did not object to *jupe* (skirt), says Farwell, "but he did object to being called *commandant* [major]. He demanded that he be addressed as *'mon colonel.'*"

"These Belgians don't even know the difference between a *commandant* and a commander!" raged Spicer to Dudley over dinner one night.

After weighing up all the evidence—the bogus Vice-Admiral's flag, the confusing array of pips and crowns on his shirt and the story of the attack on the Kent coast—the Belgians had decided Spicer was Stinghlamber's junior. Ironically, Spicer's account of his incredible heroism while sinking a German cruiser had done him no favours. They were now calling him "only the captain of a ship," as he complained in a letter to the Admiralty.

On the morning of 8 November work on the harbour came to an abrupt halt after a shocking discovery. The corpse of a young woman suddenly floated up to where the men had been working the previous day. Her legs had been bitten off by a crocodile. Construction stopped for her burial, though she was never identified. Fearful of more crocodile attacks, the men wouldn't go back to work, so Spicer put some of them on guard on the half-built harbour wall. Shankland remarks that "every now and again they fired at a dark patch, but no crocodiles were slain." Still, nobody wanted to go near the water. Eventually, Goor came scooting by in his *vedette* and threw a stick of dynamite into the water, its fuse protected by a bottle. The detonation killed plenty of fish, but no crocodiles, as far as anyone could tell. The ratings watched from the wall, while a large troop of baboons watched the ratings from the hillside above. They occasionally made loud hooting noises, as if in derision.

Also observing these farcical scenes—through a pair of binoculars while standing on the deck of the *Kingani*—was one of Zimmer's two Jobs on the lake. It was Lieutenant Rosenthal of the Imperial German Navy, who had seen service on the disabled German cruiser *Königsberg*. In spite of the terrible hardship endured by his crew and the shame of losing the German navy's most important battleship on the coast, Rosenthal could be proud of his track record. The *Königsberg* was blockaded in the Rufiji from 30 October 1914 to 11 July 1915, and it had taken twenty-seven British ships to locate her. That meant twenty-seven ships and their men were not fighting on the European front.

Now Rosenthal was itching for revenge. He had a taste for it, having seen more action since the sinking of the *Königsberg*. In September, while *Mimi* and *Toutou* were crossing the Lualaba plateau, the Belgian commander-in-chief General Tombeur had sent three battalions of *askaris* north from Elizabethville with the aim of taking Ruanda-Urundi (Rwanda and Burundi, then unified) from the Germans. The *Kingani* was one of several German ships that had transported six *askari* companies north from Kigoma as part of the counter-offensive. She might have been less than half the size of the *Hedwig von Wissmann*, and tiny compared to the vast *von Götzen*, but Rosenthal's ship had played her part. His immediate superior Gustav Zimmer was pleased with him.

Zimmer's lake-steamer fleet had also supported raiding parties along the Belgian coast of Lake Tanganyika, with Rosenthal again distinguishing himself by cutting Belgian telegraph lines, then cutting them again as soon as they were repaired, in a series of successful raids. On another occasion, Rosenthal and a crewman named Müller attempted to disguise themselves as Africans so as to scout out the Belgian camp at Lukuga (just before *Mimi* and *Toutou* arrived). But the boot polish with which they had blackened their faces washed off in the water, so they abandoned the plan.

The purpose of Rosenthal's mission—and the reason why he was now spying on the Lukuga camp—was to establish just how far the Belgians had got in constructing a slipway for the formidable *Baron Dhanis*. Holo-holo informers had now told the Germans that the steamer's numbered sections were at the railhead at Kabalo. According to Shankland, the Germans had also "heard a rumour some time ago that the English were trying to drag boats across the Mitumba Mountains, but they had simply laughed, believing it to be impossible."

Telling his stoker—a tall young African called Fundi—to lay off for a while, lest the roar of the *Kingani*'s engine or the smoke from her chimney alert the Belgians to their presence, Rosenthal let the boat drift towards the shore. He was watching the aftermath of the detonation of dynamite in Lukuga harbour. Dead fish were floating to the surface and the Africans were eagerly collecting them in their dugout canoes. A white man in what appeared to be a skirt was pacing up and down the breakwater, wildly gesticulating. Other white men were sitting or lying around on the beach or on the half-completed wall. After a while they stood up and began to go back down into the water with their shovels and pickaxes. It was as if they had been on strike and the man in the skirt had persuaded them to up tools again.

Rosenthal took the *Kingani* as close to the camp as he dared, jotted down some observations in his log, then decided to come back later. He wanted to confer with the other Job, Job Odebrecht, who commanded the *Hedwig von Wissmann,* and with their mutual ranking officer Zimmer. Odebrecht knew a little more about Lukuga—during a raiding party earlier in the year he had destroyed some Belgian dhows and whalers that had been moored there.

Odebrecht had also tried to sail into the mouth of the Lukuga in a dinghy, but it was difficult to navigate through the shoals and reedbanks, so he had turned back.

It was nearly three weeks before Rosenthal returned, chugging along in the *Kingani*. After conferring with Zimmer and Odebrecht he had decided to come right into the bay in front of the Belgian camp, under cover of darkness very early one morning, to see if he could get a better look at what they were up to. He had noticed a strange flag of some type on his previous recce—white with a red circle in the corner—and then there was all the building work . . .

Rosenthal had crept within 400 yards of the shore by the time the sun had risen, but the Belgian guards spotted him immediately. They began firing twelve-pound artillery shells at the *Kingani* from the two gun emplacements on top of the cliffs. The shells landed splashing in the water near to the boat.

Realising he had underestimated the Belgians, Rosenthal quickly turned tail, heading for the open lake. He told Fundi to get a fierce fire going as quickly as possible. The noise of another shell— an unearthly moan over the water—filled their ears. As it fell to starboard, the *Kingani* began vibrating like a drum-skin as the water in the boiler heated up. The noise of the shell still echoed among the crags above Lukuga, ricocheting from bluff to bluff, then bouncing out across the water.

It was as if that great echo were pursuing them. Looking back anxiously, Rosenthal saw people running from the camp up the cliff, from where—at just that moment—the white puff of another volley of shell could be seen. Thank God for Fundi's skill with the furnace. His name meant "expert" in Swahili, and so he was proving as he hurled log after log into the fire.

Dr. Hanschell woke that morning (it was 1 December) to the sound of gunfire and he too heard the echo reverberating among the rocks above the camp. He pulled on his long leather mosquito boots over his pyjama bottoms and ran outside. In the grey light of dawn he saw the *Kingani* zigzagging across the open lake, with shells falling all around her. The large Iron Cross flag in her bows was enveloped in smoke from the funnel. Others emerged from their tents and the doctor joined them as they ran up to the bluff where the Belgian gunners were hard at work.

Bent over their twelve-pounders in postures of something like supplication, they were feeding shell after shell into the breeches. Each time the guns spoke their booming piece, gusts of white cleared the barrels. These wreaths of smoke hovered for a while before drifting along the bluff and slowly sinking down to the water.

The British ratings thought they were firing at the *Hedwig,* the ship *Mimi* and *Toutou* had come to sink—and for this reason some of them half-hoped the Belgians wouldn't get her. This hope was soon fulfilled as the *Kingani* drew out of range, getting smaller and smaller until she disappeared round the promontory of the bay. Afterwards, the British gunlayers Waterhouse and Flynn were scornful of the abilities of their Belgian counterparts, especially since they were firing from stationary gun platforms. Magee says the commander of the *Kingani* showed clever manoeuvring, but that doesn't seem to have been the view of the naval personnel.

The Belgian gunners only spoke French or Flemish, but no doubt they caught the drift of the British comments. Typically, Spicer exacerbated the situation by offering Flynn and Waterhouse's services to Stinghlamber. He suggested they man the twelve-pounders in place of the Belgians until *Mimi* and *Toutou* were ready to be brought from their inland hiding-place. The twelve-pounders were originally Admiralty guns, after all. The offer, says Shankland, "was coldly but politely refused."

The routing of the *Kingani* did not deter Lieutenant Rosenthal. The next night he returned, hoping to gain further intelligence. Donning a cork life-vest and putting his clothes, boots and hat into a rubber bag, he slipped over the side of *Kingani* into the cold black water. As he swam closer to the shore, he could see the outlines of Belgian dhows in the river mouth and a small motor boat. There was a fairly strong current and he let himself float quietly up the shelving rocky beach just to the right of the new harbour.

He lay there for a while, taking in the scene in the moonlight: the half-built wall and the two camps. One had a Belgian flag; the other flag, he suddenly realised, was British. It was the flag of a Vice-Admiral! Gaining the shore, he ran to some bushes and quickly changed into his clothes. Then he bravely skirted the two camps and carefully examined the harbour. There were no ships. But why were the *Engländers* here, if not to bring a ship? It must be inland, he concluded, and started to walk along the railway.

After several hours, Rosenthal came upon a small encampment next to the track. Avoiding a dozy sentry in British uniform, he could make out two boat-like shapes under tarpaulins in the shade of some trees. They were clearly motor launches of some kind, but it was too dangerous to go any nearer. Realising he had to get this information to Zimmer as soon as possible, he turned and looked for the *Kingani*'s signal light. There it was, winking deep in the lake. He began to walk, then run, back down to the shore.

At the lake's edge, his arms and legs cut to ribbons by thorn bushes, Rosenthal searched in vain for the signal light on the water. He checked his watch. He had been ashore for much longer than he had agreed with his shipmates, but surely they hadn't given up on him? It was almost dawn, at which time they had arranged the *Kingani* should leave. He began to panic. Finding the cork vest, he quickly put it on again and swam out into the lake, hoping that he might spot the *Kingani* beyond the promontory. There was nothing to be seen except Mount Kungwe's ominous summit and behind it the sun rising, casting pink and yellow rays over the water.

It was no use. Rosenthal swam back to shore. He would have to hide out until nightfall, when he hoped the *Kingani* would return for him. Exhausted, he staggered out of the water and sought cover near some bushes. He had just finished changing when he heard African voices. It was a patrol of Belgian *askaris*. They spotted him at once. At first they were respectful, asking him in Swahili what he was doing, until one of them noticed the black, red and white epaulette markings on his shirt and shouted *"Jerumani!"* The game was up.

Prodding him with their bayonets they took Rosenthal to Major Stinghlamber, who questioned him for several hours. What had he seen? A British flag (though he didn't say so). The new harbour (he could hardly deny that). After several days in detention, Rosenthal was escorted up the railway inland to Kabalo.

As the train climbed through the Lukuga valley, he glimpsed those British boats again. At Kabalo he also saw the rusting pieces of the *Baron Dhanis*. How ironic it was that he and his fellow officers had been so worried about the Belgian ship that they had paid no attention to the rumour of a British expedition. Well, the rumour was obviously true, but there was no way of warning Zimmer, short of escaping . . .

Chapter Fifteen

The baboons smelt it first as they loitered on Lake Tanganyika's shingle coast. Lifting their grey muzzles, they sniffed out the moisture in the air, then ran for the shelter of the forest. Out on the lake, the first sign of the coming heavy sea was an alteration in the colour of the water from blue to green as the skies darkened. Then a big thundercloud that had been hovering behind Kungwe slipped down the mountainside and rolled across the lake, whipping the crest of each wave into a fleck of foam.

The white-toothed waves increased in size as they raced towards Lukuga, their surfaces pocked with drops of icy rain. By the time they were within a hundred yards of the harbour, they were huge breakers throwing up spray in every direction as smaller eddies of wind and water attached themselves to larger ones and so on and on until, with an earsplitting crack, the thundercloud broke just above the new harbour.

Perhaps Mkungwe was angry that yet another foreign power had dared to set foot on his lands and was taking out his rage on Spicer's new harbour. Eighty yards of work was swept away and two whaleboats were thrown up onto the beach. *You big devil!* Tons of rocks that had been blasted at a quarry inland and dumped into the water were swatted to one side as if they were marbles. *You big king!* The expedition was at least thankful that *Mimi* and *Toutou* had not yet been launched. *You kill all men; let us go by.*

Wainwright, who had been sent to collect the missing stores from Fungurume, returned in the midst of the storm. The moment the weather had cleared he took charge of the rebuilding of the harbour. Gradually, says Magee, "the rock piled up and extended into the water." Wainwright now wore a large cowboy hat like that of the contractor they had used at Fungurume. He conveyed his instructions to the African labour force by miming. He shouted at them all the while in Shona (the language he had learned in Rhodesia), but since the workers understood only Swahili and their local tongue they hadn't a clue what he meant.* Wainwright swore at them until he was blue in the face, but as Shankland points out the labourers simply "smiled happily as they ran to do his bidding."

Magee records that the extension of the breakwater into the lake "gave the natives the impression that we intended to build a road across the lake to the German coast, 40 miles away, and march across." Rosenthal—now on his way to a prisoner-of-war camp—had heard the same story and he was still determined to find a way of getting a message to his countrymen.

Spicer was still sulking. He had heard about Rosenthal from the servants, but had to wait until 7 December (four days after the Ger-

---

*It can't have helped that the Swahili for "I," the first-person pronoun, happens to be *Mimi.*

man's arrest) for Stinghlamber to inform him officially. On the 8th Spicer sent a message to Commandant Goor informing him that he wanted to interrogate Rosenthal. The Belgians didn't take any notice; the prisoner had already been sent inland by then, in any case. A furious Spicer sent a complaint to the Admiralty.

The next fortnight was taken up with further work on the harbour. The necessity for *Mimi* and *Toutou* to have a place of safety became apparent when a German ship—no one was quite sure which one—came and shelled the sea-wall one night. Luckily, this attack did far less damage than the storm. Two more nights the men were called to action stations after reports the enemy had landed, but these proved to be false alarms.

It was not until 22 December, seven months after leaving Tilbury, that the first of the motor boats was launched. *Toutou* led the way this time—pushed down the rickety Lukuga railway by the little steam engine and its Belgian driver. She ran straight into the lake (thanks to a clever system devised by Wainwright whereby the rails and sleepers projected into the water) and was joined the following day by *Mimi*.*

It was Christmas Eve morning by the time everything was ready. The petrol tanks had been filled, the guns had been mounted fore and aft and the boats had been carefully checked: this was no time to spring a leak, as had happened before. *Mimi* and *Toutou* were ready to go forth and fight.

Dr. Hanschell watched the boats take to the water, with half an eye on the local bird life as usual. A curious fish-eagle inspected *Mimi* and *Toutou*, but its distinctive cry was soon lost in the roar of engines. *Mimi* and *Toutou* drove out into the bay, heading straight for Mount Kungwe on the opposite shore. Some way towards it, the guns were tested—their boom echoing across the sheet of water—

---

*Again Spicer takes credit for this operation in his lecture. "I devised a method of running [the boats] on railway trucks from their place of concealment into 10 feet of water and in each case the launching was accomplished in 20 minutes."

then the crews returned triumphant. Waterhouse claimed to have seen a crocodile swimming alongside *Mimi*.

Further trials took place that afternoon, in the course of which Spicer attempted to semaphore from the Belgian barge to *Toutou*. George Tasker, *Toutou*'s signalman, could make neither head nor tail of it and afterwards an irritated Spicer called him to his hut.

"What's the matter?" he demanded. "Aren't you a signalman? Aren't you qualified?"

"Oh yes, sir," replied Tasker. "It's only your semaphore I can't read, sir."

According to Shankland, Spicer's treatment of Tasker was brutal: "Spicer gave orders that he was never to enter the office hut, and he told CPO Waterhouse not to take him afloat again."

On Christmas Day Spicer was still in a bad mood, though it had nothing to do with his semaphore. He had begun to accept the horrifying truth. As well as the 45-ton *Kingani,* which they had seen for themselves when the Belgians fired on it, and the 60-ton *Hedwig,* the only ship mentioned in the Admiralty orders, Spicer had been left in no doubt that there was another German ship on the lake to contend with, the even larger *Graf von Götzen*. The Belgians had filled in the details. With three big guns—the largest taken from the *Königsberg,* Rosenthal's old ship—and the capacity to transport over eight hundred troops, the *Götzen* utterly dwarfed *Mimi* and *Toutou*. Its biggest gun fired shells four times the size of theirs.

Dogged by doubts about the expedition, Spicer did not embrace the Christmas spirit. During his rounds he discovered that the red-haired Irish seaman had decked his part of the dormitory hut with variegated leaves—a poor substitute for holly.

"What's this?" shouted Spicer down the line of beds. "A whorehouse? Take all that down and burn it."

Flushed with rage, the Irishman knew to keep silent and do as he was told.

In contrast to this display of mean-spiritedness, Magee reports that "we kept Christmas in the good old-fashioned style," though this appears to have been purely for the benefit of the readers of *National Geographic.* Farwell says, "there was no Christmas celebration of any sort." The volunteers had a grim time of it: no alcohol, no cigarettes, no plum pudding. Not even a guinea fowl in place of turkey.

Spicer had other things on his mind. "It's not fair!" he complained to his officers as they ate tinned beef and biscuits that Christmas night. "I have to go out in the launches and take all the risks of the naval action, because there isn't another seaman among you."

He laughed crazily—then promptly disappeared to his hut, his skirt flapping about his knees.

The "time of death and wounds," in Shankland's memorable phrase, was approaching. The men were acutely conscious of their own destinies. Some couched them in religious terms. There had been bushfires along the hilly promontories of the shore around them. Lit by Holo-holo tribesmen hunting bush-rats, they were often miles long, advancing over the curving hills like a fiery army. It made for dramatic scenes at night, when the glowing ranks were mirrored on the lake below. During the day, extinguished by rain, the fires smoked. Eastwood remarked that they were being led by pillars of fire by night and pillars of smoke by day.

As Spicer's men tried their best to celebrate Christmas without him, the *Kingani* was steaming south through the night towards the British camp. *Leutnant zur See* Junge had taken command after Rosenthal failed to return. The Germans had no idea what had happened to their former captain, but thought it most likely he had drowned. Junge's orders from Zimmer were exactly the same as Rosenthal's: to find out if the Belgians had built a slipway at Lukuga with which to launch the fearsome *Baron Dhanis.* Once assembled, the rusting fragments at Kabalo would constitute a ship of 1,500 tons—300 tons more than even the *Götzen.* With a boiler installed and the guns that were currently above the Belgian camp mounted, the *Dhanis* could prove invincible.

Zimmer's concern was premature. It was *Mimi* and *Toutou* he should have been worrying about, but only Rosenthal knew of their existence. The German POW had tried to open a secret channel of communication by persuading his captors to allow him to send a written message to Kigoma—the main German base on the lake—requesting his personal possessions. On the back of the letter, written in the "invisible ink" of his own urine, were detailed observations about the Allied forces. If Junge and his navigator Penne had known the letter's contents as the *Kingani* steamed sedately down the coast early that Boxing Day morning, they might well have turned around.

But they didn't. Apart from Rosenthal's absence, everything seemed normal. Below deck the engine clattered, the boiler spluttered and the ash-pans filled as Fundi expertly stoked the furnace. The Iron Cross flapped from the mast in a freshening breeze and amidships the stumpy funnel smoked and roared. From the prow another noise was heard: the bleating of a goat which the crew kept on board. Its official purpose was emergency food, but the tethered animal had become a kind of mascot. As if standing on some rocky mountain outcrop, she held her horned head high and stared unblinking at the clear blue water as the German steamer powered forwards.

Chapter Sixteen

O Eternal Lord God," intoned the man in the skirt, "who alone spreadest out the heavens, and rulest the raging of the sea, who hast compassed the waters with bounds until day and night come to an end, be pleased to receive into thy Almighty and most gracious protection the persons of us thy servants, and the fleet in which we serve."

As much as he was able, Spicer adapted his supercilious drawl to the form of prayer used in the navy. "Preserve us from the dangers of the sea, and from the violence of the enemy; that we may be a safeguard unto our most gracious sovereign King George, and his dominions . . ."

Boxing Day 1915 happened to fall on a Sunday, so the officers and men were mustered for "divine service," as it was known in the navy. They stood on the flat sandy space in the middle of the camp which Spicer had designated the quarterdeck. As he spoke with prayer book in hand, the Union Jack fluttered in the breeze off the lake. The air was cool. The northern European is always grateful for this moment of balm before the sun fully rises, although the African labourers on which his comfort generally depends are already hard at work.

The officers—Wainwright and Dudley, Tyrer, Dr. Hanschell and Cross—were wearing their strange, pearly-grey Spicer uniforms. They faced the lake with Spicer, their unsheathed cutlasses in the salute position. The ratings, facing in the other direction, wore solar topis and presented their long Marine's rifles.

"O come, let us worship and fall down: and kneel before the Lord our Maker, whose Hand doth all the secret springs command of human thought and will," said Spicer, as an African boy came running towards them, "at whose bidding the winds blow and lift up the waves of the sea. We are thy creatures, O Lord . . ."

The boy was carrying a piece of paper with a message from Goor, the Belgian naval commander. Spicer glanced at it, then continued reading from his prayer book.

". . . prevent us, in all our doings, with thy most gracious favour, and further us with thy continual help; that in all our works begun, continued, and ended in thee, we may glorify thy holy Name."

The officers began to stir as they saw the *Kingani* rounding the point behind the lower ranks in front of them. The ratings twisted their heads, trying to see what was going on. Spicer held up his hand as he finished the service.

". . . and finally, by thy mercy obtain everlasting life; through Jesus Christ our Lord. Amen."

"Amen," the men echoed impatiently.

Spicer watched the German gunboat, his hand still raised in the air. It was a few minutes before he spoke. "Chief Petty Officer Waterhouse! You may dismiss the divisions—and man the launches for immediate action!"

The men ran down to the harbour, Spicer walking slowly behind them. Waterhouse and Tait climbed into *Mimi* with Spicer following. Also with them was the big, red-haired seaman from Donegal, whom Spicer had taken a dislike to.

Flynn manned the gun on *Toutou* under Dudley's command, with Mollison at the wheel. Before letting them launch, Spicer waited for the *Kingani* to come past the camp, so that the motor boats would enter the lake between the German boat and the enemy's headquarters at Kigoma. Once the *Kingani* had cruised past, the two motor boats sped out into the lake, foam surging up their bows as the 100-horsepower engines thrashed the water.

Eastwood and Dr. Hanschell ran up to the cliff above the harbour with the other members of the expedition. Stinghlamber's Belgians joined them there, as did hundreds of Holo-holo tribesmen—the whole crowd lining the bluff 800 feet above the water.

"It'll be all right," Eastwood told the doctor as they watched *Mimi* head for *Kingani*'s starboard quarter and *Toutou* speed after her on the port side. "I've felt all along that the hand of God is over this expedition."

"Why shouldn't it be equally over the Germans?" snapped back the exasperated atheist.

"Well, you'll see," said Eastwood, slightly embarrassed. "We'll get home safely, every one of us."

The *Kingani*'s goat was still bleating away happily at the prow, the breeze off the lake ruffling its coarse hair. *Leutnant* Junge examined the coast for signs of a slipway down which the *Bula Matari*, as the Africans called the Belgians, might launch the *Baron Dhanis*. The day was bright, the view clear; surely this time he would be able to bring back to Commander Zimmer the information he required.

It would be no recompense for the tragic loss of Rosenthal, however. Hearing a roaring noise over the chugging of his own engine, Junge casually turned—and saw, to his horror, two motor boats bouncing over the waves towards him. From their bows the White Ensign fluttered impudently. Junge lifted his field glasses. He could see white men on board and a substantial gun.

Panicking, he shouted down into the engine-room, *"Die Engländer sind hier!"* The English are here!

Seeing that the two launches would rapidly overtake him, Junge ordered that the *Kingani*'s speed be increased. He also turned sharply to port and told one of the petty officers to man the ship's gun, cursing the fact that it could only fire forwards.

Down in the engine-room, Junge's Chief Engineer and his Artificers were working hard to get steam up. Fundi was reaching into the furnace with tins of oil—pouring it on to the flames. Suddenly they heard a blast and felt the ship jolt backwards.

It was the recoil from their own gun. Junge had fired on *Mimi;* but his constant circling northward movement meant she was soon astern of him. He ordered the petty officer to transfer his fire to the other boat. Penne, Junge's navigator, and Petty Officer Schwarz, who had brought up rifles from the hold, began firing at *Mimi* as she surged towards them. At six pounds, *Kingani*'s gun could fire farther than hers, which carried only three-pound shells, but the nearer she got, the more danger there was. Junge told the men to crouch behind *Kingani*'s circular iron gunshield.

The range was closing. Standing behind *Mimi*'s gun, Spicer could clearly see the German captain through his binoculars. The man, who was wearing a white uniform and a peaked cap, seemed to be very agitated indeed. Spicer clenched his jaw in satisfaction, gripping his long cigarette holder between his teeth. At that moment, a shell from the *Kingani* hit the water beside them, sousing him with cold spray. There was a lurch as Tait, who was at the wheel, pulled the boat away from the shell-flash.

Mimi pitched and yawed in the choppy water. Bullets from the German rifles flew past Spicer and the red-haired seaman.

"Sit down!" shouted Tait above the roar of the engines.

"No thank you, sir," replied the Donegal man in his deep brogue. "I can see better standing up."

Spicer started shouting at Waterhouse, who was manning the gun. He was trying to spot for him, trying to give him the ranges—but Waterhouse couldn't understand a word, because of the cigarette holder in Spicer's mouth and the noise from the engines. He fired, knowing he had missed the moment the boom of the shell sounded in the breech; the muzzle wasn't steady, pointing wildly up and down with the movement of the boat.

Up on the cliff, the doctor and Eastwood watched the shells falling around *Toutou,* which was also careering wildly. The Holo-holo were murmuring in astonishment. Then another shell boomed out and suddenly flames were licking the deck of the *Kingani.*

Down in the engine-room, the German Chief Engineer knew at once it was a fatal hit. Running up on deck he was confronted by a dreadful sight. Junge and his two petty officers had been blown to pieces: the high-explosive shell had come right through the iron gunshield supposed to protect them. There was blood everywhere. *Leutnant* Junge's leg had been ripped off at the hip and his body was leaning awkwardly against the remains of the gunshield. Penne and Schwarz were less mangled, but clearly dead. The ship's mascot bleated pitifully in the ruins. As the Engineer took in the gruesome scene, his nostrils filled with the acrid smell of explosive. Another shell whistled over and went straight through the engine-room skylight. This time there was no explosion; he realised that the shell, coming down on its parabola, must have passed right through the side of the boat.

There was a splash and he saw Fundi slip into the water and swim away. The two motor-launches were bearing down on the *Kingani* now, still firing. Water was coming in through a shell-hole in the port bunker. Flames licked the wooden deck. There was nothing to do but surrender. He began to haul down the large Iron Cross flag from the mast. He must have thrown it into the water or the flames, because it was never captured.

Seeing that one of the British boats was still heading directly for him at great speed, the Engineer pulled out his handkerchief and waved it vigorously. He could see a man in the front of the boat with a cigarette holder in his mouth and—wearing a skirt?

The boat, its engines still at full throttle, rammed into the side of the *Kingani*. The Engineer watched in astonishment as the man in the skirt fell over, then got up again at once, laughing.

The other launch came alongside and an English officer climbed aboard and took the Engineer prisoner. The officer, who announced that his name was Flynn, blanched at the sight of all the blood and pieces of scorched flesh. He eyed the goat curiously, which was still bleating away. Another *Engländer* ran up the White Ensign where the Iron Cross had flown.

The vessel which had rammed them had already turned back to shore, her bows damaged from the collision. The *Kingani* followed, under the command of the squeamish Flynn, who avoided looking at Junge's body and the blood-spattered deck. The Engineer saw the man in the skirt step on to the beach, surrounded by a crowd of Africans shouting and clapping. Guns from the Belgian shore battery fired in triumph and he felt sick to the pit of his stomach. As one of the *Engländers* pointed a rifle at him, another brought the *Kingani* into shore.

Leutnant Junge's corpse rocked with the motion of the water, his torn hip fused to the blackened gunshield. The Engineer steadied himself as the *Kingani* ran aground with a heavy list to starboard. Junge's body made a sickening lurch from its pivot and seconds later the man called Flynn fainted.

Once it was known that a German vessel had been captured, more Holo-holo flocked from the inland villages to join those thronging the paths from the bluff. As Magee writes: "They came bounding down from the trees and the hilltops, giving vent to loud whoops of delight and gesticulating wildly, simply falling over each other in their hurry to reach the beach in order to pay their homage to the new Great White Chief, our commander. There they assembled in thousands, arrayed in their brightest pigments and gaudiest loincloths, a jigging, jogging, frenzied mass . . ."

Dr. Hanschell also descended the cliff with Eastwood and Magee. Collecting his medical bag from his tent, in case there were wounded who needed treating, he went to the beach. The crippled *Kingani* was being pulled in as far as she would come and the doctor spied a goat standing with its hooves in the shallows, casting a quizzical eye on all the commotion. The German prisoners were marched away by Belgian *askaris*. Meanwhile, the Holo-holo men threw themselves on the ground in front of Spicer, trickling sand into their hair in what was clearly a sign of homage. The women crowded round him, tugging at his skirt and epaulettes. They simply wanted his gaze to fall upon them, says Magee, "regarding this as a fetish which would protect them from evil spirits."

But in Shankland's account, Spicer does not seem like a man enjoying the fruits of victory: "The Doctor went across and congratulated him: he stood there dazed and unsmiling, and only moved his lips silently as if trying to say thank you. Then he turned to examine the damage to *Mimi*'s bows . . . Perhaps, the Doctor thought, he couldn't yet adjust himself to the fact that after years of romancing he really had distinguished himself at last."

Leaving Spicer to the congratulations of the Belgian officers— expressed, says Magee, "in the usual demonstrative Continental fashion of embracing and kissing"—Dr. Hanschell climbed aboard the *Kingani*. Walking across the deck, he noticed that his boots were covered in blood. It soon became obvious there was nothing he could do for Junge, Schwarz and Penne. He went to sit on the quay with Flynn, who was still recovering from his fainting fit. The petty officer was dangling his boots in the water to clean off the blood and the doctor followed suit. Neither of them spoke for a while. All that could be heard was the jubilant hubbub of the crowds overlaid with the salutations of some *askari* buglers and drummers, who were sounding a fanfare in Spicer's honour. Some members of the band were hardly more than children.

Chapter Seventeen

The same bugles sounded that evening at the funeral of the dead Germans. Their bodies had been wrapped head to toe in white canvas and, stretched out on wooden trestles near a mound of fresh red earth, they resembled ancient mummies.

Between Stinghlamber and Goor stood Spicer, his hat under one arm and his khaki skirt revealing bare knees above brown puttees. Behind them stood the Asian deckhands from the *Kingani* wearing their loincloths; Rupia in his fez; Marapandi, Eastwood's servant; and Tom, who now affected a skirt like his master. Nearby was a shaken-looking trio of German prisoners.

On the other side of the graves stood Dr. Hanschell and the British officers. The doctor did his best to listen to Spicer as he read the burial service, but his mind wandered back to the moment when he had been sitting on the quay with Flynn. Spicer had arrived to inspect the *Kingani,* stepping over the corpses of Junge and the others to count the marks where shells had struck.

"Twelve hits out of thirteen shells," he announced. "That's a pretty good show." He went on to attribute much of this success to his own range-finding, despite the fact that Waterhouse could not understand his instructions. And then, quite casually, Spicer bent over Junge's twisted body and calmly removed the dead man's signet ring.

It was on Spicer's finger now as he read the burial service psalm: "I said I will take heed unto my ways: that I will offend not in my tongue. I will keep my mouth as it were with a bridle: while the ungodly is in my sight. I held my tongue, and spake nothing. I kept silence, yes, even from good words . . ."

The bugles sounded the last post as the sun flooded in low from the western side of the lake, turning the waves scarlet where the light touched the water. Dr. Hanschell watched the deep-red orb dip below the surface. His eye was drawn to a group of Holo-holo behind Spicer. They now knelt down whenever he passed.

Spicer's words echoed under the bluff, his skirt flapping in a light breeze, the red sun glinting on his new ring. "Man that is born of a woman hath but a short time to live, and is full of misery. He cometh up, and is cut down like a flower; he fleeth as it were a shadow, and never continueth in one stay . . ."

A rifle salute, fired by fifty Belgian *askaris,* concluded the ceremony. Specially chosen guards were posted over the graves during the night. According to Magee: "The significance of this lies in the fact that a large majority of the Belgian native troops are recruited from tribes addicted to cannibalism and some of them might have felt tempted to take the opportunity of indulging in their horrible custom if precautions had not been taken to prevent it."*

Spicer wasn't alone in wanting a trophy. Soon after he had

---

*In his lecture, Spicer used this event to display some fancy vocabulary: "A guard had to be placed over the graves to prevent the *askari,* who still retain their anthropophagous habits, from digging them up."

returned to his hut, Dr. Hanschell was visited by the red-haired Irishman. He had a little bottle of Junge's blood and wanted to pre-serve it as a souvenir. A petty officer accompanying the Irishman also had a bottle filled with blood. Holding it up to the light, the doctor saw to his horror that the second bottle contained half a fin-ger that had been severed from one of the dead. He obliged them all the same, pouring antiseptic into the bottles to stop their contents from putrefying.

Recounting all this to Shankland in the 1960s, the doctor could not remember the name of this petty officer, but the event clearly affected him deeply. It made him wonder of what, exactly, Western civilisation consisted: "When they had gone, he sat for a time deep in thought. Spicer had the Captain's ring as a trophy, the *askaris* wanted to eat the bodies, and now these two men had bottles of blood. *Requiescat in Pace.*"

A few days later, a tall, half-naked African teenager with long soft curls was brought to "Tubby" Eastwood by his Nyasa servant. Marapandi explained that his name was Fundi and he was the stoker off the *Kingani*. The boys had been hiding him in their camp since he had swum ashore during the fight. Eastwood suggested he join Cross and Lamont in the engineering workshop. Spicer agreed: he had no intention of following procedure and handing Fundi over to the Belgians after they had kept him in the dark about Rosenthal.

This decision increased Spicer's standing with his men, which had in any case risen considerably since the engagement. They liked the sweet-natured Fundi and he transferred his loyalties from the Germans to the British with remarkable ease. As Shankland reports:

Fundi soon became popular with everyone: he had some-thing of the quiet dignity of a pastoral tribesman. The other boys and the ratings supplied him with clothes, and he was put on the ration strength. The Doctor's contribution was a used razor blade with which Rupia cut a path through

Fundi's curls, giving him a nice central parting: the boys parted their hair "all the same masters," using razor blades on each other to achieve the proper effect.

It was agreed that Fundi would remain the *Kingani*'s stoker once it had been refitted. The eleven surviving members of the *Kingani*'s crew—three German engineers and eight African deck-hands—were marched away by Stinghlamber's men. The goat that had been on board was adopted by Tait, who tried to dress her up in naval uniform and take her on parade. But the goat was not as tractable as Josephine, although she let the chimp ride on her back.

Over the next few days the *Kingani* was raised and mended. The shell-hole in her hull was repaired by Lieutenant Cross. After sending out for wood from the forest, he made an iron patch over a charcoal fire with bellows. He then applied the red-hot slice of metal to the tear in the hull.

Until then the former racing driver had shown little aptitude for engineering, so everyone was fairly astonished when the patch worked. Lamont, the Glaswegian engineer with whom Cross had a difficult relationship, was full of praise and even Spicer was gracious for once. He promptly renamed the ship HMS *Fifi,* which he thought went rather well with *Mimi* and *Toutou.* It meant "Tweet-tweet" in French and was suggested by the wife of a Belgian officer (she had a little cage bird of the same name). Shankland reminds us that "HMS *Fifi* was the first German warship to be captured and transferred to the Royal Navy."

With Fundi's help, Lamont fixed *Fifi*'s engines and the Belgians handed over a large gun with which to rearm her: it was one of the twelve-pounders that had formed part of their defences on the cliff. They were happy to do this because some new guns had been brought up from Kinshasa. Also their own steamer the *Alexandre del Commune* had at last been repaired and brought out from its muddy resting place on the banks of the Lukuga. There were similar plans afoot to finally assemble the *Baron Dhanis,* which still lay in pieces at Kabalo. A boiler had been found for her at last.

The *Del Commune* now came under Spicer's command. The Belgians had optimistically renamed her the *Vengeur.* The six-pounder that had been on the *Kingani* when she was captured was mounted on the *Vengeur.* There was a delicious double irony in this, since that gun, like those of the *Götzen,* had once been on the *Königsberg,* Rosenthal's old ship. Prior to that it had been on the *City of Winchester,* a British merchantman that the *Königsberg* had captured at the start of the War. (The Germans could have celebrated with a nice cuppa afterwards, as the *Winchester* was filled with crates of the best Ceylon tea.)

Why Spicer took command of a Belgian vessel needs some explaining. Though they were hardly on friendly terms, the capture of the *Kingani* had brought about something of a rapprochement between the Allied forces on Lake Tanganyika. The Belgian and British governments had come to an understanding whereby Spicer would be in charge afloat and Stinghlamber in command ashore. The Admiralty was exceedingly pleased with Spicer's performance. His promotion to full (rather than acting) commander was relayed by Morse code through a pair of Marconi field radios that had been recently installed at Albertville. At about the same time, another message came through. Spicer read it out at a special parade: "His Majesty the King desires to express his appreciation of the wonderful work carried out by his most remote expedition."

The Holo-holo offered more than mere "appreciation." The sinking of the *Kingani* and the sending away of the German captives did not simply make him a man of power in their eyes, it elevated him to the category of divine being. Everything he did seemed to increase their reverence. "The tattooed snakes curling up his arms added to his lustre," explains Byron Farwell, "particularly when he took to semaphoring to or from the launches, even though no one, not even the signalman, could read his messages. The Ba-Holo-holo believed he was calling to his ju-ju to deliver another German ship into his hands. Perhaps he was doing something like that."

Acutely aware of his image, Spicer was not averse to a little stage management.

"You've got the devil's own luck," Dr. Hanschell told Spicer shortly after Cross had patched up the *Kingani*. "All along you've been wanting to capture one of the enemy's vessels—and now you've done it!"

"Only ignorant people talk about luck," replied Spicer. "This was a case of successful mystique."

Successful mystique. It was a strange thing to say, because the capture of the *Kingani* and Cross's repairwork were far from mystifying. Perhaps Spicer meant that he had inculcated a spirit of resourcefulness in his men by cultivating an air of mystery. This may have impressed some of them, but the majority regarded him as a figure of fun. Cross, in particular, went to great efforts not to burst out laughing whenever Spicer spoke.

But among the Holo-holo Spicer was a god. His deification had been well prepared for as news of his journey and the wondrous machines that accompanied him had spread throughout the bush. After the capture of the *Kingani,* his stock needed to be maintained: one of the ways he did this was through a ritual that became known as "the twice-weekly bath."

Every Wednesday and Saturday, just before 4 p.m., Tom emerged from his master's hut with a grass mat, which he then proceeded to unroll on the "quarterdeck." Without fail, a throng of Holo-holo gathered to watch. Many were dressed in ceremonial costumes with horn and feather adornments; some perhaps wore the slit-eyed wooden masks of the Holo-holo that are collector's items today, now that the tribe is on the brink of extinction.

Tom would return to the hut and come out carrying a green canvas bathtub on his back, which he then filled with cans of steaming water. As the Holo-holo jostled for the best view, he would place a stool by the tub on which he would set a bottle of vermouth and a toothglass. Tom would then test the water in the tub with a forefinger before going to fetch his master.

Farwell takes up the story as Spicer appears—rather like Mr. Kurtz in Conrad's *Heart of Darkness:*

> The god himself emerged from his hut wearing only slippers and a towel draped round his waist, every inch of his torso covered with tattooed beasts, birds, reptiles, flowers, and insects. He stood for a moment smoking a cigarette in a long holder while his audience clapped. When silence fell, he raised his arms and, flexing his muscles, set the tattooed snakes writhing. Then, handing his cigarette holder to his servant, he stepped into the bath. He scrubbed vigorously, using a heavily scented soap that perfumed the air. When completely lathered, he stood up while his servant rinsed him with buckets of cold water. He then dried himself, wrapped the towel around his waist, and lit another cigarette while his servant poured him a glass of vermouth, which he drank appreciatively.

Sometimes the bath rite was preceded by a series of physical jerks. Farwell doesn't mention these in detail (and Magee doesn't mention the bath business at all), but they get the full Shankland treatment: "The natives, with eyes open wide, began to sigh— 'Aaaaih . . . !' and click their tongues in time with the exercise— 'Click—Aaaaih! Click—Aaaih!' and kept it up all through the whole performance."

Shankland's 1968 account of the expedition is happily free from imperialist prejudice. The same cannot be said, alas, of Magee writing in 1922. His description of the test flight of two seaplanes (which arrived immediately after the capture of the *Kingani*)* per-

---

*Manufactured and supplied by Britain, the planes had Belgian pilots. Armed with 65-pound and 16-pound bombs and four machine-guns apiece, they were assembled at a Belgian post 25 miles south of Albertville.

fectly illustrates the rhetorical devices used to emphasise the "other-ness" of Africans.

> It so happened that at about the time the Marconi operators made a test of their apparatus the Belgian airmen down the coast, having fixed up one of their seaplanes, decided to make a trial flight. Picture, therefore, the amazement of the superstitious negroes when, shortly after the wireless had begun sending test messages, with the rasping, crackling of electric sparks, lo and behold came the answer to their prayers to Heaven, as the natives thought, in the form of a low droning, gradually getting louder!
>
> Suddenly the seaplane shot into view out of the clouds, describing circles and going through sundry evolutions over the camp. The natives stood spell-bound, gazing upward with arms extended, eyes bulging, and mouths agape.
>
> The airman then made a sudden dive downward and that broke the spell. The savages bounded off into the bush, terror lending wings to their progress. Mothers snatched up their pickaninnies and dived for the shelter of their kraals, shrieking at the top of their voices. It was real pandemonium . . .

The Holo-holo should not have been underestimated. They under-stood very well that the balance of power on the lake had shifted. As a result, German intelligence on Belgian activities withered, accord-ing to Byron Farwell: "The Ba-Holo-holo switched their allegiance from the Germans to the skirted British god, the new master of the lake. The Belgians obtained an extra bonus from the expedition: they no longer had to fear an uprising. The Germans, kept in the dark, still did not know about *Mimi* and *Toutou,* nor did they know what had happened to the *Kingani.*"

Nevertheless, Bwana Chifunga-Tumbo—or Lord Bellycloth, as the tribespeople now dubbed Spicer, in honour of his skirt—still had a lot of work ahead of him. He had yet to fulfil his orders and sink the *Hedwig von Wissmann*, which had been sighted scouting the coast after the *Kingani*'s disappearance. And then there was also the matter of the Germans' largest vessel on Lake Tanganyika: the *Graf von Götzen* was clearly a formidable prospect.

Chapter Eighteen

R ain fell heavily on the camp at Albertville in the first weeks of January 1916, filling the gullies and forming open pools in the bush. Malaria and other diseases were a serious threat and several of the ratings came down with fever. Dr. Hanschell asked Spicer to declare the Belgian camp and the native villages (to which there were many nocturnal visits) off limits. Spicer agreed. Only Magee, says Shankland, "who had no duties except as photographer, was allowed to come and go as he pleased, and he was the only one to acquire a working knowledge of the local native dialect—and dysentery."

The doctor also denounced the practice of pouring kettles of boiling water on the columns of black-and-white-striped sarcophagid flies that marched in and out of the latrines, explaining that the peculiar diet of this army of myrmidons kept the toilets clean.

Snakes were also a threat in the wet, lying in the open ground of the camp and sunning themselves whenever the weather broke. Frightened off they would weave and push themselves away, only to return a few minutes later. The doctor took care to wear his long brown leather boots while walking about, and he began rewarding those Africans who brought him snake corpses. They brought him scorpions, too, and one evening he livened up dinner by removing a large live scorpion from his shirt pocket and placing it on a plate. It caused a great disturbance, until he allowed it to lash his hand with its tail, showing how he had rendered it harmless by amputating the sting and venom pouch.

It was the season of whirlwinds, of thunder and lightning, of storms that threw the lake into a fury. One day a series of sky-tall funnels were seen wheeling across the black surface of the water. They rose hundreds of feet high in crooked stems, then spread out at the top like mushrooms—where, mounting in eddies, they joined the thunderclouds in the sky.

Spicer announced that these dark vortices were waterspouts. "Very dangerous things! Only local atmospheric pressures prevent them from moving. At sea one learns to give them a wide berth. I've seen much bigger ones off the China coast . . ."

Dr. Hanschell ventured to suggest that waterspouts occurred only in dry weather, but Spicer was warming to his theme. "I remember once, as captain of a gunboat on a passage from Hong Kong to the Yangste River—I'm expert, you know, at speaking Chinese—I warned a large junk to alter course to avoid one of these waterspouts . . ."

The officers didn't pay much attention. They were too busy crowding the windows of the mess-hut to watch the whirling tapers as they swelled and spiralled in a jagged, thickening belt nearly 30 miles long. There was something theatrical about them; they looked like giant grey turnips or spinning tops moving across a painted backdrop.

"The Chinese believe that the air is full of devils," continued Spicer, "and that particularly nasty ones run up and down the waterspouts; and so at the head of the mainmast they fix a long painted bamboo. If a devil sits on it, it breaks and he falls into the sea. Ingenious idea, but that junk would have done better to listen to my advice. The waterspout broke over it . . ."

As Spicer explained how the junk had been shattered—leaving nothing but "a little painted bamboo stick bobbing up and down in the sea"—he was utterly upstaged by the grey swirls smoking up out of the lake. It was the turn of the white men to stand spellbound, mouths agape, before such awesome elemental power. Caught up in thermals, the spouts continued to rise dramatically, one after another in a staggered line. They careered over the indigo water to where the cliffs round the lake met the weather clouds 800 feet higher. At the lip of the cliff they spilled over, before being caught up in another eddy and rising again, joining the sky-clouds as they marched over Africa's vast swathes of savannah.

Not all the gyrating spouts made peace with the sky in this fashion. Others seemed determined to escape across the water, disturbing the local atmospherics and whipping up the weather. One swept towards a beach where wet-skinned fishermen were hauling in a net, keen to get it out of the storm. As the smoking eddy enveloped them, a sing-song humming noise could be heard up in the mess.

When the tempest had abated, an exploration of the beach showed that the clouds were not waterspouts at all, but a seething mass of tiny flies, known throughout Central Africa as *kungu.* Livingstone made the same mistake, as recorded in his Zambezi journal:

Clouds, as of smoke rising from miles of burning grass, were observed bending in a southeasterly direction, and we

thought that the unseen land on the opposite side was closing in, and that we were near the end of the lake. But next
morning we sailed through one of the clouds on our own
side, and discovered that it was neither smoke nor haze, but
countless millions of minute midges called "kungo" (a
cloud or fog). They filled the air to an immense height, and
swarmed upon the water, too light to sink in it. Eyes and
mouth had to be kept closed while passing through this living cloud: they struck upon the face like fine drifting snow.
Thousands lay in the boat when she emerged . . .

"I know of nothing in Africa that more wholly astounds the
mind than the *kungu* clouds of the Great Lakes," writes Archie Carr
in his wise and engaging *Ulendo: Travels of a Naturalist in and out
of Africa* (first published in 1964). They don't bite, but *kungu* come
from the same family as mosquitoes and midges and, like them,
spend their larval stage in water. On lakes like Tanganyika, the total
mass of *kungu* larvae can outweigh all the lake's other inhabitants.
Carr thought they could become an important food source, calcu-
lating that each square yard of lake bottom would produce around
a quarter of a pound of larvae: "an imposing yield of meat." He
adds that it is "more than you can expect for beef from an acre of
cultivated pasture."

Dropped from the cloud of the previous hatching, *kungu* eggs
lurk in the suffocating mud at the bottom of the lake—nearly a mile
deep—then start to rise at an average speed of 75 feet an hour, tim-
ing their various larval stages on the way by the amount of light that
comes down on them. But nobody knows why, once they have
released their eggs, these vast swarms head off over the baked veld.
"You look at the mass of those billions of flies up there cavorting
about in the sky," writes Carr, "and the thought wells up that fun or
not, such a prodigious pageant has got to have a bearing on evolu-
tion, on the final survival, extinction, or remodelling of the race. But
just you try to tell what the bearing is."

The *kungu* cloud settles on ships like mist. Sailors get lost in it. There are stories of people choking to death in it. But what is its purpose once the eggs have been laid? Why do the flies keep swirling across the savannah for miles and miles? "It both looks like cloud and merges with cloud till the cloud is midges as well as moisture. It can take the form of the tornado in the slow vortex of an ordinary thermal, or it can mix in with real tornadoes."

Perhaps the answer lies in the weather itself. The mad dance of the *kungu* creates turbulence and is therefore of great practical importance in mixing the air. Without turbulence there would be no distribution of the sun's heat, no rain clouds, no weather in fact (weather being simply the transformation of the sun's energy into the energy of wind and storms). Far from being a pointless digression, the *kungu* are a vital element in the region's delicate ecosystem.

The great cloud having passed, billions of the tiny flies (each no bigger than a pinhead) were found lying on the water and shore. The wet linemen who had hauled in the catch were plastered with them, but they didn't mind. They simply scraped them off their skin and squeezed them into balls. Others ran down to the beach with baskets into which they scooped the insects.

The fishing was sometimes hard on Liemba (as the Africans called Lake Tanganyika) and they believed the *kungu* were sent by a higher power for their benefit. Whereas a waterspout* was very bad news for fishermen, thrashing their boats to pieces, a visitation of *kungu* was very good news indeed. It was a benison from the gods, the leeshore tribes' version of manna from heaven. They liked to add this high-powered protein supplement to their plates of *ufa* (maize meal) or *posho* (cassava).

Dr. Hanschell watched them prepare it. The squashed insects were wrapped in banana leaves and dried in the sun, then smoked over a fire for several days. Baked into a cake, they tasted like stale

---

*Waterspouts are known locally by the same word for "snake," *nyoka*. In the myths of the Great Lakes, they are connected to a raft of legends about monsters that emerge from the abyss.

chocolate mixed with old fish. Sometimes *kungu* is still served to tourists as part of an omelette or scrambled eggs (a bit like grated truffle), but the Naval Africa Expedition were offered only a plain black mass. In the words of Archie Carr, trying it in the 1950s, it looked "like a burnt loaf of bread."

None of them would eat it, not even Tait or Mollison. The doctor, however, tried some white-ant biscuits that Rupia made for him. These ants—they are termites, really—often swarm around the same time as the *kungu*. This is another memorable sight, and it must have reminded "Tubby" Eastwood of his pillars of fire and smoke, if Shankland's description is anything to go by:

> They rose in thin smoky columns from the anthills all around the camp as if the earth were on fire deep down. Soon their wings fell off, and as they crawled about to start new anthills, noisy fluttering birds devoured them, and baboons and pariah dogs came out of the woods to eat them. Rupia grilled some of them on a hot stone and brought them to the Doctor as a delicacy—they really looked very tempting. Thinking philosophically that an African visiting England might think twice about eating shrimps and other insects of the sea, he tackled them boldly and found them quite good eating. They reminded him of marrow on toast.

On 14 January, perhaps as a result of the *kungu*'s movements, there was a violent storm. *Fifi* (formerly *Kingani*) fouled *Vengeur* (formerly *Del Commune*), dragging her anchor and nearly foundering on rocks. Eventually the storm clouds subsided and the expedition weighed up their situation. *Mimi*'s bows had still to be repaired after colliding with *Kingani*; *Toutou* had sustained some damage while firing her gun; *Fifi* was not quite ready to sail, despite Cross's patch; and *Vengeur* had lost two propellers in the storm. The Belgian speedboat *Netta* had also been damaged in the bad weather, twisting two propeller shafts. With the exception of the unwieldy *Dix-Tonne* (the "Fishcake") and the other Belgian speedboat, which was useless as a fighting vessel, the whole flotilla was now out of action. Things could not have been worse.

The sky had just cleared when a second German gunboat appeared on the horizon. It was the *Hedwig von Wissmann*—the ship they had come all this way to attack. Now it looked as if it was going to attack them instead.

Chapter Nineteen

As it turned out, there was no immediate cause for alarm. *Leutnant* Job Odebrecht, commander of the *Hedwig,* had no intention of attacking the Albertville flotilla that day—mainly because he didn't know about it. He dared not come in too close for fear of bombardment by the Belgian shore batteries. That was how the *Kingani* had been lost, according to the Holo-holo spies. They had told the Germans that the sunken steamer's funnel could be seen far out at sea from the shore. Odebrecht's orders from Zimmer were to find a wreck, but he saw nothing and returned to Kigoma with no news. Except to say there did seem to be considerable activity at Albertville.

Zimmer was still uncertain as to the exact situation on the lake. Had the British somehow suborned his intelligence sources? The only thing for it, he decided, was to send out the whole fleet on reconnaissance, then regroup and start a combined operation against any naval threat they found. On 8 February he sent the *Hedwig* down to the settlement of Kungwestock, opposite Albertville, with orders to scout the opposite shore, then rendezvous at noon on 9 February with the *Götzen,* which Zimmer would command personally.

After a night moored under the mountain at Kungwestock, Odebrecht set off in the *Hedwig* across the lake towards the Belgian camp. The sky was overcast and hazy, but he felt confident. He had two six-pounder guns forward and a revolving Hotchkiss aft (like the *Kingani*'s gun, it had been captured from the British on the coast). So when, around 7:45 a.m., he spotted through his binoculars a steamer and a small motor boat coming towards him from the Belgian shore, he was not unduly worried. It had happened before: the Belgians always scattered at the last minute. But as they came closer, he saw that the vessels were flying the White Ensign of the Royal Navy and that they carried proper artillery, not light machine-guns like the Belgian boats.

So the British were here after all! The steamer looked familiar . . . rather like the *Kingani,* in fact, except that it had no gun-shield and different guns.

Odebrecht spotted the laughable Belgian barge *Dix-Tonne* lumbering along behind the British launch; behind the barge was one of the Belgian whalers. It was obvious they meant to attack, but Odebrecht remained confident. Only the size of the gun on board the steamer, which was leading the attack, gave him pause. It was very big—twice the size of his own guns, even though the *Hedwig* was larger than the approaching steamer.

There were still several miles between the vessels. Odebrecht kept going towards the Belgian shore for almost an hour, until he was about six miles from the leading vessel coming towards him. Then, at 9:30, he turned sharply to port. There are conflicting reports as to why. In "Tanganyikasee: A Gunboat War in Deutsch-Ostafrika, 1914–1916," Holger Dobold and Dennis Bishop maintain that the German captain hoped to outrun the attacking flotilla and trap them. "It may have been Odebrecht's intention to ambush the Allied fleet in reverse by drawing the Allied steamers to the meeting-place with the *Götzen* . . ."

Shankland takes his cue from Dr. Hanschell, who was watching from the bluff. He thought the German captain suddenly baulked at the size, or apparent size, of the vessels approaching him through the haze:

> The Doctor, seeing the natives gazing at the sky, looked up and saw something prodigious was happening: he made out magnified images of the *Hedwig* and of the Allied flotilla suspended stationary in the air, each vessel many times its natural size. The mirage must have deceived the *Hedwig,* for she came straight on until only six miles separated the combatants . . .

Even at the moment of attack, it must have seemed to Odebrecht that he did not have too much to worry about. When the lead boat, *Fifi,* fired at him at 10 a.m., and missed, it was clear that her big gun was simply too big. Its recoil stopped the steamer dead. Odebrecht took advantage and speeded ahead, leaving *Fifi* to drop astern. He gave orders for oil to be thrown on the wood in the *Hedwig*'s furnace to increase speed. Smoke pouring from her funnel, she pulled farther away from the line of pursuing boats.

Fifi was commanded by Spicer, with Dudley and Goor in attendance on deck and Lamont down below. Spicer gave the same order: soak the logs in oil. It didn't work, as Shankland reports, though Lamont and his new stoker did their best:

> In vain in the sweltering engine-room, Fundi raked out the ashes and piled on the oil-soaked logs until the funnel became so hot that Goor and Dudley had to relieve each other frequently at the wheel. Still the pressure in the boiler

dropped: she was making only eight knots to the enemy's nine. The *Hedwig* was escaping.

As *Fifi* slackened, *Mimi* began to gain on her. Even though the Belfast railwayman had never taken a launch on to the lake before, Spicer had put Wainwright in command of *Mimi,* with Flynn as gunner and Mollison at the helm (his fellow Scot, Tait, was on *Fifi*).

Toutou was out of commission. After smashing her bows against the harbour breakwater at night, she had sunk during another storm, but had been recovered. So at the crucial moment, *Mimi* had to go forth without her sister ship. When she eventually overhauled *Fifi*, Spicer began to semaphore from the steamer's deck for Wainwright to get back in line. Taking no notice of the gesticulating, sun-helmeted figure as he roared past, the beak-nosed Belfast man got within 3,000 yards of the *Hedwig* and opened fire.

The shots missed, but Odebrecht knew he was in trouble. His stern-mounted Hotchkiss machine-gun did not have the range of the three-pounder on *Mimi*. The German swung *Hedwig* round and let fly with his forward-mounted six-pounders. Proper artillery that could do proper damage, they fired high explosive.

"Turn to the right!" Wainwright the land-crab shouted to Mollison as the two shells sped through the air. "Over to the right!" (He should have said "starboard" but of course he wasn't a seaman.)

Mollison manoeuvred the boat out of the way of the falling shells—which flashed as they hit the water—and seconds later *Mimi* was firing again at the *Hedwig* from the side. Once again Odebrecht swung round, to give his front-mounted guns purchase. The two boats circled each other in this fashion for half an hour, neither inflicting significant damage.

Meanwhile Fundi's hard work down in the engine-room was paying off. *Fifi* was gaining again. On deck, Waterhouse fired shell after shell from her big gun. On *Mimi*, Wainwright, who was close to where they were falling, could see they were missing the target. He called off his own attack on the *Hedwig* and circled back to tell

Spicer that the range was wrong. He was greeted, says Shankland, by a storm of abuse from Spicer and more frantic semaphore: "When Spicer paused for breath, Wainwright shouted back in his piercing high-pitched Belfast voice, 'No use signalling to me, Captain. We can't read you or make any signals in reply. The *Hedwig*'s in easy range now. All your shots are going a long way over.' "

Spicer had only three rounds left. Waterhouse had shot off nearly all the ammunition. If the *Hedwig* turned again now, *Fifi* would be at her mercy. If *Fifi* could hit the *Hedwig* with one of the three remaining rounds, she might just save the day. Spicer almost called off the action, but decided to try his luck.

He gave the order to fire and Waterhouse pulled the trigger, steadying himself for the twelve-pounder's resounding boom. Nothing happened. It was a misfire. They had to wait twenty minutes before the hot shell could be removed from the breech and dumped over the side. Spicer and the others could only watch as the *Hedwig* pulled away.

When the British stopped firing, Odebrecht realised he had a chance. They were now nearing the rendezvous point with Zimmer on the *Götzen,* which would blow the British away. He lifted his binoculars and scanned the horizon, looking for the familiar massive shape of the symbol of German dominance on the lake. It was nowhere to be seen.

While Odebrecht was looking for the *Götzen,* another shell was prepared on *Fifi*. Waterhouse took careful aim this time and fired. A hit at last! It smashed through the *Hedwig*'s hull. Water started pouring into the ship as, almost immediately, another shell landed, exploding in the *Hedwig*'s engine-room and bursting the boiler. Five African crew members and two Germans were killed. A seaman named Kasemann had his hand shattered by the splinters. As steam poured out, the oily logs that had been piled up caught fire.

Overwhelmed by fatigue and frustration, Odebrecht realised the game was up. He gave orders to abandon ship. The crew donned life-vests and leapt overboard. Some tried to launch the steamer's lighter, but there were too many of them and it sank under their weight.

Odebrecht and an engineer called Mewes were the last to leave the *Hedwig,* which was now enveloped in smoke and flames. Before abandoning ship they set explosive charges to destroy her, so that she could not be captured by the enemy. They jumped overboard as the ship began to list and as they were swimming away the charges exploded. Bow first, the *Hedwig* slipped beneath the waves.

When the Allied flotilla reached the place where she went down, pieces of wreckage and cargo were coming to the surface among the bobbing heads of survivors. *Mimi* and *Fifi* picked up the remaining German crew, and as they did so, Spicer spotted a flag locker among the flotsam. He at once put *Fifi* about to pick it up. Opening it, he was delighted to find a large German naval ensign—the first to be captured intact in the whole War.

It was afternoon by the time the victorious flotilla arrived back at Albertville with its prisoners. Stepping ashore, Spicer received a hero's welcome. Stinghlamber and the other Belgian officers kissed and embraced him. The Holo-holo crowding the bluff—over a thousand in number now—roared their approval and streamed down to engulf him. As the prisoners were lined up on the breakwater and handed over to the Belgians and their *askaris,* only Spicer's sun-helmet could be seen as he was mobbed by the ululating men and women. This time handfuls of sand were sprinkled over his head—to signify, says Shankland, "the land is thine!"

"The wives of the chief came to greet me as I landed," recalled Spicer. "Their message of saluting is rather uncomfortable. The idea is to pick up a handful of earth and present it to you . . . but when, as in this case, they pick up handfuls of gravel and throw them at you it is not so pleasant."

The Belgians were elevated by association. When they had first arrived at the lake, the Africans had called them *Bula Matari* ("omnipotent force"), but this practice ceased when the Belgians began to lose to the Germans. Now they had a fighting chance of being *Bula Matari* again.

Standing on the breakwater beside Kasemann, a despondent *Leutnant* Odebrecht watched the rejoicing crowds. He felt weak with fatigue and had lost most of his clothes; he'd had to strip off in the lake to swim and was now wearing only socks and trousers. But Kasemann, cradling his bleeding hand, was in worse shape. Realising the seaman needed urgent attention, Odebrecht spoke to one of their Belgian guards. He and Kasemann were marched off to see a man who introduced himself as *"Der Herr Doktor hier."*

Dr. Hanschell decided an operation was necessary. Kasemann was taken to the large hospital hut in the new camp, where "Tubby" Eastwood administered chloroform. Odebrecht stood by to comfort him, until the cotton pad over Kasemann's mouth took effect and he lost consciousness. As Rupia held down Kasemann's arm, the doctor amputated two and a half fingers.

While Kasemann slept off the anaesthetic, Dr. Hanschell noticed that Odebrecht was exhausted and gave him a glass of hospital brandy. As Odebrecht drank, he signed his parole, which had been brought in during the amputation. It was a promise not to escape, in return for which he would, as an officer and a gentleman, be accorded certain privileges.

One of these was an invitation from Spicer to dine in the British mess, which Odebrecht accepted, subject to shoes and a shirt being found for him. There being no spare shoes in the camp, Dr. Hanschell had to give him his long, brown-leather mosquito boots ("It hurt him to the heart to part with them," notes Shankland). According to Magee, Odebrecht put on an Iron Cross medal for dinner, in which case he must have kept the precious decoration in his pocket or held it when he jumped off the *Hedwig.*

It was dark by now, but the Holo-holo were still celebrating up in the hills, beating drums in the firelight. As Odebrecht followed Dr. Hanschell over to the messhut, he saw the silhouettes of dancing figures, swaying and quivering in the firesmoke. Inside the hut, he was introduced to Spicer. The British Commander's shortsleeved shirt revealed arms covered with writhing tattoos. Odebrecht brought sharply together the heels of the doctor's mosquito boots and gave a stiff bow. Spicer bowed in return and they sat down to eat.

It was a strange meal. Barely a word was spoken, even by Spicer, and the only sound was the rush of the insect-besieged kerosene lamps and the revellers outside. Like the Holo-holo, the lower British ranks were celebrating enthusiastically. Fuelled by some wine the Belgians had sent over, they were singing anti-German songs around a bonfire. Back in the mess-hut, Spicer's servant Tom served the officers tinned soup, beef stew and coffee. There was also some broiled catfish: it was supposed to be an entrée, but came too late. As Dr. Hanschell recalled: "Tom, gazing with awe at the snakes on Spicer's arms and forgetting to serve the fish, was sharply recalled to his duties by a jab in the stomach from Spicer's fork."

Despite this delay, dinner lasted a mere twenty minutes, upon which Spicer rose, nodded goodnight to Odebrecht, and disappeared into his tent. The other officers soon followed his example. It was left to Dr. Hanschell to escort Odebrecht back to the hospital hut. The German complained of a bad headache, so the doctor administered a sedative injection. Within a few minutes the exhausted Odebrecht was asleep, relieved for a while of the terrible burden of defeat.

So ended the second battle of Lake Tanganyika. While Odebrecht slept, Spicer was busy writing up his report to the Admiralty. It had been a great success, he said, describing it as "a naval action in miniature." He even claimed to have ordered Wainwright forward in *Mimi* (rather than telling him to get back in line) and praised the Belfast man for following his orders. The news was well received, once the Morse had been transcribed back at Admiralty House. In his notes on Spicer's report, the First Sea Lord Sir Henry Jackson wrote: "I doubt whether any one tactical operation of such miniature proportions has exercised so important an influence on enemy operations." Now the joint Belgian-British advance across the lake could begin.

What the Admiral didn't know was that a few days after Spicer had made practice runs in *Mimi* and *Toutou* on the Thames in June 1915, the German supership *Graf von Götzen* had been launched on Lake Tanganyika. Spicer was all too aware of the fearsome *Götzen* and he knew it made a mockery of his toy navy. But the Admiralty was still in the dark about the mighty German warship.

Chapter Twenty

The morning after the victory meal saw Odebrecht much rested. The morphine in Hanschell's injection had worked its magic. Kasemann, too, was doing well. Over breakfast with Dr. Hanschell, Odebrecht seemed to have come to terms with the sinking of the *Hedwig,* but there was one thing that worried him: the strange pattern of the battle led him to believe that he had been bested by a bunch of amateurs. Spicer's skirt and tattoos had only reinforced this impression. So the German was much relieved when the doctor told him that despite appearances Spicer was a trained naval officer.

This allowed Odebrecht to give purely technical reasons for his defeat. In their paper, Bishop and Dobold refer to a letter Odebrecht sent to Otto Schloifer, the man who had built the *Hedwig* on the lakeshore in 1900. Odebrecht "justified his defeat by stating that he simply ran into a superior enemy force consisting of four vessels which were superior in speed and armament and which opened fire from a distance of 8,000 metres, while his own guns had maximum ranges of only 3,000m and 2,500m respectively."

Schloifer wasn't the only shipbuilder for the German naval forces in Africa. In 1913 a German shipyard run by Joseph Meyer had received an important new contract. Meyer, whose yard was at Papenburg on the Ems River, was commissioned to build a twin-screw cargo and passenger ship of 1,200 tons, with a draught (how deep in the water she sat) of four metres. The proposed vessel—about two-thirds the length of a football pitch—was due for service on Lake Tanganyika.

Mimi and *Toutou* were tiny by comparison. And with their wooden hulls made on the Thames, they were far less sturdy than the steel-plated monster constructed on the Ems. The British boats were at the tail-end of a marine-craft tradition in wood; the German ship was a modern industrial product, riveted together—in some haste, admittedly, because Meyer and his team had less than a year in which to complete the contract.

The new German ship was to be called the *Graf von Götzen* after the colony's former military governor, Count Adolf von Götzen. It was the largest order that had ever come into the Papenburg shipyard, where the Meyer family had been building boats for generations. They asked for payment in five instalments, the first payable immediately and the last on delivery of the ship to the port of Hamburg. The total cost was 406,000 Deutschmarks, the equivalent of about £20,000 in those days.

The order had been placed at the instigation of none other than Kaiser Wilhelm II himself, following information received from his government surveyor in 1910. The surveyor's agents in East Africa had pointed out that the Belgians had only smallish craft on Lake Tanganyika and the British just a few tramp steamers on Lake Victoria and Lake Nyasa. A proper ship on one of the great African inland seas would be a considerable commercial asset to Germany and an important factor in the balance of power in the territory.

Purchased through the Kaiser's East African Railway Company, the *Götzen* was not originally envisaged as a troopship, but as a commercial venture with military possibilities. The likely advent of war with Britain changed all that, however. By the time the order was sent to the Meyer shipyard in January 1913, the Kaiser and his advisers knew the *Götzen* might be used to carry troops. The pressures of the approaching war are evident in a telegram sent eleven months later by Dr. Heinrich Schnee, Götzen's successor as Governor of German East Africa:

> Accelerate by all means sending slips, shipyard equipment, for *Götzen* with the latest mounting instruments. Send with 20 skilled ship-builders, if possible employees of the Railway. Economic interests and prestige demand urgency.

At Papenburg, work on the *Götzen* went on apace, even though the yard's owners and workers were pretty much in the dark as to the Government's plans for the ship. The order stated it had to be built so that it could be transported to an inland lake and that was all the information they had to go on.

"They knew that the ship had to get there by land somehow," recalled Hermann Wendt, when interviewed for a German television documentary broadcast in 2001. His father (also called Hermann) had been a shipwright in the Meyer yard and had worked on the *Götzen*. "After a lot of thinking about the best way to do it, they built the ship in Papenburg, but all the parts were just screwed together. Everything was only provisionally fixed."

Hermann Wendt senior, along with two other shipwrights from Meyer's—Anton Ruter and Rudolf Tellmann—were requested to deliver the *Götzen* in person to the shores of Lake Tanganyika. It was proposed that the ship be broken down into its constituent parts for transport and that the shipwrights would reassemble it in Africa. They were to be well paid for their work, and as Wendt's son observed: "They went away to become rich. The three of them wanted to make money."

The shipwrights' contracts of employment provided for large cash bonuses if the operation was successful and it is no coincidence that they were signed in early November 1913, the period of phony engagement, a little over nine months before the start of the First World War. The two great powers, Germany and Britain, were already in a breathless arms race in which naval power was a key factor. The *Graf von Götzen* would be a crucial part of the German war machine.

By the end of November, the loose-bolted ship was ready. Her wood-burning steam engine was fired up to see if it worked properly. Then the steel pieces of the hull and superstructure were unscrewed and taken apart. In total, the ship broke down into hundreds of thousands of individual pieces, each of which was given a code number. Packed in five thousand numbered crates, they were sent by train to Hamburg and loaded aboard four freighters.

On 19 December 1913 the cargo ships *Admiral* and *Feldmarschall* left Hamburg for Dar es Salaam, German East Africa. They carried the hull, bulkheads, deck pillars and beams for the reconstruction of the *Götzen* in Africa—and the scaffolding upon which this would take place, once it had been erected in Kigoma harbour, on the lake. They also carried all of the rivets, which on a project this size amounted to a considerable cargo in itself.

The chronology was sensible, the planning exact. This first consignment of newly forged steel would include "all the pieces necessary to set the ship in ribs," according to a letter from the East African Company's Berlin HQ to Dar es Salaam. The freighters *Windhoek* and *Adolf Woermann* left Hamburg early in the new year, carrying further cargoes. In the *Windhoek* were stowed the masts, boilers and engine. The third consignment, on the *Adolf Woermann*, consisted of all the interior fittings: the panelling for the cabins, the installations and furniture. It also carried the deck houses and the upper works—the capstans, winches and cranes—as well as the lifeboats and funnels.

Despite war being in the air, indeed being actively prepared for by Britain and Germany, all these parts and equipment were insured by British companies. At a premium of a half per cent for a total insurance of £25,000, twelve British companies around the world participated in the risk. Lloyds of London shouldered the bulk of it, taking on £8,500. The rest was spread out between different companies in chunks of less than £2,000. That was the figure for which the Canton Insurance Office and the firm of British Dominions were responsible. The Thames and Mersey Marine Insurance Company took on £1,000. The New Zealand Insurance Company took on £500. Their policies covered "all risks including fire, while under construction and/or fitting out . . . Also all risks of trial trips."

At a total cost of £125 to the Germans in premiums, it must have seemed like a good deal. But Lloyds and its associates took no chances. The policies were also issued on the basis that the *Götzen* was "warranted free of capture, seizure and detention, and the consequences thereof or any attempt thereat, piracy excepted, and also from all consequences of hostilities or warlike operations whether before or after declaration of war."

After a journey that had taken in the Mediterranean, the Suez Canal and the Indian Ocean, the shipwrights Wendt, Ruter and Tellmann arrived in Dar es Salaam in early 1914. German East Africa was a world away from Papenburg—a world about to be shaken to its core. In under six months war would be declared. Dar es Salaam means "Haven of Peace" in Arabic. By the time the War was over, the three shipwrights would appreciate the irony of this. For the time being, they supervised the unloading and warehousing of the five thousand crates containing the *Götzen*.

They also acclimatised to being in Africa. "At first they were scared," Rudolf Tellmann's daughter explained in the 2001 documentary. "They came from here [Germany] and hadn't been anywhere else in their lives, and suddenly they were surrounded by Africans. They were frightened. Later, though, my father said blacks were willing people, they would have done anything for them."

No doubt the famous Klub Dar es Salaam, which served German beer, provided a refuge for the shipwrights. In truth, the capital of Tanzania was hardly "darkest Africa" even then and they had no reason to be frightened. Once a small, mosquito-ridden village, Dar es Salaam had been transformed by the Germans into one of the most modern cities in East Africa, with new roads and docks and buildings. One of these was the Klub, founded in 1903 when Governor Götzen, returning from furlough, brought back with him 25,000 marks to found a social club. The money had been donated by a number of industrialists "bent on the expansion of German interests in their colonies generally," as an early member of the Klub put it.

The Klub's articles of association state that one in three members of the managing committee must be a "commercial," i.e. not a military officer or government official. This was in order to diminish the "spirit of caste": the rigid hierarchy that beset German (and British) colonial life. In his correspondence with the Imperial Government, Count Götzen stressed that this evil spirit did not exist, while accepting that the rule was very desirable. This was the social world in which the three shipbuilders from Papenburg found themselves. They may have glimpsed across the room the figure of Lieutenant-Colonel Paul von Lettow-Vorbeck, the dashing commander of German troops in East Africa. But it is unlikely they would have been given an opportunity to talk to him.

Once African stevedores had loaded 5,000 crates on to a train in Dar es Salaam, the three shipwrights were ready to start the 700-mile journey to Lake Tanganyika. They had not gone far when a fire broke out in the wagons, damaging the rigging and bending the *Götzen*'s propeller shaft. "All risks, including fire," said their British insurers, but the Germans never got the chance to make a claim.

About 20 miles from Kigoma the railway tailed off, unfinished. The unwieldy crates were unloaded from the train. They would be carried on African shoulders the rest of the way. This part of the journey, which took almost three months and involved thousands of porters, was nothing less than a forced march. The porters were whipped when unwilling or unable to continue. The three ship-wrights were carried on a litter, an experience that at home would be reserved for the Kaiser and few others. In German East, it was the norm for white men to travel like this.

Reaching the half-built port of Kigoma on the shores of Lake Tanganyika, the shipwrights found many of their countrymen there. It almost seemed like a provincial German town, except that most provincial German towns do not have a small palace. The Kaiser-hof, as it was known, had been built in case Wilhelm II should come to visit his remotest colony.

The Africans servicing the new town lived in shacks on the fringes of Kigoma. Some of the original porters stayed, but most were laid off. New labour was hired, both African and European, for there were a lot of Germans hanging around Kigoma with noth-ing to do, colonial adventurers hoping to make their fortune.

Anton Ruter, the foreman from Papenburg, supervised the unloading of the crates. In a makeshift shipyard by the lake, the numbered boxes were counted, then unpacked. Each piece of sheet metal or other item that emerged was checked against the foreman's original lists. Except for two crates of deck bolts left behind in Dar es Salaam, everything was there.

Painstakingly, the *Graf von Götzen* was rebuilt piece by piece. The pattern of the dress rehearsal on the Ems River, back in Ger-many, was followed to the letter. During the rebuilding the three shipwrights lived in huts next to the shipyard, each engaging his own personal staff. For all that, it was not a luxurious life. At one point they even ran out of shoes.

Around this time the *Götzen* was officially transferred from the German East African Railway Company to the military authorities; its value at this point is stated in German documents as 750,000 marks—approximately £36,765. The rise from the book cost of

£20,000 was due to the cost of transport to and reconstruction at Kigoma.

War broke out in Europe on 4 August 1914. On 26 August von Lettow sent *Kapitän zur See* Gustav Zimmer to Lake Tanganyika to take charge of the German naval contingent: his fleet would consist of the *Kingani,* the *Hedwig* and the emerging star of the show, the *Graf von Götzen.* By the end of 1914, "the ship that came by train," as it was known, looked like a ship again. An armed ship: the two guns from the disabled *Königsberg* having been installed and tested.

On 1 June 1915 the *Götzen* was launched, making a fifty-hour journey to Bismarckburg (now Kasanga), a German-held town at the south end of the lake. In his report on this trial run, Zimmer mentioned that the British-made steering mechanism connecting the wheel to the rudder was defective, causing the ship to roll and list, but this had been rectified. A related issue was the draught, which was too shallow. Zimmer recommended it be increased by adding two metres to the length of the funnel.

Eight months later, the day after the sinking of the *Hedwig,* the *Götzen* steamed past the British camp at Albertville looking for her sister ship. Hearing shouting, Dr. Hanschell and Odebrecht left the breakfast table and went out on to the "quarterdeck" in front of Spicer's hut. They gazed at the giant steamer, the noise of her propellers clearly audible for many miles as they chomped the water.

The Iron Cross fluttered as the *Götzen* moved slowly along the horizon, spreading the foaming, twinfold ribbon of its wake over the surface of the lake. Her charcoal-burning furnace left a curlicue of black smoke above the blue water. On deck, next to bulkheads fore and aft, clusters of seamen stood round the big guns, watching and waiting for the order to fire. It was an oceangoing-sized ship, all screws and steel plate below, steel rigging and swinging derricks aloft. How had the Germans cast and hammered all that metal out here in the bush, then fitted it all together?

The doctor and Odebrecht watched as Wainwright and the crews of *Mimi* and *Fifi* ran down to the harbour (*Toutou* was still out of commission). They heard *Mimi*'s engines start up and saw smoke begin to rise out of *Fifi*'s funnel as Lamont and Fundi stirred her banked-up fires. Meanwhile, Dudley's whippet-thin figure ran to Spicer's hut to tell him that battle must be joined again. The *Götzen* drew parallel with the camp, at which point Byron Farwell takes up the story:

> Spicer-Simson, standing on his verandah, watched it intently through his glasses, while Dudley, beside him, pleaded with him to order an attack. In the harbour, *Fifi* was getting up steam and *Mimi* was preparing for battle, but Spicer let the moment pass. The *Graf von Götzen* looked formidable; he had already earned his place in history. While Dudley argued, the *Graf von Götzen* altered course and disappeared.

In the middle of the argument Spicer simply turned abruptly on his heel and went back into his hut. Cursing him, Dudley strode past Odebrecht and the doctor—and without looking at them, says Shankland, "went to the edge of the bluff and put his hands to his mouth to form a trumpet and shouted, 'As you were! As you were!' He waved to the crews to come up, and went off down the path to meet Wainwright."

Odebrecht watched the whole scene from the cliff's edge, but remained silent. Then comes the most dramatic moment in Shankland's marvellous book: "[As] at last he turned and gazed straight at the Doctor, not a muscle of his face moved. Then he walked quickly away and entered the hut where he was billeted." Three days later, Odebrecht was marched to a prisoner-of-war camp, still wearing the doctor's mosquito boots.

In the interim, Fundi had turned up at the hospital tent with terrible burns on his hands and shins from stoking *Fifi*'s furnace during the attack on the *Hedwig*. Lamont had only noticed these injuries as they were preparing for the aborted attack on the *Götzen*. Fundi's body was a suppurating mass of blisters, especially the tops of his feet. In the service of his new colonial masters, he had raked out the hot ash directly onto them. The romantic adventure of *Mimi* and *Toutou* was well and truly over.

Chapter Twenty-One

Morale plummeted over the next few days. The men wanted to go out and fight; an instinct that the reappearance of the *Götzen* rubbed raw and angry. Twice again she had been spotted on the horizon, the temptress, casually riding the swell. Still Spicer refused. He gave no reason, but perhaps he believed he had fulfilled his orders by sinking the *Hedwig* and it was foolish to pitch *Mimi* and *Toutou* (now repaired) against such odds.

It was a time of signs and wonders. Walking through the bush, Dr. Hanschell had been delighted to come across a carpet of golden butterflies that stretched for yards around. A few days later he was less pleased when he awoke to find a brown-and-pink, diamond-patterned snake near the wall of his hut. He stamped his foot and it fled outside. Curious, the doctor followed. The snake had gone. On the lakeside opposite, the sun was rising behind Mount Kungwe at exactly the point where it reached its full height of 8,620 feet; its notched, double-topped head embodying the greatest demon of the land.

A few days later news came through on the radio that Spicer (with whom the Admiralty was generally well pleased), Wainwright (for carrying out Spicer's orders to the letter) and Lamont (for running *Fifi*'s engines without a stoker) had all been awarded medals. On hearing of his award Lamont disappeared to his workshop. He emerged at nightfall, clutching a brass medal on one side of which he had engraved the words FUNDI RN (Royal Navy) and on the other HMS FIFI, 9 FEBRUARY 1916. But who would present it? As Shankland tells us:

> The Black Squad* went in a body to Spicer and asked him to present it at a ceremonial parade. Spicer gave permission for the parade, but thought it wouldn't be tactful for him to take part in it personally. Marapandi produced a broad ribbon of red, white and blue from which he suspended the medal.

In the end, Lamont presented the award himself. After it had been hung round his neck, a beaming Fundi acknowledged the cheering, clapping crowd and went round shaking everyone's hand, Spicer's included.

Not long after this spontaneous display of gratitude, Spicer abruptly left Albertville. He said he was going down to Stanleyville and left Wainwright in charge, adding that he was not under any circumstances to attack the *Götzen* unless the German ship began shelling the camp.

Spicer was away for months. The expedition heard that he had gone down to Leopoldville (Kinshasa), the Belgian capital on the

---

*The African connections of the expedition.

western Congo, more than 1,500 miles away. Nobody knew quite what he was up to, but on his travels Spicer received a telegram from General Northey, who commanded British troops in the region, asking him to attack the *Götzen*. Spicer replied that he would not, because he thought the chances of success too slim.

As it turned out, Spicer was trying to commandeer the St. George, a bullet-proof steel boat belonging to the British consul at Banana on the mouth of the Congo. Despite being overruled by Bonar Law at the Colonial Office, and contrary to Shankland's account, Spicer went ahead with this plan. Richard Dunne, a resourceful plater working for Lever Brothers in Kinshasa, was seconded to the Naval Africa Expedition. His duty was to dismantle the St. George and accompany her to Lake Tanganyika where she was to be rebuilt. In this task he was successful, completing a 4000-mile round trip no less full of hazard and incident than that of Mimi and Toutou—but the St. George arrived too late to make any appreciable difference to the outcome of the battle for Lake Tanganyika. Wainwright and Lamont helped Dunne reassemble the boat, and the plater seems to have bumped into Hanschell's Greek trader on the way, too. The trader had a steel trunk with him, and things were on the up. "When we were nearing Stanleyville, I asked him what was in the trunk," Dunne recalled in the 1960s. "He told me it was full of money and that he was going to buy native trade goods to take back with him."

It was during Spicer's absence that the statues started to appear. The Holo-holo had been so impressed by the sinking of the *Hedwig,* writes Magee, "that they moulded images of the commander in clay (and good likenesses, too) which they worshipped in their villages as their new ju-ju." Dr. Hanschell first heard about them when Rupia had burst into his hut as he was writing some letters home.

"Navyman God!" said his servant with a mysterious smile. When the doctor asked him what on earth he was on about, Rupia merely repeated, "Navyman God!—You come see!"

He followed Rupia out to a small clearing in the bush, where they found a clay statue about two feet high with short legs and arms but a well-modelled face and torso. The doctor told Shankland how he "went up close to it and found that the face was a recognisable caricature of Spicer with a pointed beard and wearing a sun-helmet. It was grasping with both tiny hands an object representing a pair of binoculars. Tiny incisions marked the tattooed snakes and butterflies on the chest and forearms, and between the squat little thighs there was a bit of native loin-cloth."

Later, the Catholic missionary from the Order of the White Fathers came to Dr. Hanschell for quinine as he prepared to return to his church at Karema (established in 1885, the mission station was formerly a vast transit camp for slaves en route to Zanzibar). The White Father confided to the doctor that these statues had been appearing all along the lakeshore and inland as well. He accused Spicer of undoing all his good work as the tribe reverted to its old ways: there had been some cockerel feathers and snakeskin on a platform before the statue and some stones smeared with blood. The elderly White Father had spent many years trying to persuade the Holo-holo to give up cruel practices and idolatry and embrace Jesus Christ—and now a fetish of a European had been set up within a few miles of his mission!

"I suppose they think of me as some kind of great chief witch doctor?" Dr. Hanschell asked the despondent missionary.

"No—that's not their name for you," replied the White Father, at last breaking into a smile. "What they call you, as nearly as I translate it, is something like 'Harmless Village Idiot.' Poor doctor! No statues for you!"

Why had Spicer, in particular, inspired such worship? The snakeskin by the statue is of relevance here, and it relates to the spirit of Mount Kungwe. Mkungwe had two troublesome sons, Katavi and Lubadyu. According to Dr. Egon Kirschstein in a 1937 edition of *Tanganyika Notes and Records*:

The tale tells of a quarrel between Katavi and his father Kungwe long long ago, whereby Katavi split the father's head. That notch is visible today. Kungwe did not pardon the insult, but ordered Katavi to leave the country. In his anger Katavi threatened to create another Tanganyika somewhere else. Old Kungwe smiled contemptuously when he heard of such a boast by the outcast. Katavi, however, fulfilled his threat and made a new Tanganyika further inland, in that part of the country which is now called the Katavi plain.

Katavi's brother Lubadyu was similarly outlawed, so enraging Kungwe that he picked him up and threw him over to the other (Congolese) side of Lake Tanganyika. "The effort was so great," according to C. C. O'Hagan,* "that Mkungwe lay down and in the early morning he can be clearly made out from the north lying on his back, his head towards the water, his knees raised with his hands clasped over his stomach."

Mkungwe has never risen again. Over on the Albertville side, Lubadyu made mountainous country, too, when he fell; but the shock of the fall was so great that he disintegrated—"so that only his bulk, but not his form can now be made out." This myth of the division of a single land mass into two parts, each with a divine authority subordinate to a greater power, may be related to a theory advanced by the explorer Sir Henry Morton Stanley—namely that early humanoids were witness to the tectonics of the Rift Valley (which produced Lake Tanganyika) and retained that distant memory in their myths and legends.

Holo-holo mythology has a strict hierarchy. Just as the spirit Mkungwe reported to the cosmogonic god Kabedya Mpungu (who does not concern himself with merely human affairs), so the errant sons reported to Mkungwe. Doubles play an important part in these legends. For instance, on appeal, the ancestral spirits of human twins (known as Migabo) would act as intercessors to Katavi and

*A British colonial official who climbed Mount Kungwe in May 1939.

Lubadyu, who would pass this appeal to Mkungwe and so on up the chain to Kabedya Mpungu. The Migabo were usually approached and called upon after a vision or dream of snakes. Seeing snakes meant that the spirits had been neglected.

Add to this a related story about a monster in the lake (which was thought of as a giant snake) and we come closer to understanding why the tattooed Spicer was so revered. The snake designs on his arms and thighs plugged him directly into the mythic consciousness of Holo-holo society.

His main claim to holiness, however, was his victory over the Germans, who were disliked by some Holo-holo for violating a sacred site. In 1925 G. W. Hatchell wrote about visiting Kafishya, near Karema on the former German side of Lake Tanganyika. Here the Holo-holo had once stored wooden images of the old kings of the people, which they brought over when they crossed from the Congolese side:

> It was said that a German, Lieutenant Bishoff, having reason to suspect that Kafishya was the scene of human sacrifice and believing that he had found human blood on the images took them away and destroyed them. Certain of the older people at Karema however believe that many of the images had been sent to Berlin.

According to Hatchell, a sect of Holo-holo women keep the skulls of the dead kings safe from any further interference at another site on the lakeshore. I heard the same story during an expedition to the lake in 2003 and it cast some light on Spicer's deification.

When their kings became infirm, the Holo-holo would kill them. This was done with full ceremony, but in secret by a witch doctor. As part of the ritual, the new king would emerge from the same hut in which the old king had been murdered and thereby take his place (the dead king's skull would then be kept as a sacred object). This symbolism may well have played its part in the deification of Spicer. Having killed the "old king" (the Germans), he took on their power. It is a variant of the Fisher King myth made famous by Sir James Frazer's *The Golden Bough* (1890–1915).

Modulations of this ritual can be found in various parts of the Rift Valley and Nile basin. While it seems to be geographically focused on the nexus of the Great Lakes, it is the wellspring of many myths of renewal that travelled far and wide. During their explorations of Lake Tanganyika in November and December 1871, Stanley and Livingstone were told a fable by their boatman Ruango which reiterated many of the cultic motifs, including fish and secret enclosures, that Jesse Weston believed underpinned medieval romances such as *Sir Gawain and the Green Knight* and were furthermore the bedrock of the Holy Grail story. Weston's *From Ritual to Romance* (1918) is said to have exerted a profound influence on T. S. Eliot.

The fish myth may have some connection to giant Nile perch (*Lates angustifrons*). Found in Lakes Tanganyika and Victoria and throughout the Nile system, they can grow as large as seven feet long and weigh up to 400 pounds (for comparison, the largest salmon ever caught was probably around 71 pounds and most salmon are 10–16 pounds). As Christopher Ondaatje writes in his *Journey to the Source of the Nile* (1998): "They were known to the ancient Egyptians, and mummified remains of the fish have been found. There is some evidence that Nile perch may have once been the object of cult worship."

Sadly the men of the Naval Africa Expedition were prevented from fishing for Nile perch by the power of another king. In colonial times, Lake Tanganyika was regarded as the private fishery of the Belgian king Albert I, so Stinghlamber forbade them from using the fishing rods they had brought all that way.

By the time Spicer returned to the lake on 12 May 1916, plans were afoot for the Belgians to take Kigoma, the German provincial capital, and the British to take Bismarckburg, their redoubt at the foot of the lake. A British column under one Lieutenant-Colonel Murray was advancing on Bismarckburg through Northern Rhodesia (Zambia). The idea was that Spicer's flotilla would support them from Lake Tanganyika and prevent the Germans from escaping by water.

Mimi, Toutou, Fifi and *Vengeur* were loaded up and prepared for the long journey. The men wanted to take the goat from the *Kingani,* but Spicer wouldn't let them. With tears in his eyes, Tait led the animal behind a hut and shot it. The goat was burnt and its ashes cast upon the waters of the lake. Eastwood's chimpanzee Josephine, however, was allowed to join Dr. Hanschell on *Fifi.*

They arrived at Bismarckburg on 5 June to find a white fort armed with cannon and a harbour in which floated a fleet of dhows in the German service.* Once again, Spicer baulked at attacking. He had no desire to come within range of the fort's guns. Dudley and Wainwright wanted to rip into the harbour in *Mimi* and *Toutou,* guns blazing, and destroy the dhows. Instead, Spicer withdrew the flotilla back to Kituta, a port in Northern Rhodesia. (According to the official history of the war, *Military Operations East Africa,* the flotilla did actually fire two shells into the fort before withdrawing. It seems likely this was a Spicer-Simson ploy by which he tried to persuade the Admiralty that he had done the right thing.)

Four days later, when Spicer and his men returned to Bismarckburg, they found a Union Jack flying from the Beau Geste–style fort. The dhows were gone and laughter and jeers greeted the navy men as they landed.

"Where the hell were you chaps last night?" called out one of the Rhodesian soldiers in the harbour. "You let the Germans get away by sea. We had the fort surrounded!"

Byron Farwell gives a good account of the precise moment when Spicer's self-confidence took a nosedive. Lieutenant-Colonel Murray was a formidable figure. His colonials, who had sustained

---

*The ruins of the fort can still be seen at Kasanga in present-day Zambia.

casualties while fighting their way through to Bismarckburg, were not the sort to be impressed by ju-ju or "successful mystique." Or by a man in a skirt.

> Spicer-Simson ordered Dudley and Hanschell to accompany him as he stepped ashore wearing his gold-braided cap, blue flannel shirt, and his skirt. He asked a young Rhodesian officer to take him to Murray, but he merely pointed to the fort and said, "Straight up there. You can't miss it. Just follow your nose." Spicer-Simson's face flushed, but he said nothing. Marching up to the fort he was greeted with whistles and ribald laughter: "Kiss me, Gertie!" and "Oh! la! la!" and "Chase me, Charlie!"

Spicer was in with Murray only for a few minutes. No one knows quite what was said, but the glowering Rhodesian was clearly furious. When Spicer stepped outside the room, says Shankland, "he was dead white, and looking as if he were not quite sure where he was, and holding out his hands as if he were half blind and must feel his way."

A few weeks later and Spicer was in trouble again, this time for refusing to let the Belgians use the Allied flotilla to move troops and supplies up and down the lake as part of the final assault on German positions. On 11 June the Belgian seaplanes reported that they had bombed the *Graf von Götzen* at Kigoma—but nobody knew if she had been put out of action. In his memoirs the ship's captain Gustav Zimmer writes that the aerial attack "did not cause serious damage," but as Dobold and Bishop point out, "The air raids certainly did have some effect on Zimmer and the Germans' morale."

The defences of Kigoma were strengthened in expectation of the coming land battle. Spicer's refusal to offer naval support to the offensive caused ructions between the Belgian and British governments. He told the Admiralty that the Belgians were trying to squeeze the British out of the picture and prevent them acquiring former German territory. The Belgians complained that Spicer was trying to stop them using their own vessels, not just *Mimi* and *Toutou*. Spicer's relations with his own officers were no better: after falling out with each of them in turn, he resorted to communicating with them only by letter.

These episodes put an end to Spicer's dreams of glory. When Lieutenant-Colonel Murray's troops marched out of the Bismarck-burg fort on 15 June, the Naval Africa Expedition was ordered to remain behind in its grim, stone-floored rooms. Spicer took to lying on his trucklebed all day, fully dressed and gazing at the ceiling, refusing to do anything whatsoever. Dudley took command of the flotilla as Spicer sank further and further into lethargy over the next few months. His mood was not helped by the discovery that the fort's guns—into whose range he had not wanted to bring *Mimi* and *Toutou*—were, in fact, wooden dummies.

In the first weeks of July, the Belgian general Tombeur's Brigade Nord began their attack on Kigoma, which they captured on 28 July. An ignominious end was in store for the *Graf von Götzen* as well. Two days earlier, a desperate Zimmer had given orders for her to be scuttled. The supership was filled with cement to make her sink, but Zimmer hadn't given up hope completely. He ordered the three shipwrights from Papenburg to grease the *Götzen*'s engines to preserve them and allow her to be sailed if she were ever raised. Then he sank her at the mouth of the Malagarasi River (one of the biggest rivers in Tanzania), so that she wouldn't be too deep to bring back to the surface.

The Times of 2 August 1916 reported: "During the same period our Tanganyikan fleet showed great activity. The defences of the port of Ujiji [Kigoma] and enemy vessels in the harbour were subjected to almost daily bombing. The German gunboat *Graf von Götzen* is reported destroyed. We have secured complete liberty of action on Lake Tanganyika." The following day's report gave more detail, though it does not mention the crucial fact that the ship was actually scuttled. "While steaming along the German shores of the lake the Belgian gunboat *Netta* commanded by Lieutenant Lenaerts surprised at 6 a.m. on July 28 the *Graf von Götzen* as she was disembarking troops. The Belgian boat immediately opened fire, whereupon the German boat attempted to escape, but was sunk in 15 minutes."

What actually happened was that when the Belgians took the river mouth, they noticed the *Götzen*'s masts sticking out of the water and sent down divers to investigate her condition. It turned out that her big guns—the very ones that had been brought off the *Königsberg* the previous year—had been replaced with wooden decoys, like the guns in the fort at Bismarckburg. Needing them for his beleaguered land forces, the German commander von Lettow had ordered Zimmer to hand them over to him in mid-May—about the time Spicer came back from the coast. So the Commander—who was still lying in torpor at Bismarckburg when this news came through—could have taken the defenceless *Götzen* with *Mimi* and *Toutou* after all.

Chapter Twenty-Two

Following Spicer's bad example, the men were also becoming demoralised. On 23 August 1916 Dr. Hanschell took the difficult decision to invalid out Spicer. He could go home. According to Shankland, "Spicer came to life at once!"

There was no great leave-taking, neither for the men of the Naval Africa Expedition nor for *Mimi* and *Toutou*. Nor even for the Holo-holo. One day Spicer was there, the next he was gone.

To his African devotees he briefly became something like *le dieu caché,* the "Hidden God" of the Christian West of whom the White Fathers sometimes spoke. What was once plainly manifested—by semaphore, by blood on the decks of ships, by the image of the snake—would soon recede into myth, since they looked for him and found him not.

Only the statues remained, but they too would eventually be drained of their occult power, becoming mere curiosities in a museum. The Holo-holo fetish was a means of evading the god's displeasure. You embody the god to appease him. If he is not there, if he is strolling down the Mall, for instance, there is no need.

Worthy fame and great renown were uppermost in Spicer's mind and he was soon up to his old tricks again. Although the medical certificate Dr. Hanschell had given him cited "acute mental debility," in his own report to the Admiralty Spicer stated that he had malaria, dysentery and various other diseases. These seemed to have cleared up nicely by the time he reached London in September 1916.

He got a mixed reception. The navy gave him his DSO (Distinguished Service Order), but also reprimanded him for not accommodating the Belgians more gracefully. For their part, the Belgians awarded him their Commander of the Order of the Crown, as well as the Croix de Guerre—perhaps recognising that officers in the tropics operate under a great deal of stress (Spicer's old adversary Stinghlamber had also been invalided out).

During 1917 Spicer claimed prize money* for sinking the *Kingani* and his story ran as a feature in many newspapers. He was "The Hero of the Gunboats" whose "Nelson Touch on the African Lake" had rightly earned him his medals. He had persuaded the newspapers of his heroism, but the navy never let him have a command again. "His tactless behaviour might have contributed to a serious disaster," grumbled Admiral Gamble, who was charged with investigating the incident. Spicer was given the same desk job he had had before the adventure began, dealing with the transfer of Merchant Marine officers to the Royal Navy.

Characters fly off in many directions from a battlefield. Some of

---

*An antiquated Royal Navy procedure whereby commanding officers receive a cash bonus for capturing an enemy vessel intact.

the Naval Expedition's members stayed in Africa; others couldn't wait to return to Britain. They came back by a different route, paddling long dugout canoes down the Luapula River, which descends gently down into what is now Zambia. (*Mimi* and *Toutou* were handed over to the army for use as transports.) The Germans weren't so lucky. Rosenthal, the officer who had swum to Lukuga, did not get home until 1920.

After Kigoma was captured, the three shipwrights, Ruter, Wendt and Tellmann, were sent to a prisoner-of-war camp in Egypt. They escaped by tunnelling with some other men and making for the Nile. As Wilhelm Tellmann's son recalled: "They swam across the Nile, but the one who was carrying the food drowned. A few days later they were caught again and brought back to the same camp." The shipwrights eventually returned to Papenburg in 1919, deeply disappointed. "I went away to become rich," complained Wendt, "and came back a poor man—and a sick man too."

Dr. Hanschell also had a terrible time of it. Wounded in the forearm by shrapnel in one of the last actions of the lake war— which took place soon after Spicer left—he developed sepsis and a malignant form of malaria. Like Spicer before him, though with good reason, he took to his bed for several weeks.

Disease wasn't the only thing to beset the doctor. The symbols of Spicer's dominance over the Holo-holo plagued him, too, as if the Commander were exerting his power from afar. One day, writes Shankland, Dr. Hanschell awoke from sleep in his stone-and-cement cell in the Bismarckburg fort "to see a three-foot-long mother snake gliding across the floor in company with six child snakes each one foot long. He staggered from his bed, seized his stick, and killed three of the children: the mother and the rest of the family got away."

The doctor's condition worsened and he was evacuated to Northern Rhodesia, after being taken down the lake in *Mimi*. On landing he was carried 14 miles in a canvas hammock through a heavy rainstorm by his servant Rupia and a team of African carriers. At one point the hammock split and the bearers abandoned the doctor and Rupia in the middle of the thunder and the lightning. Some fifty years later, Dr. Hanschell told Shankland that lying there in the bush he felt that "he had reached the end, and he wished he could have told Eastwood about the Devil's Advocate's spectacular exit from this world in blinding flashes of lightning and a strong smell of sulphur. Then he saw Rupia lying beside him, trying to keep him warm, and trying to shield him from the rain with the torn canvas."

The doctor eventually got back to England in June 1917. His daughter, Daphne Levens, remembers being bitterly disappointed to hear on his return that Josephine the chimpanzee had been sent to Cape Town zoo; Hanschell had been decorating his letters home with pen-and-ink drawings of the chimp. But she reports that her father did "let loose to slither over the drawing room carpet a small, rare, unidentified snake with a shot-silk emerald head—to my mother's horror." The snake was presented to London zoo and in return the family was allowed in free on Sunday afternoons.

Later, Hanschell met Eastwood, who told him everyone had come home safely,* then he went to see Spicer. He found Spicer in the same meagre office where he had interviewed him at the start of the expedition, sitting under a dusty portrait of the King. Even the Major of Marines who had tapped his temple to indicate Spicer's insanity was still sitting there.

Spicer was cordial, but not especially friendly. Looking down, Dr. Hanschell noticed that Spicer was still wearing the ring he had taken from the dead captain of the *Kingani*. After exchanging pleas-

---

*We had not a single casualty of any sort," said Spicer in his lecture, "unless we must count a Sub-Lieutenant who, being threatened by a German native, hit him with his fist, and, his finger catching on the native's teeth, it had to be amputated because septic complications set in." It is not clear whose finger this was. If it was Mollison (who was promoted to Sub-Lieutenant during the expedition), then he and Tait would have truly become twins, given that his fellow Scot set out from London with only nine digits.

antries, they agreed that they and their wives would meet soon, but they never did. After he left, wandering down the Mall past the statue of Captain Cook, the doctor was as mystified by Spicer as ever.

War continued to rage in Africa until late 1918. Von Lettow's forces (reduced to two thousand men) led the British a merry dance all over East and Central Africa. Field Marshal Smuts, the former Boer leader now in charge of Allied forces in sub-Saharan Africa, developed a great deal of respect for the Germans, whose officers survived by hunting big game. In the course of his adventures, von Lettow also learned how to carve wooden statues like those of the African tribes who followed him.

On 13 November 1918 a British dispatch rider carrying a white flag caught up with von Lettow and told him the war was over. Germany had surrendered. Von Lettow's endurance and brilliant application of military tactics had made him an instant hero on his return home. When Adolf Hitler came to power, he offered von Lettow the post of ambassador to Britain, but the old soldier refused. He hated the Nazis and all they stood for.

Von Lettow fell on hard times after the Second World War. In 1951, according to Judith Listowel in *The Making of Tanganyika*, "Field Marshal Smuts discovered him in Hamburg, living in poverty from the proceeds of his wood-carvings." In 1953 Smuts arranged for von Lettow to visit Tanganyika—then a British mandate territory—where he was given an honour parade by his former African troops, as well as British officers of the King's African Rifles. Unlike Spicer, whose heroism was to some extent a pose, von Lettow was the real thing, and the Africans and British knew it.

But as Listowel observes: "As the applause died away into the African night, it probably did not occur to either the English officers or to the German general that they belonged to a passing age. To an age in which men were proud to have waged a gentleman's war."

This is, perhaps, where Spicer erred. His conduct was not that of a true gentleman, which is probably why he has been forgotten.* Yet so has the theatre in which he fought for pre-eminence. Even today, the East African campaign is regarded as a relatively unimportant part of the First World War. Extensive histories of the conflict did not emerge until many years after it ended, in such books as Byron Farwell's *The Great War in Africa* and Ross Anderson's *The Forgotten Front*. The most significant intervention has been Hew Strachan's *The First World War: A Call to Arms* (2001), the first book to put the East African campaign in its full context. He describes Spicer as "one of the Royal Navy's less distinguished officers." But the story of the Naval Africa Expedition has had a life outside the history books. In *The Forgotten Front,* Anderson notes in passing how "Humphrey Bogart's famous film, *The African Queen,* inspired by an episode of the campaign, often provides its only lasting image."

That episode was, in fact, this very story.

---

*Not entirely. A Spicer-Simson tin-soldier model, complete with skirt, has been available for some years to devotees of colonial war games. This would have amused Dr. Hanschell no end. Hanschell himself became director of the Venereal Diseases Clinic of the Seamen's Hospital in London's Royal Albert Dock after the War, retiring in 1950. In 1931 he published an article in the *Lancet* on the efficacious use of acriflavine for treatment of 2,500 men with gonorrhoea, giving each of them a daily dose for five months. He died in 1968, the year Shankland's book was published.

Chapter Twenty-Three

There is an elation in victory, even when wounded men have to be borne very carefully along the jetty to the hospital tent; even when a telegraphic report has to be composed and sent to the Lords Commissioners of the Admiralty; even when a lieutenant-commander of no linguistic ability has to put together another report in French for the Belgian governor. He could at least congratulate himself on having won a naval victory as decisive as the Falklands or Tsu-Shima, and he could look forward to receiving the DSO and the Belgian Order of the Crown and a step in promotion which would help to make him an Admiral some day."

He never made it to Admiral, but in some ways Spicer-Simson accrued the glory he craved. He lived to see part of his story immortalised in a fine novel, *The African Queen* (1935) by C. S. Forester (of Horatio Hornblower fame), from which the passage above is taken. We do not know if Spicer ever read it, but if he did, he no doubt bridled at not playing the lead role. What Forester did with the facts—and what the film director John Huston did with Forester's novel twenty-odd years later—offers us a fascinating case-study of what happens when history, fiction and film collide.

Forester's novel tells the story of two mismatched companions: hard-drinking riverboat captain Charlie Allnutt and holier-than-thou Rose Sayer. She lives in a German colony in Africa with her missionary brother, Samuel. When German soldiers pillage the area at the start of the First World War, the missionary's flock is driven away. Samuel dies. Rose is abandoned and her desire for vengeance on the Germans seems like mere fantasy: "Here she was alone in the Central African forest, alone with a dead man. There was no possible chance of her achieving anything."

At this moment, fortuitously, Charlie Allnutt appears, making his usual supply run for a Belgian mine in a steam launch called the *African Queen*. The pair escape downriver in the dilapidated boat. If Charlie, a Cockney rough diamond, is at the helm at the start of the journey, Rose is very much in charge by the end, having shed her prim ways and somehow become a feisty fighter, hungering for satisfaction of every type: "A new surge of feeling overcame the weakness. She thought of the *Königin Luise* flaunting her Iron Cross flag on the Lake where never a white ensign could come to challenge her, and of the Empire needing help, and of her brother's death to avenge. And, womanlike, she remembered the rudenesses and insults to which Samuel had patiently submitted from the officialdom of the colony; they had to be avenged, too."

In the course of a desperate journey of several hundred miles, in which Charlie is beset by drunkenness and hangovers, Rose develops a plan to attack a German warship on a lake at the end of the river, using homemade torpedoes and detonators attached to the front of the boat. After many quarrels and tribulations—they shoot some rapids, endure leeches and malaria, and keep having to improvise machinery when it breaks down—the couple reach the lake, having fallen in love along the way.

A German ship, the *Königin Luise,* appears (Charlie calls it the *Louisa*). He and Rose prepare to attack that night. But then the *African Queen* is wrecked in a storm and they are captured by the Germans. Suddenly two British motor boats appear, HMS *Amelia* and HMS *Matilda*. Rose and Charlie are surrendered to a British lieutenant-commander at "Port Albert": the same Albertville, now Kalemie, where the Naval Africa Expedition had its camp, and where *Mimi* and *Toutou* were stored.

This is clearly where Spicer comes in, although the British navy officer who appears in Forester's novel does not wear a skirt. He orders an attack on the German ship. "The next day the *Königin Luise* as she steamed in solemn dignity over the lake she had ruled so long saw two long grey shapes come hurtling over the water towards her, half-screened in a smother of spray." The boats shoot off their guns and the three-pound shells tear into the bowels of the *Königin Luise*.

The name of the German ship in *The African Queen* comes from a once notorious incident at the start of the War. A former Hamburg-Holland holiday ferry called the *Königin Luise* was converted to an auxiliary minelayer in expectation of conflict. An hour before midnight on the day war was declared (4 August 1914), painted in false colours resembling those of steamers of the Great Eastern Company, the *Königin Luise* crept into the Thames Estuary and deposited her deadly cargo. She was later sunk—then one of the mines she had laid sank the Royal Navy vessel that had downed her.*

The actual *Königin Luise* happened to look rather like the

---

*The tale bears relating. At dawn the captain of a British fishing vessel reported that he had seen an unknown ship "throwing things over the side" in the Heligoland Bight (part of the North Sea). Sighting the rogue steamer through a squall of rain at about 10:30 a.m., Captain Cecil Fox of HMS *Amphion* gave chase. Hit numerous times, at 12:22 p.m. the *Königin Luise* rolled over on her side and sank. But the ship which had inflicted Germany's first naval loss would also become Britain's: at 6:45 a.m. the next morning, HMS *Amphion* struck one of the *Königin Luise*'s mines and sank.

Götzen, but the story into which Forester introduces her departs radically from the reality of Spicer's expedition. Until the ending, Forester has disguised his source and (quite legitimately) altered the historical record. There has also been a certain amount of geographical jiggery-pokery as the novelist transforms his raw material. The Congo/Lualaba River that Spicer and his men travelled up becomes the Ulanga River in the novel, and later the Bora River. It too is blocked by rapids—or "rocks an' cataracts an' gorges," as Allnutt calls them—and is full of snags and sandbanks. Yet the Ulanga-Bora seems to debouch into the eastern shore of the lake, rather than the western, which is where Spicer landed. For a long time unnamed in the novel, Lake Tanganyika appears as Lake Wittelsbach later in the story.

German East Africa is restyled German Central Africa and although the semiotic territory of the novel is sometimes a little dazzling, it seems as if Charlie and Rose must have sailed into it from what is now the middle of Tanzania. It is possible Forester had the Malagarasi River in mind (at the mouth of which, near Kigoma, the *Götzen* was scuttled), though it is more probable he just had a rough idea of the area, changed names here and there and let the tale go where it would.

For all that, many details of the original story—which Forester presumably took from newspapers—creep in, especially the scene in which "Spicer" is introduced:

> The post of Senior Naval Officer, Port Albert, Belgian Congo, was of very new creation. It was only the night before that it had come into being. It was a chance of war that the senior naval officer in a Belgian port should be an English lieutenant-commander. He was standing pacing along the jetty inspecting the preparation for sea of the squadron under his command. Seeing that it comprised only two small motor boats, it seemed a dignified name for it. But those motor boats had cost in blood and sweat and

treasure more than destroyers might have done, for they had been sent out from England, and had been brought with incredible effort overland through jungles, by rail and by river, to the harbour in which they lay.

Other fragments of history can be found in Charlie Allnutt's estimation of the "strategical situation"—how the "sweating generals" of Britain's East African forces would attack German Central Africa: "One thing's sure, anyway, miss. They won't come up from the Congo side. Not even if the Belgians want to. There's only one way to come that way, and that's across the Lake. And nothing won't cross the Lake while the *Louisa*'s there."

Even Admiral Jackson's original order giving permission for Spicer's expedition ("It is both the duty and the tradition of the Royal Navy to engage the enemy wherever there is water to float a ship") hovers in the background: "The lieutenant-commander paced the jetty impatiently; he was anxious to get to work now that the weary task of transport was completed. It was irksome that there should remain a scrap of water on which the White Ensign did not reign supreme."

But this is also a topsy-turvy world in which Spicer is no longer the oldest lieutenant-commander in the navy: "Tomorrow he had to lead a fleet into action, achieving at this early age the ambition of every naval officer, and he had much to think about."

While the motor boat operation, as Forester presents it, replays the attack on the *Hedwig* in many of its details, some elements of the *Königin Luise* are reminiscent of the *Götzen*, which Spicer never attacked. The captain of the *Königin Luise* scuttles the ship, just as the captain of the *Götzen* did: "The *Königin Luise* very suddenly fell over to one side. The commander had done his duty; he had groped his way through the wrecked engines to the sea cocks and had opened them."

But if Forester has conflated several accounts, the sinking of the *Hedwig* provides the climax of the novel. The story of Spicer and the

Hedwig's German flag is retold without mention of the flag locker. "The *Matilda* and the *Amelia* came rushing up just as the German ensign, the last thing to disappear, dipped below the surface."

The African Queen can be read as a critique of the ethos of "striking a blow for Britain" and the futility of much First World War heroism. Strictly speaking, Charlie and Rose fail in their mission, and if it's a happy ending it's a highly nuanced one. "So they left the Lakes and began the long journey to Matadi and marriage. Whether or not they lived happily ever after is not easily decided."

It would certainly have been a long journey. Matadi is far over on the western side of Congo. Nevertheless, it is rich in associations with this story and those that touch on it. Evelyn Waugh wanted to fly to Matadi when he was stuck in Kabalo in 1930; Spicer passed through Matadi during his disappearing act, on his way to Kinshasa in 1916; Matadi also figures in Conrad's *Heart of Darkness,* when Marlow finds dying Congolese, exhausted from working on the new railway to Kinshasa—something Conrad had personally witnessed in 1890.

It's another long journey from Joseph Conrad to Katharine Hepburn, unless you go via John Huston, who displayed some Kurtz-like (and indeed Spicer-like) characteristics during the filming of Forester's novel in Africa in 1951. Like Spicer, Huston was obsessed with hunting, often disappearing for days with his rifle. The difficulties of the production are now legendary, as detailed in Katharine Hepburn's *The Making of the African Queen: Or How I Went to Africa with Bogart, Bacall and Huston and Almost Lost My Mind* (1987). However, a harsher portrait of Huston had already appeared in Peter Viertel's novel *White Hunter, Black Heart* (1953), which was made into a film by Clint Eastwood in 1990.

Forty years before Eastwood was to play Huston, interest in *The African Queen* as a movie project was by no means assured. "A story of two old people going up and down an African river—who's going to be interested in that? You'll be bankrupt." So said Alexander Korda, the British film mogul, to Sam Spiegel, the American producer who in 1950 bought the rights to Forester's novel for

Huston—who was then just finishing an adaptation of Stephen Crane's novella *The Red Badge of Courage.*

The African Queen already had a chequered history as a film property. As Huston says in his autobiography *An Open Book* (1980), "Columbia had bought the rights years before from C. S. Forester, planning to make a film starring Elsa Lanchester and Charles Laughton. For some reason they didn't make it. Then Warners bought the property from Columbia for Bette Davis. They, too, never followed through. Warners were willing to sell the rights to Horizon for $50,000. Sam [Spiegel] and I together had nothing like this amount."

Eventually Spiegel borrowed the money from a sound equipment company. Meanwhile, James Agee (the novelist and film critic who also wrote the text for *Let Us Praise Famous Men,* Walker Evans's classic photographic record of the Deep South) was working away on the screenplay. Before it was finished, Agee (a heavy smoker) had a heart attack. Huston roughed out the film's conclusion before leaving America, then finished it off at Entebbe in Uganda. Huston continues:

C. S. Forester had told me that he had never been satisfied with the way *The African Queen* ended. He had written two different endings for the novel; one was used in the American edition, the other in the English. Neither one, he felt, was satisfactory. I thought the film should have a happy ending. Since Agee's health never permitted him to come to Africa, I asked Peter Viertel to work on the final scenes with me. He and Gige joined us in Entebbe before we started shooting, and together we wrote my ending—the ending we later filmed.

Huston's triple-decked solution to the finale is clever. At first the film ending, like the English edition of the novel, appears to be an indictment of foolhardy heroism. Charlie Allnutt (Humphrey Bogart) and Rosie Sayer (Katharine Hepburn) are captured by the Germans after the *African Queen* has sunk in the storm. They are condemned to death by hanging for spying. A bittersweet taste is then induced when the German Captain agrees to marry them, even though the nooses are round their necks. The final twist comes when the hull of the *African Queen* rises to the surface with a pair of Charlie's homemade torpedoes clearly visible.

After a wonderful long shot dramatising imminent collision (filmed from the point of view of the *African Queen* itself), the *Königin Luise* sails smack into the risen hull. The impact sets off one of the percussive detonators Allnutt has constructed from revolver cartridges, nails and blocks of wood—and the torpedo explodes. Covered in flames, the German ship tips over and the newly married couple are catapulted clear. There is no mention of any British motor boats like the *Mimi* and *Toutou* clones in the novel, nor does a Spicer-Simson character appear.

Yet there is a vestigial connection to the Naval Africa Expedition, whose exploits gave rise to Forester's story. Much of *The African Queen* was filmed in the Upper Congo—on a tributary of the Lualaba, the same river that Spicer and his men went up. Huston established a camp at Biondo on the Ruiki. As he wrote: "A narrow winding river with trees and heavy vines arching overhead, it was ideal for our purposes." The site, near Ponthierville (now Ubundu), was about 300 miles north of where Spicer's men were operating on the Lukuga and about 50 miles south of Stanley Falls. This was where Conrad was heading on his 1890 river journey, which he fictionally transmuted into the Inner Station in *Heart of Darkness*—where Marlow finds shrunken heads on the poles outside Kurtz's house and has to come to terms with the imperial enterprise on which he is engaged.

The ending of Huston's movie was filmed near another great waterfall: Murchison Falls, at the source of the Nile in Uganda. There was also some filming at Butiaba on the shores of Lake Albert. It was at Butiaba in 1951 that Huston (who had been flying all over

Central Africa scouting for locations) had found the half-wrecked hull of the boat that would become the *African Queen*. It was almost certainly the former *Kenia,* a 40-foot steam launch "manned by a crew of jolly Swahili tars smartly dressed in white breeches and blue jerseys," upon which a young Winston Churchill had sailed before the First World War (see *My African Journey,* 1908).

After crossing to the Congo side of Lake Albert, the *African Queen* was brought down to Ponthierville by lorry and thence to Biondo under her own power. Bogart and his wife Lauren Bacall arrived by train from Stanleyville, along with Hepburn and Spiegel. Much of the filming would be done on a mock-up of the *African Queen* that had been built on a raft. There were about fifty people in the crew.

Huston writes that at the Ruiki site they had "what must certainly have been the strangest flotilla African waterways had ever seen." But then, he didn't know about Spicer—unless the use of that navy word "flotilla" (which would eventually supply the title of Shankland's account) is a sign that someone had told him the story behind Forester's novel. Whatever the case, there were certainly echoes of Spicer's adventure during the shoot:

> The *African Queen* would furnish the power to pull four rafts—we hoped. On the first raft—and this was my idea— we built a replica of the *Queen*. That raft itself became our stage. We could put cameras and equipment on it and move around, photographing Katie and Bogie in the mock-up with as much facility as we'd have on a studio floor. The second raft carried all of the equipment, light and props. The third was for the generator. The fourth was Katie's, equipped with a privy, a full-length mirror and a private dressing-room. This turned out to be one too many for the little *Queen* to tow, so we had to drop Katie's raft. Katie had to use the jungle toilet like the rest of us. Her full-length mirror got broken very quickly; those two halves were bro-

ken again, and finally she was reduced to using hand-held pieces of mirror while she did her make-up.

Huston and Bogart—whom Hepburn would characterise as "jerks . . . two over-male men" in her own book on the experience—used to write suggestive words in soap on the mirror. Huston's nickname was "the Monster," because of the way he treated cast members and crew, all of whom were already suffering from dysentery and insect bites and other illnesses (Jack Cardiff, the film's brilliant first cameraman, went down with malaria). Huston says he and Bogart escaped illness by always drinking Scotch with their water; Hepburn says they just drank Scotch.

The business of shooting film of the moving boat was somewhat reminiscent of the Naval Africa Expedition's journey up the Lualaba. As Hepburn recalls:

> John would scream—Bogie and I would jump—and the boiler would be tipped over, or nearly. The canopy would be torn off. The camera or lamps or whatever was caught by the overhanging shrubbery on the banks. Or we would be going along nicely—hit a submerged log and catch on it. Or the sun would go in. Or it would rain. The hysteria of each shot was a nightmare. And there was always the uncertain factor of Bogie and me and whether John thought we'd done a scene well. Or the engine on the *Queen* would stop. Or one of the propellers would be fouled by the dragging rope. Or we would be attacked by hornets. Or a stray pirogue would suddenly appear in the shot.

Another difficulty was soldier ants, whose nightly forays into the camp were prevented by lighting trenches of kerosene. The biggest potential disaster was when the *Queen* sank.

"We got her up eventually by sheer manpower," wrote Huston, "patched the holes in her, and she continued to function." In the film, when the *Queen* goes over a waterfall, wooden models were used at half-scale. These boats were carved by monks in Pon-thierville; nuns had the responsibility of making miniature Hepburns and Bogarts to fit inside the boats. The nuns and monks were presumably chosen because they had skill in carving religious statues.

When about half the filming was done, they moved back to Butiaba, on Lake Albert. This journey was made on an East African Railways and Harbours paddle-steamer called the *Lugard II,* whose Captain Phimister had methods similar to those employed on the Lualaba by Blaes (the choleric Walloon with whom Spicer fell out). "We got to the edge of Lake Albert," wrote Hepburn, "and seemingly there was nothing ahead but a huge field—swamp—high reeds. Phimister would back us up, then ram into the reeds at full tilt. After a few rams we pushed forward into open water."

The crew lived on the *Lugard* when it got to Lake Albert, and it also played the *Königin Luise* in the film. The exact details of which ship performed this role have always been something of a mystery, despite *The African Queen* being one of the most studied location shoots ever (along with *Apocalypse Now* and *Fitzcarraldo,* for not unrelated reasons). According to an interview with the still photographer on the shoot, Arthur Lemon: "We lived on an old paddle-steamer called the *Lugard II* which had been art directed to look like a German gunboat—the one that eventually gets blown up in the film."

The *kungu* seem to have put in an appearance, too. As Lemon explained in an interview for *Better Photography* magazine: "Each evening, as the sun went down, lake flies would hatch out and swarm everywhere. Everything on the boat had to be shut up tight. They only survived thirty minutes or so and then died and fell back onto the surface of the water. Great for the Nile perch who would swim along like vacuum cleaners and scoop them up for dinner. Some of these fish were huge."*

Dinner was not something the cast thought much of while living

---

*There is one moment in the film when Bogart is enveloped by a swarm of insects, but these seem to be mosquitoes rather than *kungu.*

on the *Lugard*. Everyone save Bogart and Huston (who both "came to the table well fortified," according to Hepburn) went down with amoebic dysentery and diarrhoea. It was discovered that the boat's water-filters weren't functioning properly. There was always a queue for the toilet, where the runs turned out not to be the only problem, as Huston recalls:

> One day Kevin McClory [the film's boom boy, later a Hollywood producer] came out of it headlong with his pants down his ankles, shouting "Black mamba! Black mamba!" He had been sitting there when he looked up and saw a black cylinder moving above his head. The black mamba is one of the few really aggressive snakes around, and quite deadly. We all got a glimpse of it as it slid down out of the toilet into the elephant grass . . . From that moment all symptoms of diarrhoea in camp disappeared.

A large motor boat called the *Murchison* ferried the cast and crew around during this period and was also used to transport supplies between the filming location and the village of Butiaba. The *Murchison* had another moment of fame three years later when it was waved down by Ernest Hemingway after his plane crashed during an African safari. The pilot had clipped a telegraph wire after swerving to avoid a flock of sacred ibis.*

It wasn't the only vessel to have a curious afterlife: the boat that played the role of the *African Queen* is now berthed outside the Holiday Inn, Key Largo, Florida, as a tourist attraction. But the strangest survival of all was one much more intimately connected with Spicer-Simson's quest to be a hero . . .

---

*The *Murchison* was chartered by a Scottish surgeon called Ian McAdam (later Sir Ian McAdam), who, after training a generation of East African doctors, was expelled from Uganda by Idi Amin in 1972. McAdam picked up Hemingway and his wife and took them to Butiaba—where they caught another bush plane and promptly crashed again. Hemingway, who ruptured his liver and one of his kidneys and suffered paralysis of the sphincter muscle as a result of the second crash, was reported worldwide as having died. He was a great admirer of the author of *The African Queen* ("I recommend Forester . . .").

Chapter Twenty-Four

Deo Gratias stood on the deck of the *Liemba*, his prisoners at his feet. I leaned on the rail, studiously casual. Nobody spoke. I was trying to ignore the handcuffed men and the way they were kneeling and shivering. We were in the tropics, it was hot, but they were huddling together. It was fear, of course, that permanent trembling motion, and the deep furrows in their brows were marks of dread.

I had fallen silent wondering why these heavily scored lines in the men's foreheads were more disturbing to me than the more obvious knife-gash across the throat of the one with tufty hair and up-staring eyes. The edges of his wound had been sewn together with spiky stitches—recently and roughly, too, by the look of it.

The engine churned as the slow grey surface of Lake Tanganyika rolled beneath us. We could still see the Tanzanian shore, but the Congolese side to the west was lost in a haze of mist. Finally I asked Deo Gratias what crimes were most commonly committed on the *Liemba*. Mainly stealing, he told me, lisping like a schoolgirl.

"And *lape*," he added, grinning now, spittle flying excitedly from his lips. "You know *lape*? It is when you go inside."

He made a sign with his hand, sighing gleefully.

His full name was Deo Gratias Webiro. He was twenty-seven. Wearing a red baseball cap and a linen suit and carrying a leather satchel, he was employed by the Tanzanian Ministry of the Interior. He was to be distinguished from the khaki-clad *askaris* on board. They were just ordinary policemen. Uneducated men, as he described them to me. *Uneducated men,* I wrote in my notebook.

Deo Gratias's two charges were crouched with their backs against a capstan. One was grizzled and had a stricken expression that reminded me of sinners in Renaissance paintings. The other one—with the sewn-up throat—was wild-haired, trampish, like a reggae star fallen on hard times.

Deo Gratias pointed to him. "This one, he keeps trying to cut his own throat." Then he pointed at the grizzled sinner: "He murdered a friend, beating him with sticks. This one will be hanged, I think."

Nearby, a man in a skullcap had unrolled his mat and begun to pray. Above him I spotted some graffiti written in black felt-tip on the ship's white paintwork. The Swahili words read *Wapi Mama Shakira?* ("Where's Mama Shakira?"), apparently a reference to the *Liemba*'s most famous prostitute, now dead. Also scrawled on the wall were the words *Good Lucky Kajembe* and, in a different hand, *Al Qaeda*.

A woman in a print dress, her breasts heaving, rushed up to tell us that someone had started brawling in the hold. Deo Gratias went off to investigate, his satchel bobbing on his thigh. Now he was gone I slipped the murderer a bottle of mineral water, setting it down on the steel deck by his uncuffed hand. Brand name:

Maji Poa. Good water, pure water. He did not acknowledge me, but simply stared out across the forbidding grey waves of Lake Tanganyika.

The date was 13 August 2003. I had boarded the ship at Kigoma, the port town that had been captured from the Germans by the Belgians eighty-seven years earlier. The *Liemba* was a cargo-and-passenger ship that every week made its way up and down the lake—when it eventually got going. The loading of the vessel was a chaotic business that lasted the best part of three hours. But eventually, once the interminable sacks of dried fish and the pinch-beaked chickens, the cobs of maize in their bright green sheaths and the heavy pineapples had all been stowed away, once the fog-horn had sounded and the sinewy stevedores cleared the gangplank—and the gangplank itself had been lifted on board by the ship's crane—we got under way.

My principal purpose in making the journey was to investigate the bizarre naval episode that had wrested the lake from German control, and to find out what legacy—if any—those tumultuous events at the far edges of the Great War had in the memory of local people. One of these memories I knew about, because it took physical form. The *Liemba* had been a German warship in a previous incarnation. I was standing on the *Graf von Götzen.*

Astonishing as it may seem, Spicer's nemesis is still afloat.

By the time I emerged from my cabin, night had fallen. Having an appointment with the captain, I followed the maze of pipework and narrow corridors that made up the *Liemba*'s double-deck structure. The whole place stank. People were lying about everywhere on mattresses, amid piles of fruit and the long white sacks of *dagaa* (dried fish), which were the ship's main cargo. Many of the passengers had yellow plastic jerrycans of water and thin steel mess-tins. A large proportion of the travellers were refugees from wars in Congo and

Burundi, hoping for a better life in Zambia, the ship's destination at the southern end of the lake.

The gangway was tight. One woman, sad-faced and cuddling her ten-year-old daughter, asked me in French for money as I squeezed by. *"Voudriez-vous, monsieur, nous faire une contribution matérielle?"*

I gave her five US dollars.

"C'est rien," she said. Then, to my amazement, she handed it straight back.

The bridge, as I entered it—after asking permission of the bearded crewman on guard outside—was a place of almost total darkness. A radar screen showed the ship's course as a straight green line; its glow was more or less the only light in the room. A mass of soft curves on his stool, the moon-faced captain had no desire to talk about the past. He was looking ahead into the night—watching for whalers, watching for canoes.

"It is all written down in the books," he said slowly, but with some irritation.

As he spoke, one hand gripped and ungripped the polished wood of the wheel. The wheel itself seemed rigid, fixed. It must be on autopilot, I thought, imagining some kind of clamp down below.

"This is the ship of history," the captain said. "It is well known."

He glanced down at the radar.

"No," I insisted. "Only the white man's side of the *Liemba* story is written down. Not your side."

He looked at me, perplexed, then shook his head.

I peered through the gloom at the other instruments, oddly illuminated by the radar's spectral light. The captain moved his hand slightly and the wheel moved accordingly. No autopilot.

Back in my cabin, I scolded myself for expecting that anyone should be interested in the tale. The African *askaris* and carriers who had fought in the War had suffered great privations on behalf of the belligerent colonists; but that didn't mean their descendants were obliged to remember it all. Certainly, I thought as I went to bed, they could not be expected to do so to satisfy my craving for more detail.

Tanzania's national museum is a poor place, down at heel and badly lit. I visited it before leaving for Lake Tanganyika. Walking through the section called "Africa," I found myself looking at a display of amulets. One was a small piece of lion skin (about the size of an envelope), upon which were written some protective Arab verses. Near to it was a statue of the kind anthropologists call a fetish object. A rough, red-clay model of a human figure holding outsize goggles to its eyes, it stood about two feet high. Not goggles, binoculars. I studied the fingermarks in the clay. Beneath the exhibit was some writing on a card in Swahili: *Wazungu wanaweza kuona mbali kuliko watu wengire* ("The European can see beyond the range of other people"). The *fundisho,* or moral, was also explained: "Beware of Europeans, they put glasses in their eyes and can see a person on the hill opposite."

The only hill opposite right then was a plaster of Paris model of Tanzania's geological strata, stretching down through time. I experienced a bizarre feeling of tumbling as I recalled a native fetish made by the Holo-holo in 1915. Like this one, it had a large head and was kneeling. Like this one, the figure grasped a pair of binoculars in its tiny hands. It also had small incisions on its chest and forearms. They marked the tattoos on the body of the man in whose tracks I had come: Commander Geoffrey Basil Spicer-Simson, RN.

Navyman God, as Dr. Hanschell's servant Rupia had called him. Lord Bellycloth, as he was known to his Holo-holo followers. Bwana Chifunga-Tumbo. A very remarkable person, in spite of his failings. Here, as they would on the *Liemba,* the ghosts of the past were whispering.

Another of the museum's attractions was "The Hall of Man"—

an echoey tunnel in which were displayed model skulls from different eras of human antiquity. These included the seminal discoveries made by Louis and Mary Leakey in Tanzania's Olduvai Gorge in the 1960s and 1970s. I was pleased to see these ancient ancestors, but however many times I read about it or hear it explained, I always forget how the story goes. Some ape-human creature (*Australopithecus?*), then the tool-user (*Homo habilis*), then us (*Homo sapiens*)—is that it? And the Neanderthals a red herring, a cul-de-sac—off the main drag and possibly wiped out by our ancestors? Was that today's thinking? I couldn't remember.

There were several cabinets of minerals and metals in "The Hall of Man," which seemed like a category mistake, but then again not. In lumps of rock, gold pyrites glittered. Precious motes were sprinkled on the surfaces—the jagged edges, the smooth faces—like expensive pepper. Yet the lumps also seemed to shine from deep within. A geologist could tell the story of these fragments. I stared at them in the semi-darkness.

The section entitled "Europe in Africa" was designed to shame the European. Railways and time-management are not the civilising benisons they were once thought to be. Among cabinets of curios and curling photographs of imperial soldiers of one sort and another, I discerned a chilling modern version of the genocide of the Neanderthals: Germany's extermination of the Herero tribe in South West Africa in 1904 and its equally ruthless suppression of the Maji-Maji rebellion here in Tanzania.

The same Swahili word that was on the plastic bottle I'd given to the prisoner—*maji,* water—gave its name to this rebellion. From 1905 to 1907, the Africans of this region revolted against German rule: against hut taxes, against forced labour, against a stated policy that made them economically dependent on the white invader and his cash crop, cotton. Foreign seed was imported and planted under duress.

The word *maji* in this context refers to a political movement whereby a secret communication about driving out the invaders was

passed from one individual to another. The secret was that a powerful medicine had been found that would make the white men vulnerable. The special water was carried about the person in small
containers made from maize or millet cobs. Before battle a little
would be drunk and sprinkled about the body in order to ward off
bullets. Under its charm, the enemies' rifles would spurt only water
and bullets would trickle like raindrops from the Africans' bodies.

But *maji* let them down. Anyone suspected of involvement in
the rebellion or displaying the slightest resistance to the new agricultural schemes was hanged and a scorched-earth policy imple-
mented.* Close to 120,000 Africans were either executed or died
from the famine that followed. It wasn't just a case of black and
white. While Indian traders—of whom by 1905 there were nearly
7,000 in Tanganyika—were accused by the Germans of fomenting
the rebellion, a number of Papuan and Melanesian troops were
drafted from German possessions in the Pacific to help put it down.

The man responsible for the "mild administrative pressure" (as
he called it) that sparked a rebellion—and the bloody countermeasures that suppressed it—was Count von Götzen, military governor of German East Africa from 1901 to 1906. The ship I would
travel in had once been named in this man's honour.

I stared at the exhibit: a large Iron Cross flag and a ship's wheel.
It was the original wheel of the *Graf von Götzen*. A sign told me the
ship had been salvaged from the bottom of Lake Tanganyika by the
Belgians after the War, but it said nothing about what had happened
to her before or since.

On the *Liemba/Götzen*, after a few beers in the bar and a plastic
dish of beef and rice, I had fallen asleep with stories of Hutu bandits
in my head. There had been recent threats that they would attack

---

*A technique Götzen learned from the British containment of Afrikaners during the
Anglo-Boer War (1899–1902).

the ship, but I hadn't given them much credence. So when the screams awoke me, I thought that was it. Finally, years of travel in Africa had caught up with me; this time I was for the chop, in a place where the machete was the weapon of choice.

Out of the night came a ritualised screaming, a caterwauling woman's voice. "*Pata rowe! Pata rowe! Pata rowe kwa samaki!*"

I stirred uneasily on the leather couchette which, when I'd come in, had been slick with the sweat of others. Now it was wet with mine.

Someone banged on the door. "*Katlesi ya samaki!*"

It was Swahili, but I couldn't catch their meaning. "*Pata rowe! Pata rowe!*" Then, tailing off, "*Katlesi . . .*"

It wasn't just one woman, I soon realised. Numerous voices were shouting all over the ship. The noise even drowned out the dull thud-thud of the engines. I glanced at my watch. It was about one in the morning. Slowly I became aware of something else: the ship had stopped and the engines were just idling. There were more shouts. I went to the window to see what was happening, but all I could see were dark shapes and the occasional flicker of light. There was nothing for it. I would have to go out.

I unlocked the door and turned the handle. The door wouldn't budge. I had to push hard—into a flowing mass of people—to get out on to the walkway. I really had to put my shoulder into it, like a prop forward.

Tumbling out of the cabin, I saw that the crowd covered the decks and extended down the side of the ship. Some 200 feet long, 30 feet down, more or less the whole side of the *Liemba* was covered with climbing figures. Some were climbing down, some up. There was fighting on the way: punching, pulling, kicking, stamping. It wasn't entirely selfish—there was some altruism, some handing me up and handing me down—but the atmosphere was mostly Darwinian, there was no getting away from it.

There were boys as well as women, and they were shouting too. "*Pata rowe! Samaki-samaki-samaki!*"

Someone fell, cracking a rib on the side of a boat down below. Others ate their dinner. Groggily, I began to comprehend what was happening. We were at a fast-food station, that was all; even though it was the middle of the night, in the middle of the lake. I asked someone what *Pata rowe kwa samaki* meant. Fish with cassava-flour puddings. And *Katlesi ya samaki?* Fish cutlets.

Because of the threat of ambush and a lack of natural landing places, the *Liemba* avoids stopping close to the shore during its weekly 800-mile round trip. Instead, it halts at "stations" in the middle of the lake. Boats come out from the shoreside villages to sell food, trade with passengers and enable others to embark or disembark. This is what was happening; chop was in order, but not the kind I had imagined.

Having sold their fish, the boys in the boats were up for fun. They sped round and round the *Liemba,* gunning the outboards on their whalers and calling out ribaldries at the girls on board. Plumes of exhaust hung in the air. It was a bit like a big party in the night now, but also still like a kind of fight as people jumped from craft to craft, clambered up and down, stuffed fish cutlets into their mouths or tried to catch bananas thrown up from the boats below and throw coins back.

Perhaps thirty boats were visible on the turbulent black water, caught in the *Liemba*'s spotlights. Most were dugout canoes; some were wooden rowing boats. There were also five or six Boston whalers carrying between twenty and thirty people each. Powered by roaring outboards, they kept ramming the dugouts out of the way to get a better position alongside the *Liemba.* Furious arguments were taking place.

A man in a red loincloth had his rowing boat knocked over; perhaps not quite over—I struggled through the crowd on deck to get a better view. Water was pitching in . . . The man was standing up and howling, just on the edge of the pool of light. I watched as he slowly sank. As an afterthought he started bailing frantically, but it was no use. The boat started to slip beneath the waves and he jumped out. I caught a glimpse of his arms waving in the spotlights.

Young men jumped out of other boats to swim towards the sinking one. They grabbed it and started to shove it from side to side. Eventually enough water was slooshed out over the gunwale for the man in the red loincloth to climb back in. With more bailing, buoyancy returned. His boat had been saved. It was a small victory for civilisation, but such scenes were rare. The noise and mayhem continued for a good hour—all at a banshee scale, echoing out across the waves. The *Liemba*'s lamps shone out over it all, casting crumpled sheets of light over the chaos.

Finally the fog-horn sounded and the boats scattered. Once the anchor was raised, with an unutterable midnight rattle, we continued on our way.

An hour later and the *Liemba* cast anchor again. At about 3 a.m., with the same attendant chaos as before, my own station had arrived at last. I climbed down into the whaler that would take me to dry land. I feared for my footing as I leaped into the rocking black hole. The driver gunned up the engine and we sped off into the night. As the lights of the *Liemba* receded into the distance, we soon began to struggle against larger and larger waves.

Each time we whacked down on to the lake, water spurted in through cracks in the gunwale. A veil of grey-black clouds rolled in. Moonlight, its intensity rapidly decreasing, now provided the only illumination. A storm was coming in and I was in a leaky boat in the middle of a very large lake.

The rain came down fast and hard. The driver's assistant, a boy in a spotted bandanna, was feverishly bailing away in the depths of the boat with a cut-out plastic bucket. Either side of him, through the driving spray, I could just make out my fellow passengers. They included a bearded Afrikaans brewery manager and his family, three village women in shawls, two bespectacled Japanese tourists on their way to a chimpanzee reserve and a sullen young Tanzanian soldier in full camouflage and slouch cap. In one hand the soldier held his AK-47, its magazine bound with gaffer tape, in the other a pineapple.

It was two hours before we approached the military post which was the soldier's destination. By now I was soaked to the skin. The storm was at its roughest and the driver could hardly control the boat as—swinging from side to side between heavy waves—he tried to hold steady by the shore and not run aground. All around us, protruding ten feet above the waves, were large tussocks of leafy cane. Their shaggy shapes had a fierce and occult aspect, as if they were sentinels of the kind of lost city in search of which Rider Haggard's explorer Allan Quatermain set out, leaving the placid English countryside behind him. "The thirst for the wilderness was on me; I could tolerate this place no more . . ."

Holding his rifle above his head, the soldier pitched over the edge. The black water covered him up to his shoulders. He staggered forwards. I could not see the land he was heading for, just darkness and the vicious storm. The wind gusted down between my freezing ears and wet hair, hellhound loud. At one point the whaler seemed to squat in a trough of water, like a fat man going down on his haunches.

Before the soldier could be consumed by the dark places of the night, while his outline was still visible to us, struggling through the water, the boat turned and we headed out once more into the interminable lake. I began to worry about my own landfall, whenever that might be.

Fortunately by the time it arrived, another two hours later, the sun had risen. I could see the beach where I would camp for the next few days. From here I would make my forays to villages along the shore of the lake, enquiring after Spicer and the Holo-holo. I had heard that the tribe was now almost extinct.

The storm had knocked the stuffing out of me. But sitting on the sand drinking coffee, facing the Congo over the water, with the towering shape of Mount Kungwe behind me, I began to feel confident again. For a moment, surrounded by stunted acacias on the stooping lakeshore, the leafy ones looking like "umbrellas in a crowd," as Burton wrote of the same place in 1860, I could even imagine myself one of those old-time explorers.

Dawn became day. I looked out at the lake, sipped some coffee, then made some more, spooning in the powdered milk straight from the tin. It was a taste from childhood that I had forgotten. Caffeine notwithstanding (and there isn't much in African coffee, all the good stuff being exported), I turned in and slept for most of the new day. It had been a long journey. Tomorrow I would begin scouring up and down the lake in a boat with an outboard, to interview the oldest man in each village. I would ask him about his memories of the battle between *Uingereza* and *Ujerumani*, or the First World War, as we like to call it. The Great War, as it was dubbed by those who lived through it and never expected to see its like again. A conflict in which Spicer's expedition was only the smallest of sideshows—a "naval action in miniature," as the man himself described it.

Rising sheer from the lake, Mount Kungwe is the mountain that Spicer saw when he arrived on the other side. If you want good fortune, you must sacrifice something to its spirit, Mkungwe, or at least pay him homage. Perhaps Spicer should have done so. It was opposite here, across Kungwe Bay, that he watched the *Götzen* through his binoculars and refused to go out and fight. It was under this mountain that he metamorphosed from hero back to eccentric failure.

Why did Spicer lose his spirit? Why did he decline so rapidly after the initial successes with the *Kingani* and the *Hedwig*? At first I just thought he was a coward, as well as a braggart and a fantasist. Then I made a discovery that changed my perception of events. On Sunday 26 September 1915, Captain Noel Spicer-Simson of the Royal Garrison Artillery 21st Anti-Aircraft Section was killed in action in France. He was Spicer's younger brother (born in 1881), and it seems certain that some time during the expedition he would have been informed of his loss.

News of Noel's death, whenever it came, may put the whole story in a different perspective, but by the time Spicer gave his lecture at the Royal United Services Institute in 1934, his decline had been airbrushed over. He claimed that he had summoned the seaplanes to Tanganyika and even goes so far as to suggest he flew on them: "One morning, however, when we went over to bomb her [the *Graf von Götzen*] she was not in harbour any more." His inactivity during this period is forgotten, too: "For the next three weeks we were feverishly searching every bay, harbour and mouth of a river along the Lake from end to end, being fired at from the coast because the natives had got it into their heads that everything afloat was German." This description suggests the strong feeling and physical restlessness which are the customary attributes of the classical hero, as opposed to the social or moral qualities of the imperial hero, that Spicer so clearly obviates—but the fact is, he was just lying on his bed in his room at Bismarckburg the entire time.

After a few days in Kungwe's shadow, I was beginning to feel like a failure too: no one seemed to know anything about the naval hostilities that had caused such a stir in 1914–18.

I found battles of another kind, however. The area round Mount Kungwe is one of the last strongholds of wild chimpanzees on earth and the Kungwe group are especially known for their fierceness. One afternoon, coming back from another fruitless search for remnants of Spicer and his expedition, I watched a group of thirty chimps kill a red colobus monkey, screaming with excitement as they did so. I could hardly look as, tearing it to pieces, they began eating it in the trees above me. I tried not to think of it as an omen. Sometimes things are just what they are.

At the Askari Monument in Dar es Salaam the roads radiate out like the spokes of a wheel. Images of British and African troops stand out in metal relief on a granite plinth in the centre of the roundabout:

> To the memory of the African troops who fought, and the carriers who were the feet and hands of the army: and to all the other men who served and died for their King and Country in the Great War 1914–1918. If you fight for your country, even if you die your sons will remember your name.

At first I wondered at the sheer brass of it, this work signed "Myranda, Sculptor, 1927." It seemed like a violation—one that compounded the injustice of making the black man die in a quarrel in which he had no part. Then it struck me that in the last line there may have been some exhortation, conscious or not, never to let it happen again, or even to revolt against colonialism.

I later discovered (from Kevin Patience's book *Königsberg: A German East African Raider*) that the words were written by Rudyard Kipling—an author whose relationship with colonialism is much more complex than often assumed—for the Commonwealth War Graves Commission. Ironically, the monument stands on the site of a statue of Herman von Wissmann, the German explorer whose wife was commemorated in the *Hedwig von Wissmann,* the ship Spicer sank in Kungwe Bay.

Tanganyika's Africans were still a subject population when this monument was brought out from London. They didn't get independence until 1961. Perhaps the only good thing about the War in this part of the world was that it taught Africans that the mutual cohesion of Europeans—that racial solidarity which was one of the foundations of imperial power—was nothing but a myth.

Being several, the Europeans were vulnerable. They were not invincible. They did not have to be worshipped. And time would cast a cold light on the heroes as well as the sham heroes. For as John Iliffe has pointed out, even "Lettow-Vorbeck's brilliant campaign was the climax of Africa's exploitation: its use as a mere battlefield."*

A Modern History of Tanganyika (1979).

With the help of local guides, I continued my search along the lake for old men who might remember something—anything at all—of the First World War. One day we had been walking in single file for a couple of miles inland towards the village of Kalumbe, when we entered a forest of palms. I was being stung by insects, but these astonishing palms made up for it all. As sturdy as English oaks—almost as wide as them at the base, but tapering at the neck—they seemed to march towards us in a steady stream. There must have been thousands of them and this was a hopeful sight—it was good to see they had not yet been cut down.

My guides promised me it was not much farther. Every now and then the forest opened up to reveal human dwellings. Black and scarlet chickens strutted across the path, heralding the revelation of a hamlet or small village. Here a woman crouched in her hut—stirring a basin of *ugali,* a coarse white porridge of maize meal, with a wooden spoon. Here were three more, peering into a drum of boiling palm oil. Always the women working. The men just sat around—but still they had the power and held on to it.

The man I came to see at Kalumbe could tell me nothing. He shook his head sadly. No, he did not know any history. Too long ago.

Everywhere it was the same. The oral tradition in Africa is in crisis, a trauma brought about by the advent of modern technology, the growth of towns and the spread of AIDS, which has devastated two generations of Africans now. In every town you see the coffins piled up in the marketplace, their newly planed red wood still wet with sap. Of the young men that remain, few want to listen to tales of the past. They want computers and radios and mobile phones. And they want to leave: to accelerate into the global future. Nairobi! London! New York!

It is—I grumbled to myself, tramping back through the forest to the lake—not so very different in Britain. How many young Britons know anything about the First World War or even think of it at all?

I strode through a village full of pye-dogs with fox-like ears and amazing patterns in their coats. Black and white and chocolate. Yapping away ten to the dozen, they seemed to be the village's only occupants.

We came out of the palms into open country and immediately the temperature rose. There is a difference, a discernible difference—I said to myself, I told myself, wiping my face. It is that we in the West have been writing down our history for centuries. Most Africans have no access to books at all and in most cases the right books do not exist anyway. The living history Africa is losing was once passed down by voice, structured on the genealogy of the tribe and on records of military victories and migrations. It lived in the telling, not in the tombstone of a book; and now that the habit of telling has gone, the history is passing away.

From the boat, on the way back to the campsite, I saw bushbuck on the beach, hippopotamus in the water. A croc slid off a rock. At one point I went onshore to look at a place where a Belgian barge carrying cement sank in the 1950s. The cement bags had petrified. They looked like strange rock formations now. Clambering about among them, I found a lump of quartz about the size of a football. It was full of veins of gold, or so I reckoned. I carried it back to the boat, stumbling on the faux-rocks, wondering whether my gold was genuine.

We set off again with the lump of quartz in the bottom of the boat. The outboard spewed its wake behind—chaotic white foam. I looked back at it and realised I was in the remotest place I had ever been; remote in time, it seemed, as well as in geography. As we made our way back to the campsite and the mountains of which Kungwe is chief, the landscape grew greener and more populous. Splinters of quartz and granite gave way to lush expanses of bush and the occasional village.

I was watching one of these groups of thick mud huts roll past in the distance when the outboard motor started to spit out puffs of blue smoke. There was a series of puttering coughs, then one great big puff followed a last valedictory hack. And then came silence. The motor had conked out.

While the boat-driver, Abu, tried to fix it, I read my copy of Burton's *The Lake Regions of Central Africa*. Only a large ship passing us marked the difference between his time and my own. I saw that it was not the *Liemba*, but a freighter taking fuel to Burundi, where, it said on the radio, there had been fighting this week. Its wake sent us back, rocking to and fro. At that moment something connected, the outboard kicked, and we were on our way again. During the journey, a plane flew low over us, heading west. It was a UN aircraft, Abu told me, taking supplies to Uruguayan troups stationed in Congo.

The following morning, at the village of Lagosa, I found Mr. Malyamungu. He was ancient, a tiny man in a flowing red robe under which was a dirty T-shirt with CHIMP HAVEN on it. Moustaches—long, thin and twirled—poked out either side of his nose, exactly in parallel with the drooping straw roof of his hut. He sat in a deckchair, smoking cheroots, and we spoke through two translators: from English into Swahili, then from Swahili into Tongwe, the local language.

Mr. Malyamungu told me that as a young boy he had narrowly escaped conscription by the Germans. "My father was a powerful chief and he avoided it," he said through the translator, trimming another cheroot with his penknife. "Yes, during that time I heard of some small boats that chase the *Liemba*. But they never catched her. They were sinking two other boats of the *Kijerumani*.

"I was growing up at this time and I cut wood for *sitima* [steamer]." That is, he collected timber for the *Götzen*'s woodburning engine. "The *Kijerumani* and after the *Kingereza* would ring a bell on the cable and we would go out into the forest with our machetes and bring bundles of wood to the station." There was great competition to get the woodcutting contracts. "Sometimes there was fighting between groups and people were killed."

Had he ever heard of Bwana Chifunga-Tumbo, the Englishman

in a skirt? "I have heard of that man, but I never saw him." Later, he added, another white man had come and told them not to be afraid, the War was over and the *Kijerumani* and the *Beljiji* could not hang them any more. Did the Germans and Belgians really hang them? "Yes, they hung us and they whipped us and were very cruel."

Crueller than the British? He put out his cheroot by crushing its glow between finger and thumb. "Yes, but the Holo-holo were the cruellest."

I asked him about Holo-holo fetishes. "Those people who made those statues are gone away now," Mr. Malyamungu told me.

In 1915 thousands of Holo-holo were settled along the Tanganyikan shore of the lake. They had originally sailed over in canoes and established discrete family units down the lake. Now there are scarcely any on either side of the lake. In his book *Aux Rives du Tanganyika* (1913), Bishop Adolphe Lechaptois—the senior White Father of the area—argues that this depopulation was in part caused by the Holo-holo practice of killing newborn babies: "Since the Europeans took over the government of this land, this custom has disappeared to a large extent. But in the remote villages, too far away or too small to be visited by the authorities or the missionaries, the practice continues in secret, only instead of throwing the babies into the lake or exposing them in the bush, they are made to disappear by the simple process of sticking a needle into the brain."

A later bishop, James Holmes-Siedle—writing in 1948 about a trip down the lake in the *Liemba*—calls the Holo-holo country the Southern Wilderness, "because the whole place is practically uninhabited." He adds that there had been recent cases of ordeal by poison among the tribe. A census taken in the same year listed 4,410 Holo-holo in Tanganyika.

"Their language is very old," said Hamidu, a researcher into chimpanzees who had hitched a lift in my boat on the return journey. "They came here long ago, before the railway was built. They enslaved people for the Arabs, and then they worked for the Germans and the British." He revealed that his grandfather was Holo-

holo. "Now they have been absorbed into the Tongwe. There are very few pure Holo-holo left. They were very good fighters. In those days if you did not move off your lands when the Holo-holo came, he would kill you. But if you obeyed them and left the land they would not kill you."

Have any words of Holo-holo entered into Tongwe? "Only one I know. It is *msampwe*. Prisoner."

We made our way back to camp. Mist sat on Mount Kungwe above. I spotted a refugee camp on the shoreline, its tents of green polythene torn and flapping. I went in to investigate, but some soldiers waved me away. Through my binoculars I watched a tall naked man with a stomach like a drum stoop down to the water, cupping his hand to drink.

The following day I travelled to Kalilani, a village full of Congolese refugees from the 1960s. It was noticeably poorer than the Tongwe villages nearby. Here, I had been told, lived one of the last pure Holo-holo along this side of the lake. His name was Seif Rusesa and he came out to greet me, smiling, the sun gleaming on the beads of his Muslim skullcap.

Now about sixty-eight (he couldn't remember the exact year of his birth), he had paddled over here from the Congo in 1964. His wife, four children and a chicken came with him in the canoe. We sat on stools in the middle of the village and I asked him why he had left the Congo.

"There was too much fighting. There were European mercenaries there."

Seif and his family had set off in the morning and arrived at three the following afternoon. There was no village before he came. Now there were about five hundred people, mainly Congolese from the Bembe tribe. He speaks to them in Swahili or their own language. He doesn't speak Holo-holo any more, and has forgotten most of it.

Was he always a Muslim? "No. On the other side we Holo-holo

worshipped a spirit called Migabo. Then they became either Christian or Muslim. But I am the only Holo-holo left now."

I remembered that the Migabo were the ancestral spirits of twins who interceded with Mkungwe on behalf of humans. Round us, children were beginning to gather, draping themselves over an old tree trunk. I pressed him on the Holo-holo religion, even though it made him uncomfortable to talk about it.

"There was a hut where the *waganga* [witch doctors] would call down the spirit. They would smear white soil on their face. Like suntan cream you whites put. They were members of a spirit society and you went inside the hut to see him, and they bring the spirit down into you."

The children around us were terrified; he told them that he had seen this ceremony with his own eyes as a child. "They don't know any of these stories," he explained. "They cannot capture it any more. In the old days they would sit round and listen." I suddenly realised that in coming here to research the oral tradition, I was encouraging a rare demonstration of it.

I asked Seif if he could remember anything about the ceremony which brought down the spirit. Could he show it to me? At first he was reluctant, putting his head in his hands and saying it hurt to remember. Then he sent one of his wives to fetch a cloth. He put the cloth over his head and started to shake, putting out his arms.

"They shook gourds with stones inside," he said through the cloth, "and they sang."

He began to sing in Holo-holo, dredging ancient words from his memory: "*Nangisane babo, nangisane kulingamira, nanjata kulugo . . .*" It was the spirit-possession song of the Migabo cult, and hearing it chilled me a little, though the translation was innocuous enough. "I am coming to you, I am coming to see, I am going home . . ."

Why call down this *nzimu*, this spirit? Seif pulled on his fingers, making the list. "It is to make a sick person better, to explain something that has happened in the past, or to say what is going to happen in the future. And it is also to kill somebody."

I wrote down Seif's answers as carefully as he had given them to me. As I was doing so, a motor boat buzzed across the bay. Like Spicer ninety-odd years before, I took out my binoculars and looked. It was one of the boats from the chimpanzee reserve, donated by the Frankfurt Zoological Society, whose logo was printed on the side.

I thanked Seif for his help and tried to give him some money for his efforts. He refused it, pointing at my binoculars. "When you come back, bring me some of those."

In June 1919 Spicer was a Royal Navy delegate at the Paris Peace Conference, probably on account of his skill in speaking French. The following month he organised an International Hydrographic Conference in London, for which he was also official translator. Those attending included Commander Yamaguchi of the Japanese navy and Lieutenant-Commander de Vasconcellos of the Brazilian navy. They were joined by British dignitaries such as Sir William Napier Shaw, Director of the Meteorological Office, and Sir Francis Younghusband, the explorer of Tibet. To entertain the delegates, Spicer took them to a performance of *Chu Chin Chow*—a spectacular musical based on the story of Ali Baba and the Forty Thieves.

Briefly Assistant Director of Naval Intelligence, Spicer later became the first Secretary General of the International Hydrographic Bureau in Monte Carlo, an organisation dedicated to the sharing of technical information about the world's oceans. A note in the autobiography of Baroness Orczy, the Hungarian-born novelist who wrote *The Scarlet Pimpernel* (1905), mentions Spicer in glowing terms and also a lecture he gave to the town's Société des Conférences about his mission to Lake Tanganyika.

The Baroness clearly enjoyed Spicer's talk. "He showed us some wonderful magic-lantern slides that he had taken and developed himself." Later in the season, the Baroness herself tackled the subject of literary frauds in a lecture (Chatterton and Macpherson and suchlike). Had her friend Spicer—who wore a chestful of medals and heavy ceremonial gold epaulettes on such occasions—told the whole truth in his lectures? It seems unlikely. For one thing, Magee, the journalist and "Petty Officer Writer," had taken the pictures, not Spicer. Perhaps it didn't matter. Within the glittering confines of the British expatriate community on the Côte d'Azur, Spicer could live out his fantasies with all the props.

In 1937, as the storm clouds of another war approached, the man who had been Bwana Chifunga-Tumbo resigned his post in Monaco. Settling in Canada, Spicer lived in Courtenay, British Columbia, until his death on 29 January 1947, at the age of seventy-one. He was survived by his wife, Amy.

His elder brother Theodore, who was interned by the Gestapo in France during the Second World War, lived much longer. Moving to the United States in 1946, he achieved some celebrity with his work as a portrait medallist. By the time he died at Coconut Grove in Florida in 1959, many prominent figures on both sides of the Atlantic had sat for him, including Wilbur Wright, James Joyce, Joseph Conrad, Winston Churchill and several US presidents. Theodore had made a medal of Geoffrey in 1903 (twelve years before the expedition to Tanganyika). It is interesting, to say the least, that both brothers were consumed with the idea of the heroic, for that is certainly the quality that Theodore's medals strive to express. Perhaps it all goes back to those gold sovereigns their father dealt in.

The *Graf von Götzen* had been twice sunk and twice raised by the time Bwana Chifunga-Tumbo died. The Germans never got the chance to come back and raise her. After the First World War, it was the Belgians who salvaged the *Götzen* and towed her to Kigoma harbour—where she sank again at her moorings during a storm not long afterwards. In 1921, back in the job of First Lord of the Admiralty in the post-war Liberal government, Winston Churchill ordered that the *Götzen* be raised once more and reconditioned under the auspices of Britain's new League of Nations mandate territory of Tanganyika. The long period of immersion in water had less effect than might be expected. Once Zimmer's grease had been removed, the steam cocks and engine parts shone brightly. Astonishingly little damage had been sustained. On Monday 16 May 1927 she sailed again, registered as the *Liemba:* the name given to Lake Tanganyika in Livingstone's time. A luncheon of seven or eight courses was served to the dignitaries on board, with champagne and liqueurs.

Down at the other end of the lake, George Tasker, the signalman whose semaphore Spicer professed not to understand, settled in the Abercorn area of Northern Rhodesia, living there until at least 1967. He was well known as a member of the *Mimi* and *Toutou* party, donating a White Ensign from one of the ships to a local museum. Spicer himself seems to have kept another flag used on the expedition; together with his ceremonial cocked hat, epaulettes and gloves, it weas inherited in 2000 by his great-nephew Hugh Brading.

Fifi/Kingani also survived after the War, though not for so long as the *Götzen*. Known as "the government steam launch," she maintained a passenger and cargo service between Kigoma and the southern ports on behalf of the Marine Department of the Tanganyikan government. The fare in 1922 was 2½ cents per mile for Africans, 9 cents per mile for Europeans. In 1924, deemed unseaworthy, she was towed three miles out of Kigoma and sunk in 200 feet of water.

After Tanzanian independence (1961), the *Liemba* fell into disrepair. It became the obsession of a hard-drinking Irish engineer called Patrick Dougherty, who spent years working on its hull and engines. He was rather like the character played by Bogart in *The African Queen*. There was a great celebration in November 1976 when Dougherty finally got the ship running again. Nowadays the *Liemba,* which was converted from steam to diesel in 1978, is the lifeline of the lake, binding poverty-stricken communities together. In the harvest months, when people are transporting crops to market, it carries up to one thousand passengers.

As for *Mimi* and *Toutou* themselves, nobody knows what happened to them. On my return to Kigoma I received permission to look for them in the military docks, where the old German railway still comes right up to the quay. There were plenty of iron hulks there and a few old wooden boats, but I didn't think any of them could be *Mimi* or *Toutou*. Their mahogany hulls would surely have rotted away by now.

But just as I was leaving, Musa Hathemani, the chief executive of the port authority, called me in to his office. He had once been told that the wreck of HMS *Toutou* (he called her "Tow-Tow" like the ratings on the expedition) was submerged off a village called Kabalangabo. I took a whaler taxi there, thinking it was too good to be true. This could be the gold I had been looking for—a physical historical connection to the Naval Africa Expedition . . .

A fisherman directed me to an area of pea-green water about 20 feet offshore. Stripping off, I dived and swam as hard as I could. But it was too murky to see and I could not stay down. In fact, I got nowhere near the bottom. I came up spluttering and staggered back to the shore. Pulling on my T-shirt, I quizzed the villagers, who had lined up along the beach to watch my ridiculous antics. They had never heard of *Toutou*. But yes, a boat could be seen there until a few years ago—yes, it was a boat from the Great War between the Germans and the English.

Apparently some part of the superstructure used to stick up, but it was now covered by sand. Whether it had belonged to *Ujerumani* or *Uingereza,* they did not know.

It was just the boat of some white men who had fought near here, long ago.

Catalogue of Vessels

showing their relative sizes

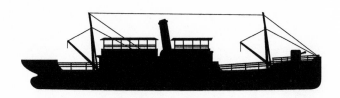

Graf von Götzen/Liemba

Length:	220 feet
Beam:	30 feet
Weight:	1,200 tons
Engine output:	2 × 250hp = 500hp
Speed:	8–9 knots

Hedwig von Wissmann

Length:	120 feet
Beam:	20 feet
Weight:	57 tons
Engine output:	1 × 60hp
Speed:	6–7 knots

Kingani/Fifi

Length:	56 feet
Beam:	15 feet
Weight:	45 tons
Engine output:	1 × 60hp
Speed:	8 knots

Mimi and Toutou

Length:	40 feet
Beam:	8 feet
Weight:	8 tons
Engine output:	2 × 100hp = 200hp
Speed:	15–19 knots

Bibliography

Anderson, Ross. *The Battle of Tanga, 1914.* Stroud, 2002.

———. *The Forgotten Front: The East African Campaign.* Stroud, 2004.

Bishop, Dennis, and Holger Dobold. "Tanganyikasee: A Gunboat War in Deutsch-Ostafrika, 1914–1916." *By Jingo* September, 2003. www.geocities.com/cdferree.

Burton, Richard. *The Lake Regions of Central Africa: A Picture of Exploration.* London, 1860.

Cameron, Lt. Verney Lovett. *Across Africa.* London, 1877.

Cane, Col. L. B. "SS *Liemba.*" *Tanganyika Notes and Records* 23/31. Dar es Salaam, 1947.

Carr, Archie. *Ulendo: Travels of a Naturalist in and out of Africa.* Gainesville, 1993.

Churchill, Winston. *London to Ladysmith via Pretoria.* Longman, 1900.

Corbett, Sir James. *History of the Great War: Naval Operations,* Vol. 4. London, 1928.

Davis, Richard Harding. "Saw German Army Roll on Like Fog." *New York Tribune,* 23 August 1914.

Driberg, Tom. *Swaff: The Life and Times of Hannen Swaffer.* London, 1974.

ECO Media TV-Produktion. *Die lange Fahrt der Graf Götzen.* Documentary broadcast on ARTE, 2001. 45 minutes. Directed by Stephan Lamby.

Estes, Richard. *The Behavior Guide to African Mammals: Including Hoofed Mammals, Carnivores, Primates.* Berkeley, 1991.

Farwell, Byron. *The Great War in Africa (1914–1918).* London, 1987.

Forester, C. S. *The African Queen.* London, 1935.

Geddie, John. *The Lake Regions of Central Africa: A Record of Modern Discovery.* Edinburgh, 1883.

Götzen, Graf G. A. von. *Deutsch-Ostafrika im Aufstand, 1905–6.* Berlin, 1909.

Hatchell, G. W. "Maritime Relics of the 1914–1918 War." *Tanganyika Notes and Records* 36/1. Dar es Salaam, 1954.

Hodges, Geoffrey. *The Carrier Corps: Military Labour in the East African Campaign, 1914–1918.* New York, 1986.

Holmes-Siedle, Bishop J. (W. F.). "Down Lake Tanganyika in the *Liemba*." *Tanganyika Notes and Records* 25/72. Dar es Salaam, 1948.

Horndern, Lt. Col. Charles. *History of the Great War: Military Operations East Africa.* London, 1941.

Huston, John. *An Open Book.* London, 1994 (1980).

Iliffe, John. *Tanganyika under German Rule.* Cambridge, 1968.

———. *A Modern History of Tanganyika.* Cambridge, 1979.

International Hydrographic Review. Monaco, 1947. Obituary of Commander G. B. Spicer-Simson.

Lechaptois, Bishop A. (W. F.). *Aux Rives du Tanganyika.* Algiers, 1913.

Listowel, Judith. *The Making of Tanganyika.* London, 1965.

Magee, Frank J. "Transporting a Navy through the Jungles of Africa in Wartime." *National Geographic* XLII/4. Washington, October 1922.

Ofcansky, Thomas. "A Bibliography of the East African Campaign, 1914–1918." *Africana Journal* 12/4 (1981).

Ondaatje, Christopher. *Journey to the Source of the Nile.* Toronto, 1998.

Patience, Kevin. *Königsberg: A German East African Raider.* Published by the author (PO Box 669, Bahrain). Bahrain, 1997.

Pigott, J. R. *The Crystal Palace at Sydenham, 1854–1936.* London, 2004.

Popham, Michael. Article on Hannen Swaffer and Frank Magee. *World's Press News.* London, August 1938.

Sayers, Gerald F. (editor). *The Handbook of Tanganyika.* London, 1930.

Schnee, Heinrich. *Deutsches Kolonial-Lexicon.* Leipzig, 1920.

Shankland, Peter. *The Phantom Flotilla.* London, 1968.

Spicer-Simson, Commander Geoffrey Basil (editor). International Hydrographic Conference London, 1919. Report of Proceedings. London, 1920.

———. "The Operations on Lake Tanganyika, 1915." *Journal of the Royal United Services Institute,* Vol. 79. London, November 1934.

Spicer-Simson, Theodore. *A Collector of Characters.* Miami, 1962.

Stewart, Graham. *Burying Caesar: Churchill, Chamberlain and the Battle for the Tory Party.* London, 1999.

Strachan, Hew. *The First World War, Vol. I: A Call to Arms.* Oxford, 2001.

Waugh, Evelyn. *Remote People.* London, 1931.

Young, Frances Brett. *Marching on Tanga.* London, 1917.

Acknowledgements

This is a fugitive tale, and I have employed a large number of sources in pursuing it. By far the most important of these is Peter Shankland's marvellous *The Phantom Flotilla* (1968). I hope that I have been able to add usefully to his account. I would also like to recognise the generous assistance of the individuals who have aided me during the writing of this book, in particular Rowland White (whose idea it was), Derek Johns, Ian Pindar, Steve Caplin, who compiled the "Catalogue of Vessels," Sarah Day, Elisabeth Merriman, Katy Nicholson and Terence McNamee of the Royal United Services Institute. Imtiaz and Sextus from Kigoma Hilltop were of invaluable help on a difficult journey in Tanzania. Brian Furner of the London School and Hospital of Tropical Medicine and Andrew Crymble of the Royal Society of Medicine assisted me in tracking down an obituary of Dr. Hanschell. Thanks are also due to Ian Jack of *Granta* and Sarah Spankie of *Condé Nast Traveller*, Sandra Piscedda of Murenga Ridgebacks, Hugh Brading, Nevill Joseph, Daphne Levens, Chris Dunne and Linda Costa. The book would be a much lesser thing without its illustrations by Matilda Hunt.

The author and publisher are grateful to the following for permission to reproduce copyright material: quotations from *The Phantom Flotilla* by Peter Shankland © Peter Shankland (1968) reproduced by kind permission of HarperCollins Publishers; quotations from *The Great War in Africa (1914–1918)* by Byron Farwell

Acknowledgements

© Byron Farwell (1987) reproduced by kind permission of Penguin Books; quotations from "The Operations on Lake Tanganyika in 1915" by Geoffrey Spicer-Simson (*RUSI* Journal, Vol. 79, November 1934) reproduced by kind permission of the Royal United Services Institute; quotations from *An Open Book* by John Huston © John Huston (1980) reproduced by kind permission of Da Capo Press; quotations from *Remote People* by Evelyn Waugh © Evelyn Waugh Settlement (1931) reproduced by kind permission of PFD (www.pfd.co.uk) on behalf of the Beneficiaries of the Evelyn Waugh Settlement; quotations from *London to Ladysmith via Pretoria* by Winston Churchill © Winston Churchill (1900), reproduced by kind permission of Curtis Brown Ltd., London, on behalf of the Estate of Sir Winston Churchill; quotations from *Die lange Fahrt der Graf Götzen* © ECO Media TV-Produktion (2001) reproduced by kind permission of Stephan Lamby.

A Note About the Author

Giles Foden, who grew up in Africa, was for three years an assistant editor of *The Times Literary Supplement* and then joined the staff of *The Guardian*. In 1998 Foden won the Whitbread First Novel Award for *The Last King of Scotland,* which was followed by *Ladysmith* and *Zanzibar.* He lives in London.

A Note on the Type

The text of this book was set in Sabon, a typeface designed by Jan Tschichold (1902–1974), the well-known German typographer. Based loosely on the original designs by Claude Garamond (c. 1480–1561), Sabon is unique in that it was explicitly designed for hotmetal composition on both the Monotype and Linotype machines as well as for filmsetting. Designed in 1966 in Frankfurt, Sabon was named for the famous Lyons punch cutter Jacques Sabon, who is thought to have brought some of Garamond's matrices to Frankfurt.

Composed by North Market Street Graphics,
Lancaster, Pennsylvania

Printed and bound by Berryville Graphics,
Berryville, Virginia

Designed by Soonyoung Kwon